WRITING VIETNAM, WRITING LIFE

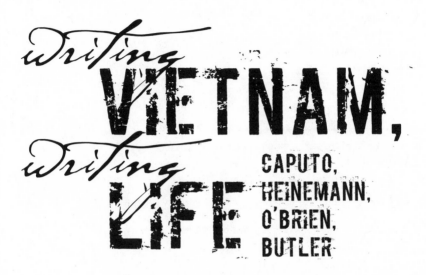

writing VIETNAM, writing LIFE
CAPUTO,
HEINEMANN,
O'BRIEN,
BUTLER

by Tobey C. Herzog

University of Iowa Press, Iowa City

University of Iowa Press, Iowa City 52242

The University of Iowa Press is a member of Green
Press Initiative and is committed to preserving
natural resources.

Printed on acid-free paper

Library of Congress Cataloging-in-Publication Data
Herzog, Tobey C.
Writing Vietnam, writing life: Caputo, Heinemann,
O'Brien, Butler / by Tobey C. Herzog.
    p.   cm.
Includes bibliographical references.
ISBN-13: 978-1-58729-631-4 (cloth)
ISBN-10: 1-58729-631-4 (cloth)
1. Caputo, Philip—Interviews.   2. Heinemann,
Larry—Interviews.   3. O'Brien, Tim, 1946– —
Interviews.   4. Butler, Robert Olen—Interviews.
5. Vietnam War, 1961–1975—Literature and the war.
6. War stories, American—History and criticism.
7. Novelists, American—20th century—Biography.
8. War correspondents—United States—Biography.
I. Title.
PS228.V5H43 2008   2007030602
810.9′358—dc22

08 09 10 11 12 C 5 4 3 2 1

This book is dedicated,
with admiration, to my
fellow Vietnam veterans
who have made the best
of a difficult situation and,
with love and hope,
to my granddaughters,
Mia and Elle

CONTENTS

ACKNOWLEDGMENTS

I especially wish to thank the four soldier-authors who agreed to be interviewed for this project: Philip Caputo, Larry Heinemann, Tim O'Brien, and Robert Olen Butler. Without their encouragement and support for this project, this book would never have materialized. All generously shared their time, stories, personal details, and living-writing spaces with me and did so with such graciousness that I will forever be indebted and will forever value their friendship. I also wish to thank Wabash student-intern Matt Tanney for his long hours and his attention to detail involved with research for this book and, most important, with his transcription of three interviews. Thanks also to Megan Johnson for her superb transcription of one interview. I was able to complete this book because of the generous financial support of Wabash College through its Student-Intern Program and its Coss Fund for Faculty Development. I also acknowledge the significant contributions over the years from Wabash students in my Vietnam freshman tutorials and my modern war literature classes. These students have provided valuable questions, answers, insights, and enthusiasm for my study of war literature and its authors. A note of thanks to Joseph Parsons, my editor, for his encouragement and advice about this manuscript, and a special thank you to two friends who have aided this project and others in many ways—my Texas friend Marilyn Knapp Litt and my London friend John Heuston. Finally, my deepest debt of gratitude goes to my wife, Peggy, whose unwavering support and love for me as I embark on these writing projects make all of them possible.

I also wish to thank the following who have kindly given permission to use copyrighted material:

Portions of the interview in chapter 3 are based on previously published material by the author that appeared in the *South Carolina Review* 31 (1998): 78–109, copyright © 1998.

INTRODUCTION
WAR STORIES, STORYTELLERS, AND AN iPOD

"This is what I saw; this is what I did; and this is what I became."
—Larry Heinemann

You are about to read conversations concerning war, life, and the careers of four prominent American soldier-authors who fought in the Vietnam War.[1] As a result, you will find many questions and answers, life stories, and observations about writing and the teaching of writing. In addition, as suggested by Heinemann's terse summary of his time in war, you will encounter many personal war stories. Specifically, you will read what these four soldier-authors did in war, what the war did to them, and why they wrote their stories. A character in Chinua Achebe's *Anthills of the Savannah* (New York: Anchor, 1989) judges the war story to be "chief among his fellows because it is only the story that can continue beyond the war and the warrior. It is the story that outlives the sound of war-drums and the exploits of brave fighters. It is the story, not the others, that saves our progeny from blundering like blind beggars into the spikes of the cactus fence" (114). Having spent much of my life hearing, living, telling, reading, watching, and teaching these stories (many filled with the horrors of war; others with noble exploits), I am intrigued with their widespread personal and public importance. At a personal level, my changing associations with these stories and their tellers have paralleled evolving stages in my life—son, soldier, father, and college professor—with each stage bringing new questions about the tales and the narrators. Along the way, these accounts have indeed outlived the warriors and the storytellers; the form, content, and the quality of the telling have differed; and the battlefields and machinery of war have changed. At various moments in my life, these stories have given rise to fantasized adventure, catharsis, emotional highs and lows, insights about human nature, and connections with the storytellers.

Whether these stories have saved me or anyone else from "blundering like blind beggars into the spikes" is still a matter of debate. However, one constant throughout my life journey accompanied by war stories has been my abiding fascination with the storytellers' lives and minds. Nabokov once noted about stories and their tellers that "the good, the admirable reader identifies himself not with the boy or girl in the book, but with the mind that conceived and composed that book . . . the individual genius who imagined and created it" (qtd. in Michael Roemer, *Telling Stories*, Lanham, MD: Rowman & Littlefield, 1995, 204). Particularly regarding war stories, I indulge such an identification with and curiosity about the storytellers. Why do they tell their tales? Are their stories original or part of oral traditions? How have the tellers merged memory and imagination to construct these stories? And perhaps the most fascinating question for me: how can the particular stories and the individual narrative voices together open windows into the lives and souls of the storytellers? These questions and others, some formed early in my life, shaped my four conversations with Vietnam soldier-storytellers Philip Caputo, Larry Heinemann, Tim O'Brien, and Robert Olen Butler.

Growing up listening to war stories, I contemplated simple questions about the genre and the art of storytelling. As a baby boomer born in postwar America in 1946 to an American war bride and a U.S. Army First Sergeant, I listened to my father's and my mother's stories from their World War II experiences. I first heard war stories from my father, who was stationed with the 8th Army Air Corps near Norwich, England, from 1943 through 1945. Proud of his service, proud of his country, and nostalgic about the camaraderie within his unit, he related simple noncombat accounts (he was always stationed in England) of the events and friendships characteristically arising in the military's rear areas. His stories emerged in private father-son moments but also in more public forums when he took me to the local American Legion Hall where he and other veterans swapped stories about their war exploits and briefly reestablished those relationships forged in war. Early on, his narratives had more to do with the landscape and people of England—travelogues with my dad as soldier-tourist. Also included were brief character sketches about particular commanding officers or enlisted men with whom my father had bonded and kept in touch after the war. Later, as I reached my teens, the war stories seemed more pointed toward teaching me life lessons: as his unit's first sergeant, one of his duties was to dispense prophylactics to the enlisted men as they left camp on leave. Today, knowing the storyteller better, I am sure this account was his oblique way of satisfying the requirements of a father-son talk about sex, but at the time the message was lost on his young, naïve audience.

Since my father wasn't much of a writer—either during or after the war—his oft-repeated stories were perhaps his version of spoken letters or a journal, and this oral form allowed for unlimited revisions. With an embellishment here, a digression added, a new character introduced, and a deletion there, the tales seemed always to be evolving. Even when I was young, I wondered how close to the original event was the fourth, fifth, or twentieth iteration of the story. Did my father consciously evoke this process of revising his stories, or were the facts and fictions all tangled together in his mind and impossible to separate? Was he, like any good storyteller, simply enhancing the listener's pleasure with these changes, as well as making the events clearer and more accessible to his audience? In the course of his storytelling was he attempting to enhance his own character—creating a more appealing public persona (the image of the tough first sergeant as father figure)? How much of his private persona was exposed through these yarns? With each retelling was he reaching a clearer understanding of himself (who am I?), of the event, and of his role in it? Why were some of the stories better than others? And finally, why did my father, raised by a single mom, rather seamlessly move from war stories into wider-ranging life stories, ones frequently including a subtext of a search for a father figure?

Recently, with both my mother and father dead, I have thought more about my mom's war stories, which were really broader life stories. She told fewer— probably because I didn't think to ask her; perhaps because she didn't think these narratives, compared to my father's, were real war stories; and certainly because at the time in our small provincial hometown a woman's homefront war stories were not deemed all that compelling and significant. But what I did hear from her were, as I realize now, tales every bit as compelling and relevant as my father's. During the war, she was a thirtyish professional woman (secretary) working in a large office in a midsize city (Indianapolis, Indiana). She met my father while traveling on a train to Chicago in 1942, married him six weeks later at Camp Atterbury, Indiana, and then didn't see him again for over two years, until a few months after V-E Day. Unfortunately, in telling her occasional story, she consciously or unconsciously never moved much beyond the surface details of this narrative outline: the life of a married woman working and living alone in an urban environment while her husband, more of a stranger than an intimate companion, was off fighting in the war. If I had been more inquisitive, if Mom hadn't been so reticent, if society at that time had validated such stories, her war stories would have been just as interesting and instructive to me as my father's. In a pre-feminist world, the subtexts of her accounts suggested personal liberation in wartime, as well as constraints imposed by society's expectations for a woman in her position. I am now left with considering the possibilities suggested by the realities of this portion of her life and with more questions I should have asked both my mother and father about their war and life experiences. Answers to these questions and more stories may have helped me further know where the stories came from and why they were told.

Years later, for twenty-one months (1969–1970), I unexpectedly gathered material for my own war stories as an army draftee stationed first at Fort Gordon, Georgia, and later at Long Binh, South Vietnam. Unlike my father, I have written records of some of my war activities in the form of saved letters written to my wife. Reading these letters has helped me factually reconstruct portions of my one-year tour in Vietnam for the war stories I occasionally tell my sons and others. The letters frequently read more like journal entries, only with another reading audience in mind: a list of daily events to give my wife a sense of a routine day on a large military base in South Vietnam, descriptions of other men in the unit who happen to be friends or unusual characters, the usual comments about missing my wife and wanting to be home with her, and occasionally the mention of rocket attacks on our base or descriptions of nighttime perimeter guard duty in a fortified bunker on the jungle's edge. I now wonder why I included these latter events, potentially upsetting for my wife. Although real, they were somewhat out of context. While performing perimeter guard on about fifteen occasions during my entire tour of duty, I never once saw the enemy, never once fired any of the weapons in anger, and mainly slept and talked. Was I inventing a heroic persona, one that might off-set the rather unheroic job designation of personnel specialist? What persona emerges as I tell my own war stories today? What window into my life and soul do the listeners, particularly my sons, gain from these stories? What truths emerge? Who am I?

Finally, over the past thirty years of teaching college students, I have introduced them and myself to a host of war stories (prose, poetry, drama, and film) created by soldier-artists and noncombatants ranging from Erich Maria Remarque, Wilfred Owen, and Virginia Woolf to Anne Frank, Norman Mailer, Bao Ninh, David Rabe, Oliver Stone, and Anthony Swofford. These war stories, ranging from memoir to fiction, more often than not are life stories about the tellers and their characters. Some are superficial, more travelogues and event-centered; others are deeply personal, at times confessional. However, across time, wars, homefronts, battlefields, cultures, and advancements in military technology, many of the stories' themes, confessions, horrors, evils, acts of courage and cowardice, and moral dilemmas are strikingly similar and expose the souls of the writers and their characters affected by war. Admittedly, my questions now about these stories and storytellers are more sophisticated than the ones I pondered when listening to my father and mother tell of their wartime experiences. Yet underlying these new questions remains my basic curiosity to know more about the geniuses behind the stories, the relationships of tellers to the narrated events, and the attributes of a good war story.

So what do these personal ruminations about war stories and storytellers have to do with this book? They partially explain its origin—a listener's, participant's, reader's, and teacher's ongoing inquisitiveness about the lives and craft of soldier-storytellers—and the questions it contains. But the other impetus for the book emerged over ten years ago during a personal encounter with soldier-author Tim O'Brien. Beginning in 1979 with my first Vietnam War literature course, I have repeatedly taught his award-winning novels *Going After Cacciato* and *The Things They Carried* (recently named in a *New York Times Book Review* poll as one of the best works of American fiction of the last twenty-five years). In researching O'Brien's life, I also identified with this author. Both of us were born in October 1946, drafted into the army soon after graduating from small liberal arts colleges in the Midwest, served in Vietnam at approximately the same time, and upon discharge entered Ph.D. programs. In 1994 the relationship became personal. O'Brien accepted my invitation to visit Wabash College, and during his two-day stay (soon after the release of his war novel *In the Lake of the Woods*), he met with my war literature class, presented a public reading, and graciously agreed to a future interview for a book I was writing about him (*Tim O'Brien*). Subsequently, in July 1995, I traveled to Cambridge, Massachusetts, to interview O'Brien in his apartment—two days of intense and frank conversation about his life and his writing. The interview focused on three key stages of his life: son, soldier, and author. As we chatted, I became intrigued with the life stories and war stories he shared, but more important, I valued the candor and passion with which O'Brien talked about conflicted relationships in his life and with his writing career. Suddenly, I glimpsed the "individual genius" who had created the books: a young O'Brien dealing with a complicated father-son relationship, a soldier and veteran feeling guilty about his Vietnam service, a writer wishing to avoid the narrow label "war writer," and a fellow human being constantly searching for love. I was also struck by one of his answers to a question about the interplay between memory and imagination in his life and in his art: "Everything that I am doing flows out of the life I have led. And the life I have led is a life of finding it hard to distinguish within myself and without about what's true and what's not."

Several years after this pivotal interview experience, I began planning this book of conversations with American soldier-authors connected to the Vietnam War. My curiosity grew about unexplored connections between O'Brien's life and his war stories, the relationship between an author's memory and his imagination, and the significance of Saul Bellow's categorizing fiction as a "higher form of autobiography." Furthermore, as I taught other authors in my war literature courses, I wondered more and more about these individual geniuses who had created war stories. Old and new questions surfaced. Did their war and life experiences make them writers? Why did these soldier-authors choose to write war stories, either as memoir or fiction? How many of these stories directly emerged from their roles as soldiers and veterans? As their writing careers evolved, did the war stories fade into the background, and did these soldier-authors move seamlessly into depicting a broader human landscape in their books, but with war and its related issues always lurking beneath the surface? Since I had already initiated a meaningful conversation with O'Brien, had published portions of our 1995 interview, but had generated many more questions since our first visit, my plan to include him in this proposed book of interviews with Vietnam soldier-authors seemed a natural starting point. But the major unresolved questions were how many other authors and who?

Quickly, some very arbitrary but practical criteria involving literary merit and author accessibility emerged for this selection process. The first of these was to choose writers of Vietnam War–related books that readers and teachers judge to be of high quality—the proverbial "books standing the test of time." Within the war genre, such works contain serious events and themes of the Vietnam War in particular and of war in general presented in a sophisticated, artistic, and honest fashion. More important, the books transcend the immediate battlefield experiences and explore the broad continuum of war and life. The second criterion emerged from the first: demonstrated praise for the writing in the form of a prominent national writing prize for the author, such as O'Brien's National Book Award in Fiction, or widespread critical acclaim for a particular book. The third measure, closely connected with the first two, was career longevity. Not only are the authors' books related to the Vietnam experience still being read, but the particular soldier-authors are continuing to write and publish. The next condition, a non-literary one, seemed pertinent to a project involving war stories. I wanted to pick soldier-authors with varied military experiences in the Vietnam War—differences created by branch of service, military rank, military occupational specialty (MOS), location of their tour of duty in Vietnam, and, most important, their dates of service in Vietnam.[2] The final criterion was perhaps the most difficult to gauge but the most practical. I wanted to select writers who would be accessible to me, would be willing to sit down in *their homes* with a relatively unknown college professor placing a 20-gigabyte iPod with Griffin iTalk recording attachment in front of them, and would submit to two days of in-depth interviews probing their roles as son, soldier, and author. This last criterion seemed the most daunting to meet.

After researching the lives and writing careers of living Vietnam soldier-authors I had taught in my Vietnam literature classes, everyone from James Webb, Stephen Wright, and W. D. Ehrhart to John Del Vecchio, Lynda Van Devanter, and Michael Herr (a quasi-soldier), Caputo, Heinemann, and Butler best met all the criteria for inclusion with O'Brien. Each had entered Vietnam at a very different point in the war's history; each subsequently, directly or indirectly, had written about his life and war experiences; each had crafted one or more highly acclaimed war stories, fiction or nonfiction, still widely read; and each had recently published or was about to publish a new work: O'Brien's *July, July* (2002), Butler's *Had a Good Time: Stories from American Postcards* (2004), Heinemann's *Black Virgin Mountain* (2005), and Caputo's *Acts of Faith* (2005). Finally, I had or was about to have connections to all four.

I first taught Philip Caputo's nonfiction *A Rumor of War*, paired with Graham Greene's *The Quiet American*, in an undergraduate literature class called "Classics of the Vietnam War: Innocence, Experience, and Aftermath." In the innocence segment of the course, Caputo's war memoir introduced my naïve draft-age students to the seductive and, at times, destructive nature of military adventure as Caputo recounted his voluntary Marine Corps experiences in officer training and later in Vietnam. While still in college, he had enlisted to escape the boredom of a suburban existence and to fulfill romantic illusions of heroic adventure, medals, and service to his country. The book is a war classic, with some critics regarding it as the best memoir to emerge from the American experience in Vietnam. Nevertheless, the Pulitzer prize–winning Caputo did not receive a national writing prize for this book; instead, he was recognized for investigative reporting while covering Chicago politics in the early 1970s (a different type of warfare) for the *Chicago Tribune*. My only personal contact with Caputo had occurred at his 1986 reading at Purdue University, where I introduced myself as a fellow Vietnam veteran and someone who was teaching *A Rumor of War*. He graciously signed my first-edition copy of the book.

My initial contacts with Heinemann and Butler were equally modest. I taught their fiction in the second and third segments of my Vietnam literature course, specifically the experience and aftermath portions of soldiers' and civilians' war encounters. For the experience segment, Heinemann's *Close Quarters*, which fits Paul Fussell's label of a "first novel" (written in the first person and based heavily upon the author's own experiences), introduced students to the routines and horrors of the battlefield. Influenced by World War II soldier-author James Jones, Heinemann's book portrays the activities of war, combat psychology, and unit dynamics, but with a gripping realism, gruesome detail, vulgarity, and angry voice characterizing much of Vietnam combat writing in general and Heinemann's in particular. In the aftermath section (postwar adjustments), I used Heinemann's *Paco's Story*, which depicts a Vietnam veteran suffering from PTSD and searching for a physical and emotional home in the midst of an indifferent and, at times, antagonistic American society. This second novel won the 1986 National Book Award for Fiction, selected with considerable controversy over Toni Morrison's *Beloved* (the latter recently named in a *New York Times Book Review* poll as "the best work of American fiction of the last 25 years"). My only direct contact with Larry transpired in 1980, after I had published a review essay for *College English* surveying the emerging literary landscape of prominent books exploring the American experience in Vietnam. Larry sent me a signed copy of his first novel, *Close Quarters*, which I had not mentioned in my article, and noted that "you might find my Vietnam novel of interest. Paul Fussell has called it an 'admirable' book." Five years later we met briefly in a hallway at an international conference called the "Effects of Vietnam on American Culture," held at Manchester Polytechnic University in Manchester, England. I introduced myself as the author who had not mentioned *Close Quarters* in a review article; he seemed to remember.

My introduction to Robert Olen Butler also initially arose through teaching one of his books in the aftermath section of my war literature course and later by attending one of his public readings. Providing my students with a very different perspective of the Vietnam War's after-effects, Butler's *A Good Scent from a Strange Mountain* (a collection of fictional stories in multiple first-person voices) describes the complicated lives of Vietnamese immigrants in America who must negotiate two cultures and cope with the fallout of, for them, a very different "American War" experience. Butler received the 1993 Pulitzer Prize for Fiction for *Good Scent*. A few months after the announcement of this prize, I attended a University of Notre Dame–sponsored conference called "The United States and Vietnam: From War to Peace," where Butler read his short story "Salem," an aftermath narrative in which a North Vietnamese veteran contemplates the American soldier he killed years earlier. As Butler read, I was struck with his powerful use of the first-person narrative, his obvious immersion in Vietnamese culture and language, and his sense of a reading as performance art. Ten years later, when Wabash's English department selected our first visiting writer in a newly endowed writer's series, I invited Butler, based on his long and distinguished career as a writer and as a teacher of creative writing. Over three days on campus, Butler read from his work-in-progress (*Had a Good Time: Stories from American Postcards*), talked with Wabash English majors about his unique views on reading literature ("thrumming to the work"), and conducted for high school English teachers a workshop in teaching creative writing. The morning after his reading at Wabash, in the midst of a Hoosier biscuits-and-gravy breakfast at Uncle Smiley's restaurant in Crawfordsville, Indiana, Butler became the first of the four proposed authors to agree to participate in this still developing book project.

With Butler on board, I turned my attention to securing the other writers' involvement. Quickly, in what I viewed as a validation of a positive experience in our earlier interview, O'Brien, via email, consented to meet once again. This time, we would get together for one session to clarify some points in the 1995 interview and to discuss details of his life and writing since our visit in Cambridge. Several months later, Heinemann agreed to be part of the book during lunch of pasta and beer at the Coco Pazzo Café in downtown Chicago. Finally, an email to Caputo secured his somewhat reluctant participation as he noted that he was a "bit stale about Vietnam and its literature" but had said yes to an earlier request for an interview and therefore would honor mine. With the soldier-authors secured, an unobtrusive iPod recording device purchased (something to make me look efficient and technologically savvy), and tentative dates and itineraries mapped out, I finalized the structure and content of the interviews and sketched a tentative table of contents for the book. My curiosity and insecurities increased each day as I waited to visit each author in his writing space.

I conceived the four interviews as being organized around a core of questions related specifically to each author's role as a son, soldier, and writer and generally to each individual's development as a writer. I planned to ask these same basic questions of the four authors in order to establish significant similarities and differences among their lives, war experiences, and views on writing. I also wanted to interview these individuals (and later organize the interviews in the book) in the order of their arrival in Vietnam—earliest to latest. Underlying such questions and intentions is a major subtext: the relationship of each author's life experiences to his writing and thus the intersection of memory and imagination in his works. Thus, I initially assumed many of my questions would elicit the four soldier-authors' views on life-writing, that somewhat nebulous, controversial, and now very popular genre encompassing all forms of letters, journals, diaries, memoirs, autobiographies, biographies, and even autofiction. But early in my first interview, and later when I asked the other authors the obligatory question about life-writing, I discovered that such a narrow focus on this broad and ambiguous topic was not something that the four subjects wanted to discuss directly. As O'Brien noted in our conversation, "All writing is life-writing; I can't imagine a work that wasn't related to life." Quickly, my plans changed, and the conversations (for that's what they became) settled into a intriguing array of life stories, war stories, discussions of each writer's creative process, political commentary (past and current events), candid views on teaching creative writing, analysis of individual works, and the bottom-line message from all four authors that a good war story is really just a good life story. Interestingly, however, along the way we did manage indirectly to discuss some aspects of life-writing within broader contexts. Also, with the first interview, I quickly realized that there is considerable missing information and published misinformation related to key events and people in the authors' lives. Therefore, some of my questions and later research gathered information appearing in the chronologies, which are an important feature of this book.

Each subject received the script of questions a few weeks in advance of our conversation. But each mentioned, at our first session, that to make the discussions more spontaneous and meaningful, he either had not reviewed the questions or had given them only a cursory glance. For the most part, I followed the scripted questions. Obviously, however, follow-up questions often differed from interview to interview based on the initial answer to a pre-selected question or information gained in previous interviews. In many cases, my questions led to unexpected stories and digressions that took our conversations in serendipitous directions. Because we had not previously engaged in a Q&A situation, Caputo, Heinemann, and Butler seemed cautious during the early portion of each first-day session as they tried to get a feel for what I was up to and how I would be using the information. Not surprisingly, the issue was one of trust. On my part, the feeling was uneasiness. I was very aware that I was intruding upon these well-known people's private spaces and lives and impinging upon their very valuable writing time. Quickly, however, their wariness and my uneasiness dissipated, and the sessions settled into stimulating, occasionally humorous, meaningful conversations. The one constant in all four interviews was the graciousness with which the four well-known writers patiently, thoroughly, and candidly answered my questions. Emerging from these exchanges was a mix of the expected and unexpected; the trivial and the revealing; the light-hearted and the disturbing.

Finally, here are some general guidelines for reading these conversations.[3] For each author, the chronology and interview together provide a mini-biography: an overview of each writer's life, the relationship of these life experiences to his writing, and the path of his writing career. Taken together, these four life stories also offer a mini-tableau of a fascinating and troubling time in '60s and '70s America, a time of social and political upheaval fronted by a controversial war. Naturally, because of the four writers' life and literary connections to the Vietnam War, questions as to what each soldier-author saw and did in the Vietnam War and what he became as a result are central to each discussion. All four agreed that their war experiences made them writers, influenced the content of several of their stories, but also unfortunately pigeonholed them with the misleading label of "war writer." Perhaps the best advice for reading these interviews comes from the writers themselves. All cited the pitfalls of the biographical fallacy in directly linking an author's life with his or her works. But Caputo admitted that one purpose for such an interview is to "find out what made the person write a particular book, or what makes him or her write at all." Heinemann confided in his typically blunt way that "one of the last things 'lifers' don't get is that. . . writers always get the last word." O'Brien urged readers to pay careful attention to the narrative voice emerging in each interview, because it's the same writer's voice (language, tone, underlying values) present in his books. And Butler observed that such interviews can be helpful in revealing how writers' "unconscious selves are formed": "to see the relationship of the writer's life experiences to the way in which the writer invents other self-contained worlds is certainly interesting and can throw a light on the legitimate creative process that goes into the making of these works of art."

My personal goal for these conversations was to hear more war stories and to know more about the storytellers (answering the basic questions of where the stories are coming from and who the storytellers are). My professional goal was to provide my readers with a thorough and helpful introduction to each author's life and writings. My personal goal has been achieved. I hope as you read the rest of this book, you will find a similar satisfaction in having some of your questions answered and learning more about the lives, souls, aesthetics, and craft of four prominent sons-soldiers-authors. Finally, one cryptic cautionary note: my purpose for the conversations was, borrowing terms from Tim O'Brien, less on discovering "happening truths" and more on learning "story truths."

NOTES _____

1. Throughout this book I have used the labels "conversation," "interview," and "discussion" interchangeably. Although the published format follows that of a typical Q&A interview, my sessions with Caputo, Heinemann, O'Brien, and Butler frequently became informal conversations as we occasionally discussed personal and career topics unrelated to the particular focus of this book or we exchanged "war stories" that are not presented in this book.

2. In thinking about the importance of dates of service in Vietnam, I speculated that tours of duty during the early stages of the official war (1965–1966), middle stages (1967–1969), and final stages (1970–1975) would differ according

to participants' attitudes toward the war, public sentiment toward the war, military strategy, and nature of the combat. Such an assumption proved particularly true in comparing the tours of Caputo and O'Brien.

3. Each of my recorded interviews with Caputo, Heinemann, and Butler occurred over two days in 2005, with sessions generally lasting three and a half to four hours each day. The most recent (2005) O'Brien interview lasted three and a half hours on one day. Soon after each interview was completed, my intern made a verbatim transcription of the audio recordings, and I then checked each transcript for accuracy while listening to the recordings. For the edited version of each interview, I eliminated dated information, the author's off-the-record comments, some information appearing in the chronology, and exchanges unrelated to the focus of this book. I also edited some of the responses and rearranged the sequence of some of the questions to improve clarity, conciseness, and coherence. After completing the final edited version of our interview, I gave each author an opportunity to review the manuscript and suggest changes or additions.

conversation with
PHILIP CAPUTO

Caputo reviewed the final edited version of our June 2005 interview and made no changes to the manuscript. He noted in an email, "I am pleased with the results. Nice editing of a conversation—I sounded coherent."

Our meetings took place during the mornings of June 21 and 22, 2005, at the author's home in Norwalk, Connecticut. Upon arriving for our first session, I found Phil in his writer's cottage (located in his wooded backyard a short distance behind his two-story Cape Cod home) busily working to eliminate a computer virus. This writer's spot is a sparse but functional one-room wood structure with small windows, plenty of desk and computer space, and several wall hangings. The latter include photographs from Caputo's many travels as a war correspondent, writing awards, and a framed shadow box with his military decorations and a picture of Marine Lieutenant Caputo. The interviews on both days occurred in the book-lined den of the Caputo home, which he shares with his wife, Leslie Ware, who is managing editor for *Consumer Reports*. We talked on the first day for three hours, and then casually chatted over lunch in nearby Rowayton at a popular sandwich shop situated on a small boat harbor near Long Island Sound. During the next morning, we talked for two and a half hours with Phil beginning our conversation by recounting his previous night's reading (in nearby Darien, Connecticut) devoted to his recently released novel *Acts of Faith*. Our session ended with my giving Phil a ride to the nearby train station so he could catch a commuter train into New York City and tape an interview with Charlie Rose to be aired on PBS the next night. Phil's trim, muscular appearance befits someone who was a college wrestler; enjoys the outdoors, including sailing; and until very recently spent considerable time, first as a war correspondent and later as a freelance journalist, in some of the most dangerous areas of the world. During our interview, Phil's responses to the scripted and unscripted questions, perhaps because of his journalism background, were direct and precise. But he punctuated them with laughter, self-deprecating comments, and numerous life stories. What struck me in the interview is Phil's ongoing personal and authorial fascination with moral questions and moral quandaries when guidelines are not clear. Also apparent was that despite his earlier reservations, Phil proved to be anything but "stale" on the subject of his war experiences and war literature.

SON

H: You have used the phrase "commonplace middle-class upbringing" to describe growing up in a Chicago suburb. Talk about some of your activities and interests as a child and teenager.

PC: I had a great interest in outdoor sports and pastimes. From the time I was virtually an infant, until I was eighteen, every summer my dad would work somewhere in northern Wisconsin, Michigan, or Minnesota fixing the machines that Continental Can sold to canning factories. He would actually work there from May to October, and when school would let out in June, my sister, my mother, and I would then join him until school started again. So I grew up around the Northwoods, lakes, and places like that and developed a great interest in things like hiking, camping, canoeing, fishing. Also, because Westchester [Chicago suburb] at the time that I grew up was right on the border of rural landscape (as a matter of fact, there were still some working farms within the town limits), in the fall I used to hunt pheasant and rabbit out there.

H: Did you have any other interests at this point in your life?

PC: Well, we played some Little League baseball, but in those days most of it was kind of disorganized. There were sandlot pick-up games, but I remember playing a lot of it. I played football for two years in high school, on the junior varsity. I was on the boxing team (they had boxing teams in the Catholic league in those days) for three years. I tried the swimming team. I was actually a pretty good swimmer, but some of those other sports, like the boxing and the football, really militated against being a top-notch swimmer because I developed all these tightened-up muscles.

H: Did you have any relatives in the military, and did they talk about their war experiences with you when you were young?

PC: My father was not a veteran. My dad was first given a draft deferment [WWII] because I was born. They were taking married men, but without children. The second time he got drafted, the work he was doing for Continental Can was called "critical industry," and he was a very skilled machinist. So they kept him out. . . . I had one uncle who was in the Seabees at Tarawa, among other places in the South Pacific. He would not talk about it at all. Later on, not when I was a kid or a teenager, but much later, he told me about one of the things the Seabees did with beach construction and even beach preparation, and he talked about being on Tarawa where you could hardly breathe for all the dead bodies. . . . But I had another uncle who was in the Army Air Corps, and he didn't say much either. Then oddly enough [a great uncle], Uncle Sam was his name, was at Iwo Jima, and he told me a few things. I remember he had a lead-cast model of Iwo, and as a matter of fact, I still have the K-bar knife that he carried. It's scratched in there "Iwo Jima, February–April 1945." It's out in the garage. And he told me some funny stories.

H: Did you play games of war as a child?

PC: Yes, we did that kind of thing where you'd chase each other around in the woods and try to hit each other with clods of dirt.

H: The precursor to paintball.

PC: Yes, they were almost like paintball games, except with fairly deadly stuff. I remember we'd just throw rocks at each other; everybody looked like a bunch of cavemen.

H: Did you read a lot when you were growing up, and what were your favorite books?

PC: The time immediately before high school, I read mostly science fiction, and I read an awful lot of sporting and men's magazines: True, Argosy, Sports Afield, which still exists, Field & Stream. I read a lot of those before high school and into high school, too.

H: At a young age, were you interested in becoming a writer?

PC: I first got an inkling that I might like to do it about age fifteen, but I can't say that I had an idea of doing it as a living. We had to write a short story as an assignment in high school, and I remember I really liked doing it. I was fairly good at it.

H: During your childhood and teenage years, did you have any particular heroes, including political figures?

PC: Yes, I'll try to pick categories, just like Trivial Pursuit. In sports, it would have been Stan Musial, and you may not remember him, but a Chicago Cubs first baseman named Phil Cavarretta. Also in sports, because being of Italian American ancestry, Rocky Marciano and Carmen Bassilio, boxing heroes. And Teddy Roosevelt I much admired as a kid, and still do, even with all his warts. I just read his biography. I realize there was a lot about the guy that was not terribly attractive, but overall, I still find him just a compelling figure. As a matter of fact, I remember reading in one of those men's magazines an account of his last big expedition to South America, when he almost lost his son. I remember reading that when I was about fourteen or fifteen and being captivated by it.

A literary hero I had was Hemingway because I went to school in Oak Park, and I knew where his house was. I'll have to admit I was more captivated by Hemingway's legend than his writing, not because I didn't like his writing. But what really drew me to him was his "living large," as they call it.

H: It's interesting that you mention in A Rumor of War that John Wayne was a hero who influenced you through his movies.

PC: I can't say that John Wayne was actually a hero of mine, because he was an actor. He played heroes. It was the idea of John Wayne.

H: How did these movies influence your attitudes toward war, your attitudes toward heroism and patriotism?

PC: Well, the earliest war movie I saw, my dad took me to see it. It's one of the most vivid memories of my childhood. It was a cold February day, and I reckon it must have been when the movie came out because we went to a theater to see (so I would say 1949) the Sands of Iwo Jima. I remember being captivated by Sergeant Striker and swept away by the strains of the Marine Corps Hymn as they charged up the island of Iwo Jima. Of course, as I said, my great uncle had been there, even though he wasn't with that first wave. And I think it was a very great influence on me, even on into a more mature age, because my conception was that the United States stood only for what was true, good, and right and that we were the great liberators of the world from totalitarian tyranny. So I was very influenced more by these movies than anything else.

H: Did your family spend a lot of time discussing books and politics?

PC: Not a lot, no. Certainly not books. This was a real blue-collar family, and it was newspapers and stuff like that. Politics, though, was touched on only lightly. We were a Democratic family of the old nuts-and-bolts New Deal–type of Democrats, especially my father, who to this day (he's still alive at ninety) thinks that long before Pope Paul should be canonized, FDR should be.

H: Was religion an important part of your upbringing?

PC: Yes. It wasn't that strong on the part of my father. A little bit stronger on my mother's part, and most of it came from those parochial schools that I attended.

H: What did you take from your Catholic education that is present in your life and writing today?

PC: Well, I think when you're raised Catholic, you almost absorb a reverence for history and tradition. Even to this day, there's something about the long history and the long tradition of the Catholic Church that makes me feel in some way superior to these parvenu Protestants, and the only [Western] religion older is Judaism, unless you want to include Zoroastrianism. I also think you come away with a certain desire for order in life and a desire to impose order on life. It's that medieval tradition of Catholicism, going back to St. Thomas Aquinas, where everything is schematic. And there's a place for everything, and everything in its place. Even though that isn't true, you tend to want it to be true. Then, of course, I think what you come away with is a concern with, even obsession with, moral questions and moral quandaries.

H: Good versus evil?

PC: The relationship between good and evil. Also, I must say—not so much at the middle school or grammar school level, but on the high school and college levels—that you come away with a rather rigorous way of thinking, a rigorous logic that you apply to things. It's generally called a Jesuitical approach, which I have realized over the years I do unconsciously. . . . I remember having a discussion of some issues with a reporter from *People* magazine. It was a casual discussion; she wasn't interviewing me. And she said, "You were trained by Jesuits." "How did you know?" I asked. And she said, "Because you're trying to put me on your little Jesuitical railroad track; I won't get on it."

H: Describe your father and your relationship with him during these years of growing up at home?

PC: Well, we went through different stages. I would say from prepubescence to early adolescence it was fairly good. It was, not like now, more distant. He was the authority figure. Also, he worked very hard, and he worked long hours. So I didn't get to see a lot of him. Then, I went through the rebellious period when I thought that he didn't know a damn thing and that I knew it all. And so we butted heads quite a bit when I was in high school and even in college, and I would say even beyond that. Then, sometime probably by my late twenties, early thirties, we established a fairly good relationship. I still call him once or twice a week. . . . So I would say it was a good relationship, and it was a healthy relationship, but not a real-close-buddy kind of relationship.

H: What did you learn about life from your father?

PC: I learned the value of hard work and craft. He was and, in some ways, still is (although he doesn't work anymore) so conscientious about his work. So in the days when he was a machinist, if he fixed a machine, that bloody thing would work, period. And when he was that technical troubleshooter type, he was sent all over the world, to Germany and Hong Kong and places like that, to solve problems in various kinds of breweries and canning factories. And when he solved problems, they were solved.

He was an amateur carpenter, which is to say he never made his living at it. And he paneled a room that I was in with [real] paneling, not fake paneling. And he had to finish one part of the room where eves came down in a triple angle. Well, if you didn't measure those angles precisely and cut the panels very precisely, you'd have one board sticking out. And even if it was an eighth of an inch, you would have to put molding over it to hide it. He wouldn't do it, and he said that somebody had once said something to the effect that [molding] hides a lot of sins that good carpenters don't commit. I would put it all under the category of honesty; he really taught me honesty: intellectual honesty, honesty in your work, honesty with your self, honesty with your craft. That's what I admired and still admire most about him.

H: Did you consider enlisting in the military immediately after your graduation from high school?

PC: Yes.

H: Who or what dissuaded you?

PC: My father. He did more than dissuade me; he forbade it.

H: Were you going to enlist in the Marine Corps?

PC: Yeah, I wanted to go in. I really wanted to just get out and see the world, see the action.

H: Did he tell you to go to Purdue and become an aeronautical engineer?

PC: Yes. Well, first of all, he was absolutely determined that I was going to graduate college, no matter what happened. I could have run away from home at eighteen and gone and done what I wanted, I suppose; but his influence on me was such that [enlistment] was only a theoretical option.

H: Are there additional details about your family and upbringing from this period of your life that might give people an insight about you as a person and your development as a writer?

PC: In high school I was very influenced by an English teacher named Robert Hlavin. He was the one who had us write stories, and he actually saw some spark in me and encouraged me privately. He had me write for some story contests and once had me write for a radio drama.

H: At Loyola, did you take any creative writing courses?

PC: I took a one-semester night course. It was given at what was called the University College [Loyola-Chicago], which was basically an adult education program, and it was given by the man to whom I dedicated *Horn of Africa*,

Stan Clayes, a very good course and the only one I took, aside from the standard composition courses.

H: Did you do any writing outside the classroom at Loyola—college newspaper or literary magazines?

PC: Yes, I wrote for the literary magazine and the college paper.

H: At this point, were you thinking of journalism as a career?

PC: Yes, but not very seriously. . . . When I say not very seriously, in those days you knew the draft was on; you knew that you had to do that. The Vietnam War was not on; this was '63 and early '64. This is before Gulf of Tonkin [August 1964]. But you knew that you were going to get drafted, or you were going to end up going into the service. So any plans I had for a career were in something of a hiatus.

H: You mentioned an awareness of the draft during this time, but from 1960 through 1964 at either Purdue or Loyola was there much discussion of American involvement in Vietnam?

PC: No, there was none. The big subject was the Cuban Missile Crisis, that and the Soviet Union. I would say that in 1963, if you had asked me where is Indochina, I would have had no idea where it was.

H: During your time in college, what were the most significant books you read? For example, in many interviews you mention the influence of Conrad on your writing.

PC: Yes, but I didn't like him when I was in college. I believe we had to read Lord Jim for a course I took in my senior year. I took a graduate level course in the English novel, and I found Conrad just very difficult to get through. So in college, he was not any significant influence. I would say The Sun Also Rises, The Possessed [Dostoevsky], and The Brothers Karamazov. I remember being really captivated by The Heart of the Matter and The Power and the Glory [Graham Greene] and Moby-Dick.

H: At this point, had you read any war literature, for example A Farewell to Arms?

PC: Yes, I had read it. I know in college I read All Quiet on the Western Front.

H: Any of Wilfred Owen's poetry?

PC: Yes, except it didn't affect me then. It affected me later. I did read Wilfred Owen and Siegfried Sassoon. I really, really liked The Thin Red Line [James Jones]. I did like From Here to Eternity, but I liked The Thin Red Line even more.

H: Why?

PC: Even though From Here to Eternity is probably the better novel, I liked The Thin Red Line because there was more action in it. It was an actual war novel, whereas the other one was almost like a social novel, where the society being examined was the army.

H: You didn't read Mailer's *The Naked and the Dead?*

PC: Not then, I read Mailer later on. I wasn't too taken then with *The Naked and the Dead,* and I'm still not. Mailer is a genius, I think, as a journalist . . . *Armies of the Night* and *Executioner's Song*—those I thought were just magnificent. I read a lot of Jack London when I was in high school and college and really loved that stuff. I was listening to a Jack London tape on a cross-country drive earlier this year, and I was amazed at how good I thought he still was.

H: Any other events from this period of your life that influenced who you are and contributed to your development as a writer?

PC: Indirectly. I had a doomed love affair when I was twenty-one. It went on until I was in Vietnam, and I actually took up again with this woman for a while after I got back. I've never written about it, but there was (I wrote some poetry to her, which I would not show to a living soul now) something about that. I think it affected me in some indirect way—that first lost love.

Also an indirect shaping influence would have been the Cuban Missile Crisis [October 1962]. I took some classes in what was called the downtown campus of Loyola, and I was in the student union during the height of those thirteen days. All of a sudden the fire alarm went off, that claxon-like thing, and everybody was glued to radios and TVs because that was when the Russian ships were still coming toward Cuba, and our ships had set up the blockade. I remember this claxon goes off with that startling, horrible noise, and the whole union (it must have been six or seven hundred students in there at least) just went dead silent. Everybody had the same thought: that the balloon's gone up, there are nuclear missiles headed here, we're here in downtown Chicago, we're nineteen years old, and our lives are about thirty seconds away from ending. It was more than a sobering experience; it was, in a way, an embittering experience, I think, for someone that young. You had this sense that not only my petty little existence, but everything here, doesn't mean a goddamn thing. And the alarm turned out to be, by the way, a crossed wire in a circuit somewhere that set this thing off. But I remember that, and I think that must have given me, perhaps, a certain sense of doom or gloom, or something in my psychology, because I remember it so distinctly.

H: How did this sense of doom and gloom influence you as a potential writer?

PC: Let me put it this way. I said doom and gloom, but I think it made me think of things that nineteen-year-olds don't usually think of: what does my life mean, what is death, what is the matter with the human race that we have come to such a point here that we may now, the two biggest nations on earth, annihilate each other and perhaps a whole lot of other people?

H: Any other shaping experiences or influences?

PC: I think I had a bit of a chip on my shoulder that came from growing up in this sort of working-class, blue-collar family. Though I grew up mostly in suburbs, these were mostly working-class suburbs. . . . You still had to be kind of a tough guy to hold your own. Even the baseball games we used to play often would end up in fights. But I was aware of another world out there that I couldn't quite gain admittance to, the world of the privileged middle-upper class, or even middle class in some cases. A world of people who were more sure of themselves than I was because they had certain advantages that I didn't have. They knew that if things went wrong, Dad's money, Dad's position, or Dad's power would at least provide a cushion, if not prevent them from stumbling entirely. I don't know how much this would [help people] understand me as a writer, maybe as a person, because I've still got it. I still have that chip on my shoulder. I'm still that way about some of my colleagues, fellow writers, who I think have not taken their knocks. Maybe in some ways I feel they haven't really quite earned what they've got.

H: Did some of this chip-on-the-shoulder attitude come through with the character Nick DelCorso in your novel *DelCorso's Gallery?*

PC: Oh yes, it obviously did. It sure did. I'm aware of that—that was not unconscious.

H: For example, I'm thinking of Nick's relationship with his "classy" wife, her rich father, and Nick's boxing background in Chicago.

PC: Yes, there's a little bit of that, especially with my first wife. She was an elegant woman, a very well-educated woman. I think a lot of times around her (and she would remind me of it, too, every now and then when she felt like it) I always felt a little bit like I was crude and rough compared to her, and I probably was.

SOLDIER

H: What was your motivation in 1961 to join the Marine Platoon Leaders' Class?

PC: Well, partly it was the background I was just talking about. In those days, men from the higher social circles would join the navy. That was like the aristocratic service, and then the other guys just got drafted into the army. But if you were a marine, you were really somebody, so I think that that was part of the motivation. They had gorgeous uniforms. Also, one of my best buddy's uncles won the Silver Star with the Marine Corps at Tarawa, and I just thought that this guy was really cool, really a brave, tough guy who fought one of the toughest battles of World War II. And I wanted to be like that.

H: So you were attracted to the sense of adventure and the Marine Corps image?

PC: All of it—image, adventure.

H: What about patriotism as a motivation for enlisting?

PC: Oh sure. See patriotism was not, in those days, worn on the sleeve. We were in the depths of the cold war, and only twenty years had elapsed from V-E Day and V-J Day. That's not really long. So you were in constant contact with men who were now a part of the so-called "greatest generation." They had really done something, and we were aware, long before Tom Brokaw wrote about them, that they had done something that was extraordinary. I think we wanted to emulate them, so patriotism was definitely a part of it. Patriotism now has become this nauseatingly overt, artificial, canned thing—everybody with "God Bless America," with the ribbons on the cars. None of that existed then; it was almost part of your DNA. It wasn't conscious, but it was there, for sure.

H: Since your father didn't want you to enlist in the marines after high school, did he support this enlistment during college?

PC: Yes, he knew I'd finish college and I'd be an officer. A certain amount of social status was in his mind, I think—not that he was a status-conscious guy. But I think he thought it would be cool to say, "My son is a marine officer."

H: How would you respond to Tim O'Brien's comment on his decision to enter the military via the draft and later go to Vietnam, all despite his firm opposition to the Vietnam War: "I was a coward" (*If I Die in a Combat Zone*)?

PC: That's always been an interesting idea.

H: Obviously, you felt differently about entering the military and going off to war.

PC: Well, the big difference, among other things, between Tim and me is chronological. It's a peculiar chronology. I think Tim is five years younger than I am. That five years, however, was epical in the sense of the difference between an outlook that someone like him would have and an outlook that someone like me would have. I didn't feel that way because, again, no one in the early stages questioned the rightness of the Vietnam War or the rightness of going to war with a Communist government. That seemed like the right thing to do. So that kind of idea—that I would not go for reasons of conscience or principle—just was not on the radar screen. I can see his point, though. What he was saying is that all the social pressures from his small-town, midwestern background convinced him to act against his own deepest conscience. It was easier to go to war, easier to join the army and take that big step. . . . So I see what Tim's point is. I happened never to have faced that type of moral crisis, again because I was five years older than he was.

H: Once you entered the military, what were your OCS [Officer Candidate School] summers like—OCS Basic Training and OCS Advanced Course? Were you "playing at war"?

PC: Well, no. I remember it was really rigorous. It was tough, and, yes, you did war games and war exercises, which is playing at war. But the physical training and the psychological stress put on you were really pretty tough. I think we had a dropout rate of close to a third.

H: I have this image of marine boot camp from the movie Full Metal Jacket. Was your training similar?

PC: Yes, when I saw Full Metal Jacket, I remember telling my wife, "This is not a movie; this is a documentary." As a matter of fact, some of the physical training in OCS was tougher than that in marine boot camp. You weren't humiliated to the degree that enlisted men were, because they recognized that you were eventually going to be giving orders and thinking for yourself. But some of the physical training was much tougher—not just a little, but much tougher.

H: How did you manage to survive the experience and not drop out?

PC: Well, I was very healthy, because I had done a lot of sports sort of eclectically. I had played a little bit of football, played baseball. I wrestled at Purdue. I had been on the boxing team in high school. Even when I was at Loyola (Loyola did not have a wrestling or a boxing team), there was a YMCA near the downtown campus of Loyola that had a boxing team, and I joined that. I was in really good physical condition, so physically, it wasn't a problem. As a matter of fact, if I remember right, I think in OCS I scored fourth in the whole training battalion in physical fitness. Psychologically, the way I remember surviving is that during the first three days I was there [I felt] as if I had been run over by a semi-truck. I was just stunned. Those drill sergeants were so brutal. . . . It was so awful that I remember thinking, "What have I gotten myself into?" It was as if I had condemned myself to prison or something. Then I remember about day three looking around and seeing these other guys who I knew were physically softer than I was, or didn't seem to be mentally any tougher than I was. And I said, "Well, they're all bearing up under it somehow or another, and if they can, I can." It was an epiphany for me, and that's how I got through that part of it.

H: What did you learn about yourself during these first two stages of training?

PC: Basically, that I could take the worst they could throw at me, and not only survive it, but prevail.

H: So, overall, you would characterize these two summers as a valuable part of your character development?

PC: Yes, absolutely!

H: Did you choose your infantry MOS [Military Occupational Specialty]?

PC: Yes, I have a story that just shows how dumb I could be. I thought it would be a great thing to be a marine aviator, a fighter pilot. So my roommate and I took these tests to go to flight school. There was some part of this test that we did not pass to be a pilot, but we were qualified to be the guy in the back—the radar navigator, weapons officer, whatever. And my roommate applied for that and went to Pensacola. And I said, "Well, if I can't fly the fucking thing, I don't want to be in it." So my second choice was infantry. They said, "You can be an infantry officer." That's how I ended up as a grunt officer.

H: How was your experience in Officer's Basic School (summer 1964) different from the experiences of the previous two summers in OCS?

PC: By this time, you were an officer. You weren't fully an officer; but you were commissioned. We used to call ourselves "third lieutenants," but that harassment and that psychological pressure were no longer on you. Once again, by the way, the training was very, very rigorous—things like the confidence course and the obstacle course that you had to pass with a certain score. . . . So it was physically challenging. I can hardly call it intellectually challenging, but more mentally challenging, too. You had to take courses in military law, military tactics, military history, things like that.

H: At the end of the first chapter in A Rumor of War, you describe a "tableau of that innocent time before Vietnam" at the Marine Corps Birthday Ball that occurred during your training.

PC: Yes, I still remember that. It was great, though. These senior officers literally wearing blue capes with red lining and all of that. . . . The women were good-looking, and they were charming. And you were an officer who got to wear these cool-looking uniforms.

H: Was the Vietnam War discussed during this stage of training?

PC: Yes, because midway through Officer's Basic School came the Tonkin Gulf Resolution [August 1964], and that changed the atmosphere quite a bit. By that time, we knew where Vietnam was on a map.

H: Then was there a more serious approach to your training?

PC: Yes, I remember a fairly strong sense that we were going to end up in combat somewhere, and probably there [Vietnam].

H: Did this expectation excite you?

PC: Yes, part of it is that you train for this, so it would be as if you were on, I don't know, a football squad. You're constantly scrimmaging, but then you never get to play a game. You're trained for this, so you want to put that training to some use. You are competitive. You tend to make this false analogy between an athletic contest and war.

H: While you were in OCS, both the summer camps and then later the Officer's Basic School, were you reading any war literature?

PC: Yes (not in OCS because you had no time to read anything except manuals), at Basic School, because of the sense you were going to go to Vietnam, I read Bernard Fall's *Hell in a Very Small Place*, about the siege of Dienbienphu [1954]. There was a semi-manual book called *The Guerrilla and How to Fight Him*. I remember that it was by some colonel [Greene]. I read Caesar's *Gallic Campaigns* and a book about Alexander the Great, which had a magnificent chapter on Alexander's campaign against the Bactrians in what is now Afghanistan, which was counter-guerrilla warfare. I still remember being struck by a line I came across in that book that said that the insurgent's primary objective is to attack the enemy's state of mind. I remember being struck by that, and that certainly proved to be true. I read Sun Tzu's *The Art of War* and Clausewitz's *On War*.

H: So you were becoming a scholar of warfare?

PC: Yes, I was.

H: Was your motivation one of curiosity or the thought that all this reading would make you a better officer?

PC: Both. Some of this was, by the way, required reading. It wasn't as if I'd said, "I think I'll read von Clausewitz now; what a great way to relax!" That was required reading.

H: During your first few days in Vietnam [March 1965], what were your initial impressions of the land and the overall atmosphere of the place?

PC: It's such a cliché now, but my first impression was how god-awful hot it is. And my second impression was how beautiful it is. [Vietnam] didn't look as I had imagined a country at war would look. I guess I had imagined the way it ended up looking at the DMZ—shell craters, trenches, barbed wire all over the place. It was just this beautiful jade green and dark green landscape that really was captivating, especially when you saw the schoolgirls going to school, walking along the paddy dikes wearing their white *ao dais*. They really did look like angels floating across this green landscape.

H: What was the attitude among your fellow marines during these first few months in Vietnam?

PC: Oh, everybody was very gung-ho. Everybody thought that, as I wrote in *A Rumor of War*, the mere fact that we were there it [the war] was going to be over. These guys [Vietcong and North Vietnamese Army] were going to go, "Oh my god, the marines are here; we'd better quit."

H: In *Rumor* you describe a rather comic scene of some of the first marines landing in Vietnam.

PC: Yes, they came storming ashore Iwo-Jima style and got greeted by the mayor [Da Nang] and all these schoolgirls who put leis around their necks.

H: Think of the irony of that initial entrance compared with our country's ig-nominious retreat from Vietnam ten years later.

PC: Yes, juxtaposing the two is quite stunning.

H: Describe a typical day for you in the war during those first few months as an officer in charge of a rifle platoon.

PC: Well, the first couple months, a typical day was out at night checking lines, checking your perimeter. Then there'd be morning chow. Then there would be a daytime security patrol of squad-size strength, and you'd go out into the scrub for a distance and then come back and then basically do nothing. You would sit around in these foxholes and wait for something to happen. At night, there would probably be a night security patrol or two and again checking lines.

H: Do you remember the day of your first firefight?

PC: I think the first firefight was early April of '65. We landed by helicopter somewhere probably ten to twelve miles southwest of Da Nang. As we were landing, a Vietcong unit, probably of platoon-sized strength, opened fire on the landing site with small-arms fire, nothing heavy in the sense of mor-tars or rocket-propelled grenades. . . . I remember seeing the first platoon charging up this ridge at these guys and firing at them. It almost looked like a war exercise. And then Captain Peterson telling me and my platoon, Third Platoon, that we were to form up and sweep around the nose of this ridge and then envelop these guys from that flank. While we were doing that, our own mortars started firing on them. And the combination [of all of these tactics] drove them off the ridge and then down into this swamp, and then there was a bit of skirmishing back and forth going on. . . . But some of them [VC] were fleeing, and I remember suddenly (I'll never forget it) com-ing across the first person I'd actually seen killed in action. It was not one of our guys; it was one of their guys, a Vietcong. I almost tripped over him, and I remember him just lying there, the eyes staring up at me. . . . It was scary. I remember I had my pistol out, and at first I thought the guy was alive. Then, I realized he was dead.

H: After this first firefight, were you thinking that everyone and everything performed the way you had been trained?

PC: Yeah, in some ways I thought that. . . . It had that field exercise quality to it. The part that got me was seeing . . . those eyes just staring up at me from the mud with the blood and viscera coming out of the guy's body. Even though it was bad, it was the enemy, and you were just glad it was him and not you. It's a little bit of a shock. You think, "Holy shit; they don't die the way they do in the movies." And don't forget, by the way, this is pre–*Saving Private Ryan*. Guys used to die those balletic deaths in the World War II movies.

H: It's interesting that you vividly describe the physical aspects of death, which is something you constantly do in your books, for example the graphic scene in *DelCorso's Gallery* where the Christian militia are mutilated by Muslim militiamen.

PC: That actually happened. A lot of *DelCorso's Gallery* is journalism.

H: As an officer commanding a rifle platoon, what kind of relationship did you have with the enlisted men who were in your rifle platoon? Was there open officer–enlisted hostility?

PC: No. There always will be tension in any rigid, hierarchical class system; you'll always hear enlisteds say, "Those fucking officers." It happened in World War II. . . . But overall it was a fairly good-natured tension. There wasn't that murderousness, either in feeling or in actual fact, that occurred later on in Vietnam and probably, I would say, occurred more often in the conscript army than it did in the all-volunteer branches like the Marine Corps.

H: What types of relationships did you have with your own commanding officers?

PC: Some of those were good, and some of them were really bad. My second company commander, I loathed him because he was a jerk. He was cold, remote, and careless of what we were going for, and terribly concerned with his own career and where it was going. I loathed him because of that, not because he was a higher rank, because there were captains and majors whom I absolutely loved and colonels that I thought were great men and I would have, as the old saying goes, followed them off a cliff.

H: Did your fellow soldiers discuss the politics of the Vietnam War at this early stage of American involvement?

PC: Well, there weren't political discussions; there certainly were [discussions about our mission] because we were constantly getting these changing mission orders. After the first couple of weeks, we weren't sure what we were supposed to be doing over there. "You're going to defend the airfield. Well, no, now we're going to go after the Vietcong, but not really go after them. And now we're going to be doing this, and now . . ." There really was a lot of confusion as to what are we doing here. There were some grizzled old Korean and World War II vet NCOs who didn't like that place from the day they set foot on it. They took one whiff of the air and said, "This is all wrong." I remember an old gunnery sergeant named Stone. This guy had a face that looked like it'd been run over by an Amtrak. He'd been in Korea; he'd been in the battle of Okinawa. I remember him looking around one day, and he says, "You know, lieutenant, this place ain't worth one fucking life that we've got in this battalion." And that was in 1965.

H: Are there any particular places in Vietnam (cities, villages) that you particularly remember?

PC: There was this village or complex of villages west of Da Nang down this river called the Vu Gia River. These villages or hamlets were Vietcong strongholds, so we were always getting ambushed, shot at, booby-trapped, anytime you went there.

H: Is it in this area where the climactic incident, as described in the final chapters of *Rumor*, occurs involving the shooting of suspected VC near the village of Giao Tri?

PC: Near it.

H: Were this incident and its aftermath the most difficult experiences for you in Vietnam?

PC: Yes, without question.

H: What does that incident epitomize about your experience in Vietnam?

PC: Well, about my experience, it illustrates how you can become something you never thought you would become, without being aware of the transformation. That there is evil in you, or violence in you, or both—which you're not fully aware of—and that it can sneak up and in effect posses you, or snatch your soul.

H: Was this experience similar to one of Conrad's heart-of-darkness experiences that he often introduces into his fiction?

PC: Oh, yes. Absolutely. I had to read *Lord Jim* in college, and I didn't like it. But after I got back from Vietnam, I went through *Lord Jim* as if it were a comic book. It just flowed so easily. I understood levels that I had never perceived before because of that experience [Giao Tri]. In some ways the experience was close to Lord Jim's because it still represents to me a failure on my part as an officer, and so I related to Jim's perceived failure of himself as a seaman when [he and his crew] abandoned the pilgrims. This was that heart-of-darkness experience. Again, you go there [Vietnam] and think of yourself in the highest terms. You think of your mission, or what you're doing, in the highest terms, and then you find out that the mission and you are something you never thought you would be or that it would be. That encapsulated the whole experience for me.

H: Has this disillusioning experience stayed with you in your life and writing?

PC: Sure, I think in some ways. Perhaps it's not a good thing that it has because I think I'm too cynical, too suspicious of everybody's motives. If somebody tells me something or if somebody presents himself to me as a certain somebody, right away I wonder about what lies I'm being told now. And I think I might be too quick to raise those (they're not exactly judgments) suspicions.

H: Conrad in *Heart of Darkness* also comments on the inexplicable "fascination of the abomination": Although repelled by the evil, death, and horror, participants in the horror also find something attractive, exhilarating, fascinating about the whole dark experience—an adrenaline rush, a sense of satisfaction in performing well, a gratifying of primitive urges. Did you experience or observe any of these phenomena? Does this fascination ever emerge as a theme in any of your writing?

PC: Yes, I think that's what a lot of political liberals, to put the label on them, miss the point about when we discuss the subject of war, especially war literature. They want books to be antiwar; they want their journalism to be antiwar, and I've said this myself. TV should present the war for the way it really is, like the Iraq war, or the newspaper should be more graphic. But what this attitude or perspective lacks is the knowledge that, generally speaking, the more satanic something is, the more attractive it becomes. One would think that as a nightmarish, hellish, satanic experience, nothing could ever exceed World War I. Just millions of men annihilated in a space that's equivalent from here [Norwalk] to Boston, and yet when you read literature of World War I, you see that a lot of those guys who fought in it were nostalgic for it after the fact. Conrad calls it a fascination of the abomination, or there's a lurid fascination to war.

H: Does this attraction occur in the midst of the battle or is it more a nostalgic response years later?

PC: It's both, but it certainly occurs in the midst of battle. I remember seeing this valley [in Vietnam] that was just being obliterated by us. I remember standing on this hill, and there were seven or eight dead Americans in body bags lying there. Some of them weren't even in body bags yet. But they were already stiffened up, and their arms were [outstretched]. There were some wounded

Vietnamese, and then there were some wounded North Vietnamese soldiers and Vietcong who were being taken prisoner and blindfolded. I remember one guy actually had blood coming out of his blindfold across his eyes, and they were spinning him around to disorient him further before they put him on the helicopter to take him wherever they were taking him. All along this valley, these villages had been bombed and shelled because they had been attacking us and attacking our operation. And you saw these planes swooping down, and the napalm going. It was in some odd way beautiful. I said this in *Acts of Faith* where, I think, Quinette [one of the main characters] witnesses the bombing of the hospital. She says that it's as if when ugliness and horror are taken to a certain extreme, [the scene] obtains a kind beauty unto itself.

H: Certainly, this tension between the fascinating nature of war and its abhorrent evil is an important theme in *DelCorso's Gallery* with its central characters being war photojournalists.

PC: Yes, Dunlop's [the older combat photographer's perspective of war] is honor, glory, or elegy, but in some way or another seeking to evoke a higher beautiful emotion in people even if it's of a deep, deep sadness of a tragedy. DelCorso [the Vietnam veteran and younger combat photographer] is basically trying to make everybody sick, in the truest sense of the term: to look at this thing and say, "I don't care how luridly attractive this is; this is absolute horror, and no one who calls himself a human being should have anything to do with this. . . . And I want to rub your [his audience's] nose in it."

H: Moving to a different emotion curiously linked with war, what did you learn about love in Vietnam?

PC: Well, there is this love between men in battle that we call camaraderie that really is love, but 99 percent of the time anyway, without an erotic element to it. Probably because the circumstances demanded it, it seems stronger than in fact an erotic bond between a man and a woman or, for that matter, between two men. From what I've read about Alexander's army, it seemed to work there, the erotic bond that is. But I thought it [camaraderie in Vietnam] was stronger mainly because it didn't have an erotic or physical component to it; it was more spiritual.

H: Tell me about your writing activities while you were in Vietnam. I read that you kept an unauthorized diary in your footlocker in base camp.

PC: Yes, it was unauthorized.

H: Why was keeping a diary forbidden by the Marine Corps?

PC: The thinking was that should your position get overrun, the enemy could confiscate this diary and use it either for propaganda purposes or intelligence purposes or both.

H: What were you writing in your diary?

PC: I would write down what happened and my impressions of what happened.

H: Did this diary later provide the raw material for A Rumor of War?

PC: Yes, that and the letters I wrote home [to family].

H: What were you attempting to do in the letters?

PC: Well, to give them an idea without scaring them. These letters were self-censored as to what was going on over there. Sometimes, I just wanted them to see what Vietnam looked like, and I would describe the countryside.

H: While you were keeping this diary, were you planning to use this diary and write a book about your experiences?

PC: No. What I knew I was doing was partly trying to sort things out in my own mind. I forget who said that a man should know his own mind. And a good way to know your own mind is to write down what you're thinking. I knew that this [the war] was an experience that was unusual to say the least, and I wanted to preserve it. I didn't want all of those events and experiences to just pass into oblivion, which they would do eventually, although my memory of a lot of that is remarkably clear, I must say, to this day.

H: Was the diary part of this process of developing self-awareness and consciousness?

PC: Yes, I think so—analysis of the situation. It was also a way to blow off steam: pissed off at some officer, pissed off at something.

H: From your time in country during the war, what are your lasting impressions of the Vietnamese people?

PC: Well, considering my early impression was that they were very enigmatic and inscrutable, I found them to be very enterprising, very hardworking people, very disciplined. And based on my second and third trips there after the war in 1990 and 1999, they're very engaging, certainly forgiving. When I returned, it was like, "We just love you Americans even though you blew the hell out of this place," [a response] that I never could quite fathom. I love their sense of their history and their culture. They're very aware of that. I know when I went to the temple of literature in Hanoi (well, it's not strictly a temple to literature; it's really a temple to scholarship) in 1990, they staged a poetry reading at which a couple of guys I was with, like Yusef [Komunyakaa] and Bill Ehrhart read their poetry, and then the Vietnamese read theirs. The crowd that filled that hall, it was as if they were going to see rock stars. So I was very impressed by the depth of their culture and the sense of their history. Generally speaking, I like them very much.

H: What are your lasting impressions of the land?

PC: The impressions are of its captivating beauty and its sense of timelessness. I hope the place never gets too developed. I want everybody there to be prosperous and all of that. But I hope to hell it doesn't turn into some kind of Thailand coast resort. It is so magical and so beautiful with the landscape and the cities, the really good cities like Hoi An, which has this history going back to the days of the Portuguese conquerors and beyond that to the days of Japanese colonists.

H: Upon leaving Vietnam in July 1966, how were you a different person from the one who entered Vietnam one year earlier?

PC: I would say that whoever I was when I went there died and that I was reborn. We hear a lot now about born-again Christians, but that [my Vietnam experience] really was a death and a rebirth. I would say that the big difference, in a phrase, was that I was a child when I landed in Vietnam, a child not so much in the sense of innocence as lacking in self-awareness and consciousness. But after all, that's what a child is. . . . Not until you're older do you become aware of yourself as a separate and distinct being. And I think that when I came out of Vietnam, I was now aware of myself, but beyond myself, of the full dimensionality of human nature.

H: When did you decide to write *A Rumor of War*?

PC: Sometime while I was at Camp Lejeune [North Carolina]. I had written two war poems while I was in Vietnam, and they got published in a university quarterly called the *Midwestern University Quarterly* in the spring of 1966. Whether that planted the seed of writing *A Rumor of War*, I don't know. Then, when I got back to Camp Lejeune [July 1966], I wrote another one or two war poems. I remember one night I woke up in the Bachelor Officers Quarters at about two o'clock in the morning because I heard the sound that had become so much a part of me. It was that sound of artillery in the distance, or mortar fire, and I almost did a flashback. Then I realized it was a field exercise going on somewhere. But I remember I couldn't get back to sleep after that, and in my wakefulness I wrote this poem about this experience. So somewhere in writing those poems and then in that aftermath experience, evolved this idea of writing this book. And I know I had actually begun writing it at Camp Lejeune in the late winter of '67. Even then, I called it *A Rumor of War*. I don't remember exactly when I came across that quote from St. Matthew [epigraph for the book, Matthew 24:6–13], but it just struck me. It started off as a novel, and I probably wrote at Lejeune fifty, sixty, possibly a hundred [pages]. By that time, I knew I wanted to write this thing. It was a case of figuring out how to write it. What I didn't know at that time was that you had to be in a kind of a fit mental or psychological condition to write about an experience like that, and to get into that condition takes time to get the perspective you need.

H: At this time at Camp Lejeune you were CO of a company training infantry soldiers, many of whom would end up in Vietnam? Did you feel guilty in this assignment given your belief at that point that the war was "senseless" [Rumor, 15] and your knowledge of the horrors that awaited these young men?

PC: No, I didn't feel guilty. What I felt was that I've got to train these guys to survive this thing. That's part of what bothered me; it was a whole range of things. . . . The training was totally divorced from reality. It was, at times, a joke; in fact, we joked about it. . . . And the bad thing was, I knew at the time (a time when the battles that were going on were called the hill fights in the DMZ area, and as a matter of fact, my old regiment was involved in that and took very heavy casualties in those hill fights) the Marine Corps was then hitting a casualty rate that actually exceeded marine casualties in World War II. So these guys [trainees] were canon fodder. They were being fed into this machine that was just going to eat them up, and that's what I felt bad about.

By the way, the other thing that bothered me was, again, because the Corps was taking such a whacking, we were taking in guys, a little bit like now [Iraq War], who would not have been allowed into the service two years before, either for mental, physical, or some other psychological reasons.

H: Once you left the military in May 1967, other than a later war-protest letter to President Nixon, did you get involved with any war-protest groups, including the Vietnam Veterans Against the War [VVAW] led by John Kerry?

PC: None, other than the VVAW, which I did formally join. I worked [journalist] around a couple of war protests. I actually didn't like most of the antiwar people and still don't.

H: Why?

PC: Well, I thought they were a bunch of self-righteous, ignorant idiots. They hadn't been there; they didn't know what was going on. And I sensed even then a lot of this protest was just like some version of a college prank that now had a distinct political tinge to it. I didn't like a lot of their politics. . . . The war was an excuse, in their view, to revolutionize American society. I thought anybody who thinks that this country is ripe for a true revolution is an idiot, is a dangerous idiot. I didn't like them, so I didn't really get involved with them.

H: Around this time what were your feelings about John Kerry's testifying against the war in congressional hearings and members of the VVAW throwing their medals onto the Capitol steps?

PC: Well, insofar as throwing the medals, I sent my combat ribbons to Nixon [April 1971]. My feeling, right or wrong, was that I didn't think the war was right, and I thought the war at that point certainly was pointless. But only those who had been there really had the true moral right, even if others had the legal right, to protest the war and to demonstrate against it, so that's how I felt about that. During the [2004 presidential] campaign, I was reminded of a lot of Kerry's testimony when he was a young man. Looking at it now, I think some of it was true, but some of it was really intemperate. He made it sound as if everybody over there was some kind of baby-killing atrocity committer, or something like that. That was completely off base—not that he made it sound that way, but it came across that way. But when he was calling attention to some of the awful things that were going on there, he was right.

H: Do you remember what you said in your protest letter to President Nixon?

PC: The basic gist of it was (it was kind of a sarcastic letter) I reminded him (I believe I did) that he had pledged to get us out of Vietnam, and now two years later we're still there and even in deeper. I said something to the effect that this is really the Vietnamese's war to win or lose, and not ours, and something to the effect that maybe one way to get out of the war is if in fact all these guys your age, all these congressmen, are subject to the draft and all the young men come home. Then, I said, if you gotta go, I bet the war would be over in a week—something like that.

H: In your Vietnam aftermath novel, *Indian Country*, you focus on the central character's war-related post-traumatic stress disorder. During this immediate post-Vietnam period in your life, did you experience PTSD symptoms?

PC: I probably did, but didn't notice it. It's kind of like you're not sick if you don't know you are. I undoubtedly did; I called it "combat veteranitis," the spells of black depression, then anger and rage. I undoubtedly experienced those symptoms, but I think that every war veteran does.

H: Upon your return, did you talk with other Vietnam vets about your experiences?

PC: No.

H: Why not—embarrassed, hesitant to talk about them?

PC: Well, yes, a little bit, because again it might have been my peculiar experiences—having been involved in that incident [Giao Tri] and having this perception of oneself as somebody who's capable of killing somebody like that. So it was partly an embarrassment that arose out of that incident, not that I would have gone and admitted it to people. But I think the main thing is that I felt that I had come back from another planet somewhere, the features of which were indescribable to people who had remained on this planet. There was no point in even talking to them about it because they would never understand what I was talking about and they tended to look at that experience through some particular artificial prism imposed on their own eyes: "Yes, we must fight the Communists," or on the antiwar front, "We [Americans] were a bunch of imperialistic exploiters." There was always some ideological box or prism, as I say, that they were looking at it [the war] through. Nobody would understand what the emotional reality of it was, and at that point, I hardly understood it myself.

H: Was *A Rumor of War* your attempt to get people to understand the war and to see and feel it removed from that ideological prism?

PC: Yes, I wanted to recreate the experience on the page, in all of its dimensions, especially in its physical dimensions. I really did follow what Conrad had said in the preface to the *Nigger of the Narcissus*, when he said that it is the writer's obligation, or the writer's duty (however he put it), to make the reader see. And if the reader then sees, then the reader can find whatever he wants in there. I wanted readers to see, feel, and experience Vietnam as I had, as much as is possible. That's why I was so tactile in that book. I wanted everybody to feel what it's like in the heat, in the mosquitoes, in the blackness of the night, in the sudden eruptions of gunfire out of the jungle, so that, in effect, we would now say (we didn't use those words back then) they were on a virtual tour of duty themselves. That's what I would call it now. That's what I wanted to do.

H: Despite some minor PTSD symptoms and a reluctance to talk about your experiences in Vietnam, why did you adjust relatively well upon your return when other Vietnam veterans were having problems?

PC: Well, I think education was part of it. A lot of people who adjusted badly usually had a foreshortened education. And the family I came from wasn't broken up; there were no divorces. The religious background was important. Even if the universe isn't coherent, religion gives you a coherent view of the universe and at least forces you to try to make sense out of experiences. All of that, I believe, made a big difference.

H: Did you return with a continuing "fascination of the abomination" that later led you into numerous war situations as a war correspondent and writer?

PC: Yes, I think so.

H: Do participants get "hooked" on war and conflict?

PC: Yes, they do, although hooked might not be quite the right word. People call them adrenaline junkies. There was an excellent TV program about female war correspondents not too long ago. They asked one [female correspondent], "Why do you keep covering war?" She was covering Iraq, and I think she'd been captured once, held for a week and nearly executed. She said, "I'm trying to understand the nature of evil and violence, and that's what keeps drawing me back." She said, "It's like there's something here and that if I keep doing this, I'm going to understand something." I think she got to the point where she realized she wasn't going to come to this epiphany, but that's a big part of the fascination—there's this satanic evil, but it's something I should understand and I want to understand, if I can. So you're drawn back toward it. There's no doubt that the excitement is a powerful element as well. For me, however, it was always this idea that not only would I understand something on the nature of moral evil, but maybe I would also understand, as a result of that, something about human nature: In those extreme circumstances, when all pretenses are stripped away of who we think we are, we will see the naked soul, the naked self.

H: What was it like—feelings, perspective—returning to Vietnam in April 1975 as a journalist reporting on the fall of Saigon and the South Vietnamese government? After experiencing Vietnam as a combatant, were you able as a reporter to view events objectively?

PC: The emotions were there: sometimes a certain kind of anger and bitterness, also a lot of conflicting feelings—like a sense of relief that it was finally over combined with a wish that it would be over in some other way, which is to say, a way more favorable to our side. I admit that [feeling] was more for personal reasons; just thinking that all your friends died for no reason at all is a hard pill to swallow. So all of those ambivalent emotions were there, but as a journalist you control them. I did write a story that was a news feature from Saigon. It was in the form of a letter to the two guys whom I dedicated A Rumor of War, although [the book] wasn't written at that point. It was a letter to [Sergeant John] Sullivan and [First Lieutenant Walter] Levy telling them what was going on, as if I'd written to them in heaven. There was a kind of bitterness in [the story].

H: Are the scenes in your novel DelCorso's Gallery of those final days in Saigon more journalism than fiction?

PC: Yes, it's quasi-documentary. I'd call it a docudrama if it were TV.

H: Finally, what did your Vietnam War experiences contribute to your development as an author?

PC: Well, I can only speculate on what I would have done had I not gone there. In all likelihood I would have become (and I think probably a fairly good one) a journalist and may have written a couple of books, either nonfiction or perhaps a couple of rather small collections of short stories. I would not have been what I am now, so this experience totally made me whatever I am now, for better or worse. It made me the kind of writer I am, and it probably made me a writer.

AUTHOR

H: Soon after your departure from the military in 1967, you became a journalist working as a general assignment reporter, investigative reporter, and eventually a war correspondent. Did your experiences as a journalist aid you in your career as a literary writer?

PC: Yes. I think the literary writing I do is characterized by, among other things, a great attention to detail, which is vital in literature. And the training you get as a reporter trains you to observe these details and to note them down, whether in your mind or on a piece of paper. So it helped that way, and I certainly think that (not so much in hard news writing, but news-feature writing, where you try to create an atmosphere or set a scene) is very valuable for a novelist or a short story writer. . . . Too long a time in journalism works against you in the sense that you get too used to imparting information, and a novelist is really supposed to dramatize situations. You're supposed to show a situation as it unfolds rather than, as they say, tell it, and journalism is basically about telling not showing.

H: What made you decide in 1977 to give up your full-time career in journalism and turn to freelance reporting and literary writing?

PC: Part of the reason was I had gotten this contract to do *Horn of Africa*, and in fact I was not going to give up journalism, straightaway. I was going to stay with the paper or with some other paper. But I had asked the foreign editor for a leave of absence so I could finish this novel, and [the paper] wouldn't give it to me. So basically I just said, "Well in that case, I quit." Why did I quit? Well, I wanted to do this novel. I not only had gotten the advance, but it was a story I wanted to tell [based on experiences as a correspondent in Sudan and Ethiopia]. I knew from having written *A Rumor of War* while I was employed elsewhere that if I tried that with this novel I'd be working on it for ten years, especially given the kinds of schedule that a foreign correspondent is on.

H: How do you begin a literary writing project? Is there a method you use to generate the outline of the story, or does the story just come to you?

PC: Well, I have to be open to ideas, both for characters and stories. Once an idea occurs to me, whether it's for a character or a story, I'll start a notebook and start writing whatever thoughts start coming into my head. Then, at some point, I try to write to myself, if to no one else, about a one-page synopsis of what I'm going to try to do in this novel and who's going to be in it. It may be that the final book doesn't resemble that [synopsis] in the slightest. And I don't have a method, but there will come a point in this process where I become full of the character, full of the story. The story and the character or characters begin almost to demand to be let out, and that's when I'll start writing. Sometimes, I have to prime the pump to get to that moment. Sometimes I start writing and end up with a few pages in a kind of a dead end, and then I have to back up and start over again.

H: Is there usually a moral, thematic or character center serving as a starting point for your initial writing?

PC: Character or a story, and often those two are so intertwined that I can't really separate them.

H: What are your writing habits? Do you have a routine?

PC: Yes, when I'm working on a book, I get up fairly early in the morning and after a couple of cups of coffee (I usually need those to get going) start writing. I'll write six, seven, eight hours a day. Sometimes, if I'm really hot and all that, I'll write much longer.

H: Do you literally write the story or compose directly at the computer?

PC: I do journalism [at the computer], but the books I write, especially fiction, I have to write them out longhand, and it's probably a superstition at this point.

H: The journalism just flows on to the computer?

PC: Yes, it's almost as if I don't really care that much.

H: So for the books, it's the craft aspect, that attention to detail, that you are more concerned with?

PC: Somehow, I feel that I can craft sentences better and think better if I've got a pencil in my hand, rather than staring at that screen.

H: Do you work from the notes compiled in your notebook?

PC: Yes, sometimes I do.

H: What's the shortest time in completing a book? The longest?

PC: The longest time was this last one, Acts of Faith, which was four years. The shortest time was just a little under a year for the collection of novellas I did, Exile. I think I did that in about eight months.

H: Why did you decide to write in the novella genre?

PC: Well, I regret to say that it's not an American form. Europeans like the short novel, but Americans sure don't. They will take a short story, a collection of short stories, before they'll do that, but I find it just a wonderful form for me. . . . I'm not naturally a short-story writer. You would think being an ex-newspaperman, I would be, but I'm not. But not everything I think of is a full-length novel. A lot of stuff is shorter, but it's not short enough to be a short story. That's why I love that novella form. I had these stories to tell, and that was the form they took. But, good Lord, if you tell an editor or an agent that you're doing this [novella] collection, they just groan because they know they're not going to sell anything, and they don't. If you sell five thousand copies of one of those things, you consider yourself lucky.

H: What makes a good short-story writer?

PC: I think it is the ability to bring a character alive or a situation alive in a very brief period of time, and it probably comes close to being a poet. Every last word has to justify itself. There's no room in there for any excess, any fat. . . . I'm going to try it as a hobby. I want to see if I can do it.

H: How would you characterize the literary writing that you do?

PC: I'd say I'm a traditional or a classical novelist of morals.

H: Does this description suggest that your writing focuses on traditional moral conflicts—an exploration of human nature when confronted by good and evil?

PC: Yes, that's the essence of what I write about.

H: Did your experience in Vietnam of discovering that evil in yourself shape so much of what you write about?

PC: Yes, no question.

H: Compare yourself with other contemporary authors who write about war, for example O'Brien, Heinemann, and Butler.

PC: I do not consider myself a war novelist or really a war writer, even though I am associated with that genre. I have used war or warlike situations as a stage or backdrop against which these moral questions that are my chief concern are played out. And I think that would distinguish me from [John] Del Vecchio or Heinemann, who write about war qua the war. It would distinguish me from Tim in the sense that Tim also uses war to say other things, but the things he's trying to say are different from the things I'm trying to say. He seems a more emotional writer than I am. That's a funny word to use, and I don't mean Tim sits around bawling or something. There's a kind of tenderness in him and toward his characters and in the emotions he presents that I don't deal with. He'll use war as a stage, or a backdrop, against which usually some character is playing out some kind of psychological or emotional conflict, as in that officer [Jimmy Cross] in "The Things They Carried." That's such a grand story. [Jimmy is] just so wrapped up in his lost love and his love life that in effect he gets somebody killed and then realizes all that has to be put aside. If you were to describe that [story] as I have just done, it sounds like some kind of hokey theme, or something you'd write in a military manual about "an officer must not be distracted from his duty and obligations." The way he wrote that was very effective, but [Jimmy] is playing out a different sort of drama than my characters play out.

H: We talked earlier about important books in your reading life. Are there particular writers who have influenced your writing?

PC: Well, the guy right up there above your head [points to a collection of Conrad's novels on a shelf]. I am just drawn to them, and I think some of them influence me to a point that is probably not healthy in some ways for a writer. They haunt me. Conrad is one. [Graham] Greene is another one. V. S. Naipaul is another one.

H: What links among these writers appeal to you?

PC: The focus on the moral issues and the exotic settings or exotic situations. They seem to be drawn to these edgy places the same way that I am because I think in these edgy places the inner man or woman comes into a sharper focus.

H: Writing a so-called domestic story is not interesting to you?

PC: No, I've always wanted to do that. I admire people who do that, like Ann Beattie, whom I know. But the domestic drama, the story about love relationships, I've always admired writers who can do that. One of the best [novels] I've ever read like that was Ian McEwan's *Atonement*. God, I thought that was good. I'd love to be able to do that, but I can't. In other words, I don't really feel that in my marrow, and I know that. It's something that would be neat to do, but I think it would be artificial if I tried it.

H: For aspiring writers is that an important lesson for them to learn—what they can write authentically about and what they can't?

PC: There's the old saying that you should write what you know, but I don't totally agree with that. I think you should write about what moves you the most. What excites or engages your passions is what the writer should write about. For a young writer, the only way to find that out is to keep trying different things until you find someplace where you know you are expressing your innermost self. But I think forcing yourself, after you've reached that stage, to try to write something else is probably a mistake.

H: Somewhat related to your comment about writing what one knows is a quote by Tim O'Brien in our 1995 interview: "Everything that I am doing flows out of the life I have led. And the life I have led is a life of finding it hard to distinguish within myself and without about what's true and what's not." How would you respond to this notion as it relates to your own life and writing?

PC: Well, that's Tim's aesthetics, not really mine. I don't have that experience. Certainly the kind of writing I do is a direct result, yes, of the life I've led, the places I've been, the experiences I have had, and the people I have encountered. All of these experiences, places, and people have involved, in one way or another, these deep moral questions. Maybe what I'm trying to do in my writing is to find out the bedrock truth of a character or characters: exploring what about them is a false costume and who the true person is. That's what I am interested in. I've got a character in *Acts of Faith*, Fitzhugh, who reflects toward the end of the novel that each of us is a half truth, that the self we present to the world is not really the full self, that there's another self that lies within us waiting its moment to be born. And it's being in the places and the circumstances where those births take place that fascinates me.

H: Are there times through this combination of fact (real events in your life) and fiction in your writing, you are also trying to discover truths about yourself?

PC: Oh, I think that. Writing any novel is a kind of voyage of discovery. It may not be so much truths about your own character, but certainly truth about what do I really believe, what do I really think about this situation or this character? And writing a novel is an exploration. I don't think one sets out to do that, but it's an inevitable part of the whole process.

H: Related to this discussion of the relationship between your life and your writing, explain the term "imaginative autobiography" that you used to describe the narrative content of your journalism memoir *Means of Escape*.

PC: Yes, a grave error on my part. I should have never, ever said that because it really pissed a lot of people off, like Morley Safer, even though he wrote a very admirable review of [the book] in the end, and Harrison Salisbury, whom I really admire. There's a new edition of [*Means of Escape*] where I foreshorten all of that stuff. Those interchapter episodes, called the "Disasters of War," are fictional or semifictional sketches, generally semifictional. They are drawn from experiences I've had, but in some way rearranged for an emotional effect. Were I to transcribe the real experiences, they wouldn't have the emotional effect I wanted. The autobiographical parts are memoirs with whatever distortions or omissions that one will commit by relying strictly on memory. As you can tell, in even talking to you I can't remember certain dates about where I was and things like that. But even with that said, the thing that strikes me about autobiography or memoir is that you're going to have a selective process; you're going to select things that you write about, and that selection is partly a function of the imagination because you're imagining, whom am I presenting here? What sort of story am I telling here? Maybe, to a greater or lesser degree, the character of yourself that you present in an autobiographical work, one that's not fiction, is often a reflection of who you are now, maybe not who you were then. It's how you see yourself looking back, and it's bent through a different prism than you had thirty or forty years ago. I was trying to get that idea across, but again, everybody just jumped all over me on that one.

H: Such a discussion of facts, memory, selection, perspective, and imagination seems to speak also to the myth of the reporter's objectivity in journalism—any reporter is viewing an event or person through a unique prism and is selecting certain details for a story influenced by who he or she is and the situation under which he or she is writing.

PC: Or who the editor is. . . . Of course the purely objective videotape [or print story] of an event just simply doesn't exist. In fact, if it did, nobody would read a newspaper, and nobody would watch the TV news, because it would be formless and boring. You would see things blowing up or somebody doing this or somebody doing that, and you'd say, "Well, what does all this mean? What is the context?" It's the reporter who creates the context.

H: Somewhat related to all of these issues of fact and fiction is Tim O'Brien's use of the concepts of happening truth and story truth, where a happening truth involves the facts of an event and story truth focuses on the emotional truths. You seem to view your writing in a similar way.

PC: Oh yes. In fact, last night [at a reading of *Acts of Faith*] I was talking with someone who asked what my objective is as a novelist. And I said it is to convey the emotional truth of a situation.

H: How do you know when you achieve that presentation of an emotional truth? And how does a reader know if it's true?

PC: There's no objective standard or scale as far as the writer goes. I know when I write something whether it sounds or feels false. Sometimes the sound is faint, and sometimes the feeling is faint. But if it's there at all, I know I have to listen to it or I have to respond to it because it does mean that something's wrong. [It is] almost an instinct, some innate sense that something is not true. Within the context of the story, maybe I've forced the character to act out of character. Maybe I'm saying something that I think I should be saying, but not what I really want to say. Whatever the case may be, I just know when I'm writing the truth, especially an emotional truth.

I would say that probably the same thing [occurs] for a reader. When I pick up *Anna Karenina*, the reason that novel has lasted for so long is because it is so true. Anna Karenina, though her circumstances don't even vaguely resemble those of most modern middle-class, middle-aged women, is every woman who has ever desired something more than what she's got and is willing to risk it all for [that desire]. And I just know that's true when I read it. As a reader, I have an instinctive response, and as a writer I have an instinctive response.

H: Can writers be trained to develop this "truth detector"?

PC: No, a built-in, shock-proof bullshit detector is what you have to have, and I think it is built-in.

H: And its presence may be one major difference between the great writers and average ones?

PC: Yes, I think so. It certainly is one of the distinguishing characteristics.

H: Earlier, I asked you about some of your contemporary American soldier-authors; have you read any Vietnam War literature written by Vietnamese soldier-authors?

PC: I read *The Sorrow of War* [Bao Ninh].

H: How did you respond to that novel?

PC: Well, I was rather captivated by it, fascinated by it, just by seeing the other side. I'm hedging a little on my judgments of it because I don't really know how good the translation was. I have a Vietnamese friend who speaks excellent English, a postwar Vietnamese poet, and he was reciting one of his poems. It was another one of these everybody dies and the lovers don't get together, and I said, "Why is all this Vietnamese stuff so mournful?" And he talked about how [Vietnam] has been this very sad country from war to war, storm to storm. The impression I got from *The Sorrow of War* had that kind of elegiac, sad tone to it, throughout, which I very much like. But it's unusual that this is the victorious side writing.

H: What makes a good story?

PC: To my mind, a good story is a narrative about a character who engages and fascinates the reader, and ultimately, and (I'm borrowing here from a conversation I had with Bill Styron years ago) the very best of stories, whether it's a novel or a short story, [has a] character who will never be cast into oblivion.

H: Is this need for an engaging character true for a good memoir, also?

PC: Yes, it's where the creative part and the imaginative part in memoir are. You've got to make yourself an interesting person.

H: In such life-writing, how does one move beyond the facts to the emotions?

PC: Let's focus on A *Rumor of War* for a minute because it's not fiction. When I was writing it, I had these diaries and I had the letters home to refresh my memory. I would try also to remember what I felt in some particular situation. Then, what I tried to do was to recreate the sequence of events that led me to that moment. That to me is how you create the emotion without stating the emotion. The greatest example of that, to my mind, in modern literature is the opening sequence to Hemingway's "Big Two-Hearted River." I remember reading that in school, and then after I got back from Vietnam and was in France hanging around those cafés where Hemingway wrote, I was reading it again. I wondered what was going on when I had read it in school, but that scene when he [Nick] sees those trout and Hemingway says "Nick felt all the old feelings," I knew exactly what he meant. I knew that this guy [Nick] had been somewhere that just cauterized his soul and he's trying to restore himself. I still get chills when I think of that opening experience.

H: Back to the subject of memoir, is there a danger that in this type of life-writing the narrator becomes too self-absorbed, concerned primarily with confession and self-analysis?

PC: There is a danger. I just finished reading the galleys to a reporter's memoir from Iraq. He was a really funny guy, so there's a lot of black humor in it. But he was so absorbed in why am I here? What am I doing here? What am I trying to prove? This solipsism was evidenced on every page. After a while, I started to almost scream at the book, "Where's the fucking war? How about writing about something other than yourself and what particular emotional drama you're going through at the moment?" In other words, he got so self-involved that it's almost as if this event exists so we can see this man's inner turmoil, which we're not interested in.

H: We talked earlier about what makes a good story. Are the same features necessary for a good war story—an engaging character and emotions that ring true?

PC: Yes.

H: Are there additional characteristics of the good war story, for example a realistic presentation of war?

PC: It doesn't have to be necessarily a realistic presentation of war. I go back to what I said before. It's manifesting truth about the characters in the situations, which means that you have to get the inner truth or the emotional truth of the situation across. I would write it realistically because that's the way I am, but a different example is *Going After Cacciato*. This is not a realistic presentation, by anybody's standards, except for those situations of Paul Berlin on watch. But it's all true. Now what's true about it? What's true is this yearning for escape from this dreadful situation. This is Paul Berlin's fantasy that Cacciato actually made it [walks to Paris], and that's true of many warriors when they're in their particular conflict. They want to get out of it; they want to escape it somehow, even though most of them will not. [That novel] is an example of presenting an unrealistic treatment of a truth.

H: Are all good war stories antiwar?

PC: No, the *Iliad* is a great war story, and it seems to glory in the violence of what's going on, but it ends up antiwar. If you write about war truthfully, [the story] will not say this is a wonderful experience that all of you should have at some time or another. Even Homer or Virgil glory in the bloodshed, but by the time you're through, by the time Achilles is crowing over the body of dead Hector, you're just about ready to regurgitate—all of this gore and this violence. [Homer] has written about it with a great deal of emotional honesty, so it's antiwar in that sense. . . . Actually if you set out consciously to write an antiwar story, you're going to write a bad war story because it's not going to be a story; it's going to be propaganda.

H: In *DelCorso's Gallery*, Nick says that one of his goals as a war photographer is to put war photographers out of business. Is your goal as a writer of war stories similar to DelCorso's—to put war writers out of business with a brutal description of war?

PC: No. Nick was autobiographical, but he wasn't 100 percent autobiographical. That was his particular aesthetic; I think he was wrong there. He's assigning himself this grand social mission, and I would say that the same thing is true of the war writer. A war writer's task is no different from that of any other writer's task. I hate to sound so repetitious, but it is to convey the emotional truth of a character or a situation.

H: I recently read an interview in the *Chicago Tribune* ("Blind Beliefs") in which you note that the president of Loyola University credits your "Catholic imagination" with shaping so much of your writing: moral struggles between good and evil, the ambiguities of good and evil, evil arising from good, good turning into evil. Comment more about his description of this imaginative perspective.

PC: Nobody had ever told me that about myself, nor, I think, had I ever really come across it [Catholic imagination] anywhere else. But I thought about it, and I asked him to elaborate. He talked about some of the things I mentioned earlier: a respect for tradition, hierarchy, and order. But it's also a way of looking at the world that is, in its way, antimodern, or premodern, and he compared it to the Jewish imagination. So Philip Roth or Saul Bellow would be the examples par excellence of people with a Jewish imagination, but he said that where they are similar—the Catholic imagination and the Jewish imagination—is that they're imaginations that come out of a cultural context, as much as a religious context, that goes back to the ancient world. But then where the Jewish imagination seems to differ is that if you read Bellow or Roth, they can be very modern and secular in their outlook. However, I suppose with someone with this Catholic imagination (let's use Graham Greene as the epitome of that) there's always this definite religious element that goes into the writing. Even Leslie, my wife, has pointed out that religious imagery is always occurring to me, even in contexts that do not particularly involve religious issues or moral questions. It's just that I think that way, and probably the concern with these big moral questions is a Catholic concern and in some ways a premodern concern. It's not really a modernist concern. In fact, the more I read of younger writers, with some exceptions, the more I see how different I am.

H: I read an interview in the *VVA Veteran* (June/July 2001) about your 1999 backpacking adventure in Vietnam with a young Vietnamese poet during which you dreamed of a python choking you to death and then you ripped it off your chest. Later, the poet interpreted the dream for you—"The python was the past, and you have broken its grip." Does the Vietnam experience continue to haunt you as a son-soldier-writer? Or have you, indeed, ripped the "python" off your chest?

PC: Well, the answer to that is yes and no: yes in the sense that it obviously does not obsess me in the way it once did. At one point, it was all-consuming. But it is the most significant event of my whole life to this day, and as such, it's just woven into my very being. So I can never say that I've gotten over it in that sense, nor would I want to.

H: Why does the American public still seem haunted by the whole Vietnam experience?

PC: I've been asked that probably fifty times, and my thought has been it is the fascination of the lost cause. The only other example of it in our history would have been among Southerners after the Civil War. The Civil War obsessed Southerners, and in some cases still does, for decades and decades after it was over because the war was lost. You talk about the fascination of the abomination; this is the fascination of the lost cause. I think that's part of it, and it [Vietnam] was the only war that we ever did lose, even though we did not lose it in the classic sense because it was such an unclassical war. No American general presented his sword to Ho Chi Minh or General Vo Nguyen Giap or something like Cornwallis at Yorktown [1781]; nevertheless, we did lose it. And I think also that during the course of the war, we became aware that America had failed some sacred image it had of itself. And we're still trying to figure out how that happened, why that happened, and to learn more about it, even though quite recently some of us have done the exact same thing [lost our way] with Abu Ghraib, for example, and Guantanamo [Iraq War].

H: Did our experience in the Vietnam War mark America's loss of innocence?

PC: To my mind, it definitely was. But I have two caveats. One is that it was a good innocence to lose because it isn't as though before Vietnam we had always behaved virtuously. Forget slavery for a moment, but if we're just talking about wars, think of the Indian wars and what we did to the Indians. Think of some of the awful atrocities that were committed during the Philippine insurrection after the Spanish-American War. So it's not as though we had always done the right thing and acted like civilized people. We quite often acted barbarously. But there was something in the young burgeoning nation that allowed us to overlook these excesses or to ignore them, and they no longer seemed to exist by the time Vietnam came around. So, in other words, what we lost [in Vietnam] was the ability to look at our own sins and say they're not sins. But I think that the odd thing is that, to some extent, we recaptured our innocence afterward; I really do.

H: During the first Gulf War?

PC: Not just the war, I think with Reagan. When Reagan became president and said "it's morning in America," it really wasn't, but everybody said, "Yes, of course, it's morning in America." We can't bear the idea that it's not morning in America. We are a morning people, and we can't bear the idea that it might be afternoon, or twilight, or something. We created our own reality. That's what's remarkable about this country. Everybody said it is morning in America, and then it became morning in America, both in a good sense of the term and a bad sense of the term. The bad sense of the term is, I think, that with the perfect brutality of innocence we went and got involved in this goddamned war in Iraq, which I never thought we should have gotten involved in. (Afghanistan and the Taliban were a totally different issue.) And it is almost this same kind of innocence that led to our involvement in Vietnam.

H: Did a national narcissism contribute to our current involvement in Iraq?

PC: Sure, the narcissism, however, was stronger this time. I watched a lot of stuff before the invasion of Iraq and listened to ordinary citizens and ordinary soldiers saying, "Hey, we're America." I don't know what that was supposed to mean. I remember one gunnery sergeant interviewed in Kuwait said, "We're America." Okay, what does that mean? But it means that we can do anything. So, in some odd way, we recaptured our innocence [lost in Vietnam], and this innocence, I think, partly explains how we got involved in Iraq.

H: I want to end our conversation by discussing three of your books in more detail—your first book and your two most recent books. A Rumor of War, 13 Seconds, and Acts of Faith represent different types of writing, but also display certain thematic connections. How do these three works, taken together, represent your development as a writer?

PC: I think 13 Seconds is really just an example of reportage, nothing more, nothing less.

H: Although in it are sections of memoir, history, analysis, and commentary.

PC: It's kind of a salad of stuff, and I just think it's a perfectly competent piece of reportage. I wouldn't say anything more or less about it.

H: In comparing, then, your first published book, A Rumor of War, and your latest novel, Acts of Faith, how do these pieces viewed together suggest changes (evolution) in your writing?

PC: Well, I think the writing became much more sophisticated and nuanced. My confidence in my ability to create or present characters between now and then is much more developed. For example, I would have liked to have developed some of the people who appear in A Rumor of War more than I did. I was inhibited from doing that from having been this daily newspaper kind of guy: okay, there are areas here that we can't go into because you don't really know what they were thinking or feeling at that moment or what they were really like. And then partly because I'd never written a book before, I was a little inhibited by that. . . . I think that Acts of Faith represents a much more sophisticated level of writing and a much more sophisticated level of character development.

H: All three books, including 13 Seconds, deal with good and evil and significant moral issues.

PC: 13 Seconds is similar there because a moral choice was made by the governor of Ohio and by the general in charge of the troops at Kent State, and obviously some moral decision was made by the guys who pulled the trigger or triggers.

H: In A Rumor of War and Acts of Faith do you explore the moral issues in similar ways, or has your thinking on these matters evolved in some way?

PC: I think Acts of Faith does represent an evolution. A lot of the moral failures in there occur on a far different plane than does the one in A Rumor of War, which is a very specific situation. With Acts of Faith, you've got Quinette's evolution as a character, obviously from this sort of innocent abroad into this, what I call, minor-league Lady Macbeth. It's a psychological failure, as well as a kind of a moral failure. Her failure is her lack of self-awareness. She's not aware that most of what she does arises out of her egotism and narcissism. That's why in the scene where she fakes the slave redemption to raise money to pay for an arms shipment, she's able to justify that, almost without a twitch.

H: And does another central character, Douglas Braithwaite, do the same thing with some of his questionable activities?

PC: Douglas does the same thing, and I think that together these represent more subtly nuanced kinds of moral failures than you find in A Rumor of War.

H: We've talked about your focus on creating emotional truths. Were there different emotional truths that you were trying to get across in all three of these works?

PC: I would say that they're different. What I wanted to do in A Rumor of War was to recreate the war as concretely as possible on a printed page so that I would put somebody there. By the time we get to Acts of Faith, I am not so much trying to put people in Sudan; I am trying to present a cast of characters in all of their contrariness and contradictoriness. I was very concerned with that in Acts of Faith. I wanted all of these people, even the ones who ended up doing reprehensible things, to be attractive in one way or another, and I think I succeeded. Even with Ibrahim, the Arab warlord, I wanted people to sort of like him, but then he goes galloping around and shooting people and capturing slaves. The same thing with Quinette, I wanted people to be engaged by Quinette, kind of admire her and like her. Then all of a sudden, she starts to morph. But I certainly see people that way. We're full of these contradictions. Just generally speaking, because of the ordinariness of our daily lives, you don't see these other aspects of a character. Society will demand that we present some kind of acceptable self to society. But when you start going off into these exotic distant locales, and into these situations that are anything but ordinary, then that acceptable self tends to disappear.

H: Are these three works political in similar or different ways? Or are they political at all?

PC: I never had any political intention in them. Whatever intention I had was purely literary; it was to create as true a character as I could, to write as best as I am capable of writing, and, probably above all, to create as truthful a cast of characters that I could in A Rumor of War and Acts of Faith. As I said, there's not really any character development or particularly any great writing in 13

Seconds, but I'm a very careful craftsman. I try to write to the very best I can. I would say that probably stylistically I fall short of some other writers, but that's inherent talent. It's not due to any kind of laziness in my style.

H: When you say you fall short stylistically of certain writers, what do you mean?

PC: There are some writers whose styles I admire and have to admit are better than mine. And I'll tell you who I don't mean in this case. I don't mean a lot of these younger writers who have come out of these MFA programs and will indulge themselves in these "look ma, no hands" circus acts. It sticks out like a snakebite; all of a sudden, there'll be some page that'll be full of these flourishes, metaphors, or sentences of Faulknerian length. Obviously, this is somebody showing off. It takes a certain something to be able to write like that, but it's completely calling attention to the writing. Instead, I'm talking about writers who just say things so well, generally because they're so true. Stylistically, I admire very much the earlier Jim Harrison [*Legends of the Fall*] and Tim O'Brien. There's a lyricism that I don't have. I am not a particularly lyrical writer. With Jim, he is a poet, and you can see the poet in him in the way he writes.

H: These comments about writing remind me of our earlier conversation about your father who, in doing a carpentry project, refused to use molding because good carpenters don't commit sins that they have to hide with molding. Might one consider this anecdote a metaphor for identifying good writers?

PC: I think so.

H: In addition to the sin of "circus acts," are there other sins that writers commit?

PC: Well, sometimes there's cheating in what you have a character do or a situation that you'll create that doesn't ring quite true. . . . Contrivance, which is almost by definition a falsehood, is another sin. And I think what I would call baroque or "show-offy" writing is certainly yet another one. Another is the almost deliberate obscurity that some of the icons of literary fiction indulge in. The chief sinner, to my mind, being Thomas Pynchon. I have never been able to finish reading a single thing this guy ever wrote, and I almost get the impression that he loves being obscure, cryptic, and difficult to understand for its own sake. He's beloved in the academy because if the reader goes through the book and says "what the hell is all of this about?" it then leaves the professor in the role of the high priest who will interpret this sacred text for this lout down there. By the way, I have to interrupt myself. I did finish reading *Mason & Dixon*, and the reason I finished it was I have got to at least say I finished reading one Pynchon book. It was tough, almost like trekking across the Pennsylvania wilderness with Mason and Dixon.

H: In talking earlier about creative writing programs, you said you really didn't want to teach in those. But if you were going to give advice to an aspiring writer, what would it be?

PC: Well, that learning to write (you're really going to laugh about this) is like learning to build a birch-bark canoe. I learned this when I was researching *Indian Country*. How did those Algonquin-speaking Indians of the Midwest and the East learn to build birch-bark canoes, fifty-foot long freight canoes that didn't sink or tear apart? In some book I was reading about the Ojibway Indians, this old canoemaker said that you learn by observation and experience. That is to say, the young Indian boy sits at the feet of the master and watches him build a canoe. Then he is assigned little tasks in canoe building, and then eventually, he begins to build canoes himself. Undoubtedly many of them will sink and fall apart before he gets it right. To me, it's the same thing with writing; it is observation and experience. The observation in this case comes from as wide a range of reading of literary fiction, or literary nonfiction for that matter, as you can possibly do. And I would say that one ought to avoid, especially as a young writer, reading popular fiction unless you want to write it. I really think that stuff is to the mind what Taco Bell and McDonald's are to the digestive system. And then the other thing is experience, and the experience comes from writing. You must write as much as you can, in as many different forms as you feel capable of writing in. I don't care if it's poetry, short story, essay, novels, or novelettes; that's the way you learn. I would say that you can learn everything technical that you need to know about writing in a single semester's writing course, maybe two at the most. I think the only advantage to those MFA programs is that you write. So you get the experience; you're going to college at the same time; and you're going to get a degree. But I don't think someone who goes through two years of an MFA program is going to be necessarily any better of a writer than someone who takes one or two semesters of a creative writing course.

One of the things I dislike about a lot of modern fiction is I find it kind of claustrophobic, not all of it obviously, but much of it. I find it that way because so many of these young writers go from being students in [MFA programs] to teaching in them, or being TAs or graduate assistants. They've not learned anything about life, about the world, and about people. I would just say get out and go do it [live and travel].

H: One of the things that struck me in meeting you for the first time is that you're obviously in good shape. You're a physical person, and you grew up physical—boxing, wrestling, canoeing, and other outdoor sports. Does that physical nature of your life carry over into your writing?

PC: Yes, I think so. I haven't thought of it that way, but now that you mention it, I'd say probably that's true. I try to get across the way heat feels on your skin, or if you're attacked by a horde of mosquitoes, the way that feels.

H: Or how a body explodes and what the body parts look like?

PC: Yes. [Let's take] another person who's written about Africa a lot, Norman Rush [Mortals]. He is a very cerebral writer, and I would see myself, possibly because of this physical nature or something like that, as a very visceral writer. I am not a conveyor of big ideas. Basically, Saul Bellow would be one of the great idea writers of all time. I'm very visceral; I try to get across the physical reality and, through an appeal to the physical senses, the emotional reality of a particular situation.

H: You commented earlier about having a chip on your shoulder regarding some of your fellow writers who have not taken their knocks and not earned what they have gotten. What did you mean by this?

PC: Again, I'm going back to these academic careerist writers. They've gone from the academy back into the academy. They've never been in a newsroom; they've never been in a war; some of them might have gone through a divorce. But they're very stylistically accomplished, at least in a way that pleases a lot of critics, many of whom went to these MFA programs. . . . They will touch on themes that, I think, they know will be appreciated. Usually it's some dismal marital situation. Again, it's all very claustrophobic and boring, kind of like how their lives have been. I've also found this out—a lot of them know how to network; they know how to work the prize committees. I've seen them do it. That's what I was referring to. My old editor at National Geographic Adventure magazine used to be a Golden Gloves fighter in Ohio, and he was talking about the young interns they had working at the magazine. He said, "You know the trouble with a lot of these people, a lot of them have never been cut."

H: When I interviewed Larry Heinemann, he said that he viewed the world through the perspective of the "pissed-off infantrymen." Do you view the world through the prism of the pissed-off infantryman?

PC: No. It's not anger or being pissed off that moves me. I look at the world through the eyes of a guy who's trying to figure out what people are really all about. Who they really are and what they really represent. What affects me is, call it curiosity, that desire to probe the human character. I've got an edge to me. I can be just as pissed off as the next guy, but that's not the prism through which I look at the world.

H: How would you respond to the following Arthur Miller quote about the relationships among an author's life, his writing, and an audience's response
to his life and works: "That biographical thing [knowing about the writer's
life] is a laziness on the part of the viewer [of his plays]. You [the audience]
don't have to confront the material; you just have to know what it's about.
And then you think you have understood what you have heard, which is not
necessarily the case at all. Biography is a copout" ("Miller on *Picture*," interview by Chris Jones, *Chicago Tribune* October 2004, Tempo: 1).

PC: I am not quite of the generation, but I was close to that generation when the
New Criticism came in back in the '50s. I was still a child then, but there were
still people coming to college who believed in that—that is to say, you look at
the text and everything else is irrelevant. I tend more toward that point of
view. What the reader or the viewer of a play should look at is what's between
the covers. How much of me or my life is in there is simply not relevant, except to a biographer, and then a biographer will say, "Okay, he went through
this and all that." I would agree with Miller, wholly. For someone to say that
"well, I know that this happened to so and so, and he went through this, and
therefore I got it" is worse than just a laziness. You shut yourself off from insights that you probably would have if you just put all that out of your head.

H: However, having talked to you about your life and having read many of your
other interviews, I now appreciate some of your writing more. I understand
where some of the themes and characters in your books originate. For example, your focus on good versus evil and moral ambiguity, obviously
that's rooted in your life experiences and your religious upbringing.

PC: Right, but you are a scholar of literature, and so you are probably, again,
writing for other scholars. I think, nevertheless, the truth of what a writer
writes is there between the covers. I had read most of Conrad before I got
this biography [*points to book on shelf*]. And to tell you the truth, I never finished reading the biography; it began to bore me. The biographer would
note that, yes, Conrad really did take this trip up the Congo. I said, okay,
fine, but I had read *Heart of Darkness* way before I ever knew that he'd actually done that. And the story moved me; it's a story that just shakes you up,
shakes your soul. You almost feel as if you're Marlow.

H: In a previous interview, you noted that "one thing that tends to drive people
to become writers or to *need* to be writers—Hemingway talks about this—is
some sort of wound. Really happy, well-adjusted people don't become writers. At least they don't become what we think of as literary writers" ("A Rumor:
Conversation," 5). Is part of your wound your Vietnam War experiences?

PC: Not just part of it, it's all of it. . . . Vietnam was the wound of my life.

H: What constitutes that wound?

PC: First of all, at a very young age having your friends get killed. I knew sixteen guys over there who were killed in action. Then, there's the sense of having failed myself in some way, failed an ideal, both an objective ideal and an ideal I had of myself. That was a wound as well. And then just having to look into your own soul and perhaps not exactly like what you see.

H: Is this failed ideal related to the incident at Giao Tri?

PC: Partly that, but I think I would have had that sense of failure anyway because I had this picture of myself as this sort of heroic character who would be beloved by his men and win medals. The reality of the situation was so sordid compared to that, that I think I would have had this sense of failure regardless. And then as a junior officer you lose men as a result of the orders that you give. You could say that of a four-star general, but how often does he really see that actually happen? As a lieutenant or a captain you see it happen right in front of your face.

H: But going back to the incident at Giao Tri, you gave an ambiguous order. You didn't pull the trigger, and you weren't directly responsible for the deaths of those two people.

PC: No, I was not, but you are responsible. An officer is responsible for everything his men do or fail to do. They went out there on my orders, and the orders I gave were sloppy. They were not very clear. Then at first [after initial charges filed], I did not take responsibility for it. I tried to get out of it; I tried to get them [my men] out of it. That was a moral failure as well, and I recognize it as such. So you have to confront yourself on those kinds of issues, and that's a wounding process.

H: You mentioned this failure of an ideal, imagined or real. This failure seems to be a theme in so many of your books, for example characters in *Acts of Faith*.

PC: Yes, they fail the best that's in themselves, or they're not aware of the fact, or they're comfortable with their failure. Doug [Braithwaite] is, and then Quinette is. But in *The Voyage* (the sea story I did), I didn't realize what I was doing until I was done with it. But the central character in there is Nathaniel Braithwaite, who's actually related to this Douglas Braithwaite. Nathaniel has this image of himself (he's only sixteen) as a kind of stalwart heroic character. He, his two brothers, and a buddy are on a small sailboat, and they encounter a terrible storm off the Florida Keys. [Nathaniel] discovers he's not who he thought he was after all, and he has a hard time living with that.

H: Is often this failure to measure up, the failure of ideals, also caused by a lack of realistic self-assessment?

PC: Certainly. In my case, in Vietnam that ideal was movie driven; it came out of Hollywood, which by definition is nonsense.

H: It must, at times, be frustrating, when you give readings and interviews, that people always want to talk about A Rumor of War. Yet you've written so many other well-received novels and nonfiction. In an interview, perhaps expressing this frustration, you said, "I want to write a novel that would be a sister or brother to A Rumor of War" ("A Rumor: Conversation," 17). Do you think with Acts of Faith you have achieved this goal?

PC: I hope so. I'll know six months from now. But that's my hope. I knew Gloria Jones, James Jones's widow, and she said that Jim would get so tired of people coming up and saying, "You're James Jones; I read your book" [From Here to Eternity]. And I knew exactly what she meant when she told me that.

H: What does Acts of Faith have from a literary perspective that maybe some of the earlier novels do not have?

PC: I think, again, the characters are far more fully rounded than any other characters I've ever created. The story, the plot if you will, is far more complex, but I think complex in a good way in the sense that eventually all of these strands do come together. I think the book represents the culmination of everything I have learned about writing, about life, and about people. So I think it's kind of a summation of what I've been doing for the last twenty-five or thirty years.

H: A final question: when I walked into your writer's cottage located behind your house, I was struck by the framed war medals and ribbons hanging on the wall. Obviously these decorations are important to you.

PC: Yes, they are. I came to realize that. My wife, who is a very antiwar person, said, "You sent your medals back to President Nixon, and now you want them back. Why is that?" "First of all," I said, "consistency is the hobgoblin of little minds." And I said, "This is the most important thing that ever happened to me, and these little things represent that to me. I can't let them go." You can't escape [the war]; you might as well try to deny you were born for that matter.

WORKS BY & INTERVIEWS WITH PHILIP CAPUTO

Acts of Faith. New York: Alfred A. Knopf, 2005.

"Blind Beliefs" (Interview). By Patrick Reardon. Chicago Tribune, May 17, 2005, Tempo: 1+.

"Death Goes to School." Esquire, December 1989: 136–38+.

DelCorso's Gallery. New York: Henry Holt, 1983.

Equation for Evil. New York: HarperCollins, 1996.

Exiles. New York: Random House, 1999.

Ghosts of Tsavo: Tracking the Mythic Lions of East Africa. New York: National Geographic, 2002.

Horn of Africa. New York: Holt Rinehart, 1980.

In the Shadows of the Morning: Essays on Wild Lands, Wild Waters, and a Few Untamed People. New York: Lyons Press, 2002.

Indian Country. New York: Bantam, 1987.

"Interview." *VVA Veteran,* June/July 2001 <http://www.vva.org/The Veteran/2001_07/rendezvous/htm>.

Means of Escape. New York: HarperCollins, 1991.

A Rumor of War. 1977. Reprint, New York: Ballantine, 1978.

"*A Rumor of War*: A Conversation with Philip Caputo at 58." By Michael S. Neiberg, Thomas G. Bowie, and Donald Anderson. *War, Literature, and the Arts* 12.1 (2000): 1–14.

13 Seconds. New York: Chamberlain Brothers, 2005.

The Voyage. New York: Alfred A. Knopf, 1999.

conversation with

LARRY HEINEMANN

Heinemann reviewed an edited transcript of our May 2005 interviews and made some changes, which he described in an email: "After reading it [the interview] over, I couldn't believe how inarticulate I sounded, so the revisions took on the character of rewriting a short story." Larry's changes are not as drastic as his email comments might suggest, and these changes did not alter the distinct Heinemann voice present during our two sessions together. His editing involved clarification of some points, minor changes to improve flow, and, most significant, the addition of italics in several places to add emphasis to the tone and substance of his remarks. Perhaps the most telling observation in Larry's email is the following: "I swear on the heads of my children, Tobey, that this will be the last time I sit down with anyone and talk about these things. I've finally worn myself out talking about it—the war, I mean."

My sessions with Larry Heinemann transpired on May 22 and 23, 2005, in my small twenty-ninth-floor condominium in downtown Chicago with the two of us facing each other across a small round table (à la Charlie Rose) and Larry looking out over the Chicago skyline, including Sears Tower. I had offered to meet with Larry in his home in the northern Edgewater area of Chicago. But Larry, being the unassuming person that he is and a mass transit aficionado (he had recently returned via train from Boston, where he completed a promotional tour for Black Virgin Mountain), quickly suggested that for both sessions he ride a CTA bus to the interview site. Larry arrived promptly each day, and we settled into our longer-than-expected four-hour sessions with most of the conversation on the record. On the second day, we chatted over a carry-in lunch: deli sandwiches with Larry's requested "special deli mustard" (as warned by Larry, "none of that cheap yellow stuff") and a few beers from the local Goose Island Brewery. Also, in honor of Wabash College (my place of employment), Larry arrived for this session wearing a "Wabash Steel" hat. His friend Robert Olen Butler had given him the hat upon the publication of Butler's novel

Wabash, which prominently features the Wabash Steel Mill in the fictional southern Illinois town of Wabash. Larry's persona throughout the interviews was consistent with his writer's persona. He is passionate about life, past and current politics, and writing, and he is articulate in his outrage about past and current wars, political injustices, and "lifers." He is, above all, a natural oral storyteller—language, graphic detail, body gestures, rising and falling tone, frequent laughter, and an intense connection with his audience. In responding to one of my early questions as to what should be the goal of a good interview with him, he chuckled and confided, "Keep me on topic. I tend to go on tangents, what we refer to in the house as 'Heinemann automatic.'" We did go off topic on several occasions, forcing me to adjust the script of questions, but these serendipitous digressions helped me further appreciate Larry as a passionate and funny person and as a skilled storyteller.

SON

H: Did you like to tell stories when you were growing up?

LH: Pretty much. I learned to tell stories from my maternal grandfather, who lived with us for several years when I was a kid. Not only was he this remarkable character, but also a superb bullshit artist. The other habit he had, and this was like every night, he would get dressed up and put on his very snappy straw hat, walk up to the only saloon in town, the Cypress Inn, and basically be funny for drinks. So, on top of everything else, he was a barfly. I remember when we were kids, many a morning coming down for breakfast, there'd be grampa laid out on the couch, and we didn't think anything about it. Well, okay, there's grampa. It didn't occur to us until years later that this is as far into the house as he could get. Also, he would get drunk and have these pretend long-distance phone calls in the middle of the night. He'd pick up the phone standing in the living room, get into a conversation with the long-distance operator, and "call" downstate Indiana. He wanted to talk to Verna Wheat. The line was "I want to talk to Verna Wheat, and she's got a *private* line." This was the early '50s when a lot of rural phones were still on party lines, but not good old Verna. Well, of course, it turned out she'd been dead since 1923 or some such, but he'd talk to her for an hour. My dad would go nuts—long distance for an hour!—the old man is going to send us to the poorhouse, but my mom figured it out right away because the calls were never on the bill.

H: Why was he doing this?

LH: I think he just enjoyed hearing himself talk. We lived in one of those new, postwar subdivisions—young families, and kids everywhere—and they would all come down and hang around our house. Grampa Denton would be sitting on the stoop and launch into these remarkable stories of a kind that literary critics nowadays refer to as magical realism. Some real yarns. He and Pecos Bill had a cattle ranch in Texas. We had a magic horse that lived in the basement. Civil War stories. Hunting stories. North Pole stories. The whole family was horse thieves, but *he* was the only one of uncles and brothers not caught and hung. He only had one arm, lost in a coalmine cave-in. All he ever said about that was that he could hear the shovels coming for him all morning. He didn't have a tooth in his head, so his gums were part of the story, too. He'd tell the story with his whole body, stump and all. And all we kids would sit around him in absolute awe. Just wild, wild stories. And that stump. Anyway, I expect I got my storytelling from him.

H: So do you consider yourself a bullshit artist?

LH: I prefer to put the emphasis on the "art" part. My grandfather tried to write a book about a dog named Lad, and it was just terrible. He wasn't a good writer, but Lord, Lord, he could spin a yarn.

H: Did you have any relatives in the military, other than your brothers? Was your father in the military?

LH: No, he was 4-F. He had bad feet or something. Though married with a child might have done the trick. Two of my uncles served in World War II, but they were not in combat.

H: In addition to listening to your grandfather's stories, what were your other interests as a child and teen growing up in the Chicago suburb of Northbrook?

LH: Well, we messed around like everyone else—we *were* kids. I was never very athletic. I played first base in Little League and was a fair hitter, but I was never on the A-list teams. I was okay athletically, but not very competitive. I can't remember ever trying out for anything in high school. And it never occurred to me to play football. Football players were always getting whacked in the head and, well, that didn't look like a lot of fun. Plus, I was a small kid, what my grandfather would have referred to as "skinny, run down, and nervous." When I was twelve, all the horsing around stopped when I started working summers as a caddie.

H: Were you interested in music or books?

LH: Not much. I grew up in a house where there were no books, and the only music I heard was on the radio. Late at night my older brother Jimmy and I would listen to Daddy-O Daily's all-night jazz radio program on a South-side Chicago black station, and what a revelation that was. Both of my parents had come up, of course, through the Depression and WWII. In the house, the word—the rule—was "Finish high school. Get a job." Of the four sons I'm the only one who finished college, and it certainly wasn't Columbia in New York. So I don't really remember being all that much interested in anything. I do, however, recall spending whole Saturday afternoons in the public library, but for the life of me I couldn't recall for you anything I read. No doubt I hung out at the library to get out of the house.

H: Living in Northbrook and working at an early age as a caddy at a nearby exclusive country club, did you begin to form certain views about wealthy people—"these people are the enemy"? I ask this because you have a noticeable anti-establishment, anti-authority, anti-whatever tone to your interviews and writing. Did that attitude develop at a young age?

LH: Well, I've never been a big fan of authority. Where it came from, I couldn't say for sure. But one thing I *can* tell you. When I was in school, I cannot tell you the number of times I was called "dumb" to my face. Nowadays, kids like that are diagnosed with learning disabilities. I'm one of those guys who learned to read by moving his lips, and writing was an agony. School was an agony. I didn't read a book all the way through until I was in high school. Even then it was the Civil War novel *Andersonville*. . . . And I was appalled. I remember thinking, "Good God, how could people live like this?" Little did I know. The story had to do with the prison, as well as the town.

When I was in sixth grade, we had a crazy man for a teacher who basically terrorized us. Mr. Del Vecchio. I'll never forget that jasper. He was always picking on Ted Jacobs, Bert Dibble, or me for one thing or another, and we were always in trouble with him. He'd stand over you, and he was a large man with a large voice, and scream at you at the top of his lungs. And you had to sit there, burning with a shame and just take it; you're eleven, for Christ's sake—feeling numb, dead, from the waist down as if half your body is asleep. You know, that icy tingle right down to your toes. He later became the superintendent of the middle school, and dropped dead of a heart attack after I graduated high school.

My very first job, caddying, was a definite eye-opener. I was twelve. The younger kids and rookies caddied for the women, referred to as the members' wives. We'd haul these huge heavy golf bags, called trunks, for eighteen holes. At the pro shop they'd pay you your three dollars, and then make a virtual ceremony of putting your quarter tip into your hand. This after bust-

ing your ass all afternoon. "Oh, thank you, ma'am. You're too generous."
And then she'd slide into her Cadillac and cruise on back to Winnetka.

In high school I was in the Sea Cadets, an organization run by the Navy League, and very much like the Boy Scouts, only more paramilitary. They really had this thing for uniforms. Between my junior and senior year, I "won" a trip to Japan. No one in my family had been farther away from home than St. Louis, and all of a sudden I'm on a Trailways bus headed for San Francisco—three days overland across country with three other guys from Chicago, and that was an adventure all by itself. For the first time in my life I was out of the house and had absolutely not a clue. There was no money in the house, so the money my parents gave me for the trip was precious. And a lot of things the other guys on the trip could do I simply could not. It was two weeks on a ship, two weeks in Japan—and what a grand time that was—and two weeks on a ship back. It was a Navy troop ship, taking guys to Korea for a year's tour and two weeks at sea with guys coming back. They were by far, flat out, the most interesting thing on the ship. The Japanese were pretty interesting—to put it mildly—how could they not be? For a kid from Chicago, the Japanese were utterly exotic—to say the least. Drove on the left, wore these funny clothes, ate with sticks, and graceful with a style that made a deep impression on me. But on the ship, a couple of army guys I remember sitting down with had endless stories of military life and being in Korea, and that's when I decided, well, maybe this Sea Cadet thing isn't such a good idea after all. But I was also at that age when you begin to develop a bullshit detector. So, I got home at the end of the summer and dropped out of Sea Cadets. That was it.

H: Their stories turned you off to a career in the military?

LH: Well, I never had any interest in military service of any kind. Are you kidding? Yeah, you know, the stories boiled down to something like, "The army sucks; there's all these stupid people walking around, and they're in charge. Fuck the army." That was the first time I heard that phrase.

H: I am interested in the comment that "there's all these stupid people walking around, and they're in charge." This viewpoint also seems to appear frequently in your writing: anti-officer, anti-stupidity of the military establishment.

LH: Yes, sir. I'll admit it. That trip to Japan really snapped my head back. But that's what getting out of the house will do for anyone.

H: Did this attitude emerge as a result of the episode with the Sea Cadets?

LH: That was the first time I got an inkling of what it would be like to be treated like a piece of meat. But I've also come to understand it with some humor. A lot of humor actually. Later in Mark Twain's life, someone asked him why he was such a pessimist, and he responded that he didn't think he was a pessimist or a cynic. I think his quote is, "I've often been called a pessimist, but I'm not. I'm an optimist who has not arrived." And for me, that about nails it. Put me down as a Mark Twain Optimist. I think I learned early to look at authority with a skeptical, jaundiced eye.

A lot of things about authority don't have anything to do with justice, efficiency, or being fair. It's office politics and who gets to be right, regardless; cover your ass and protect your bullshit little job. The thing I came to appreciate in the military, and what other veteran writers of any generation get to, is that the guys in charge really have their heads up their ass and they're much more interested in their precious little careers than they are in anything that's going on on the ground, and all that matters is how "it" looks on paper. Take a look at Heller's *Catch-22*, or *The Good Soldier Švejk* [Jaroslav Hašek], one of the great comic novels of world literature. When you read about the Civil War and the personalities and frictions among the generals, there was a lot of petty lifer bullshit, and that hasn't changed because the military culture, conservative from crown to sole, will never change. It's the nature of the beast. I have a hard time with people who think the war in Iraq is going just fine. The lifers have nothing to say about all these extraordinary fuck-ups. But you've got to know there is more than one National Guard outfit that went to Iraq and didn't even have flak jackets, much less body armor. None of their equipment, much less the training, was state-of-the-art; we're talking the National Guard, here. And to hear a supreme, a superb lifer, like Donald Rumsfeld, say that "you go to war with the army you have," regardless of its shortcomings, well, I hope to God I'm never in the same room as that shitass because I'll give him his "army you have" upside his head. Salute this, Don.

It's the same thing that makes me bitter about somebody like Robert McNamara, President Johnson's secretary of defense. He's the guy in 1967, 1968 who was doing the math, and the math showed him the war in Vietnam was not going to end well for anybody, and he apparently started talking it up "behind his hand" when most other men in the Johnson administration were still gung ho. In 1968 he resigned, was fired. And for all those years, until he wrote *In Retrospect: The Tragedy and Lessons of Vietnam*, he never said "boo" about his opposition to the war. And I'm thinking, "You know, Bob, you take an oath to defend and protect the Constitution. Not a personal loyalty oath to the president; you take an oath to the country. And when you see something isn't working, your job is to speak up in no uncertain terms." McNamara strikes me as a remarkable coward, and maybe the dictionary definition of a ticket-punching lifer.

But my attitude *really* got nailed in the army. I was flat-out astonished. I have never encountered so many stupid people in one place in all my life. What on earth are you people trying to get to? It about irked me to distraction to have to kowtow to people that I understood full well were not my betters. Some lifer, it seemed, was always fucking with us. Chickenshit harassment is just chickenshit harassment for the sake of chicken shit.

H: Moving to a less emotional issue, during your time as a child and teenager, did you have any particular heroes, including political figures?

LH: Probably [Chicago Cub] Ernie Banks for the most obvious reason. . . . He had great wrists. He was a slender man with a vicious swing. Played shortstop. He had great wrists, hit a million home runs. You could count on Ernie. . . . Just this wonderful man, always cheerful and had great wrists. His classic quote was always, "It's a beautiful day in the Friendly Confines, let's play two."

H: It's interesting that in other Vietnam War memoirs Philip Caputo and Ron Kovic [*Born on the Fourth of July*] frequently mention John Wayne's characters as heroes influencing them through war and cowboy movies. Did you see any John Wayne movies as you were growing up, or other war movies? Did these movies influence your attitudes toward war, attitudes toward courage?

LH: I think John Wayne was perfect for the time, because Americans, like now, really needed to be reassured about these things. You're twelve. It looks like fun. Horses. Gun play. Big talk. I mean the whole phenomenon of the Western. It sounds so dumb to say it out loud, but the whole "Western ethos": that Americans can do no wrong and the Indians are not simply caricatures, but cartoons. Not to mention in the way. There were a lot of war movies of all kinds, overloaded with the kind of testosterone that any teenager would thrive on. Blood and guts and glory. (They still do.) I don't remember many of John Wayne's movies, even the *Sands of Iwo Jima*, which is apparently his greatest cinematic performance. I don't even remember *The Green Berets* all that well. All I remember is that by the time I saw that movie, I'd had "John Wayne" up to my eyeballs. What bullshit.

H: Did you play war games when you were growing up?

LH: I suppose we did. . . . There was a cow pasture at the end of our block with the woods and railroad right there, and to the east of us was an abandoned nursery that may well have been abandoned in the Depression, because the trees were enormous. . . . So we'd go out there and play tag and hide-and-go-seek, and as we got older, the games got a little rougher—war games, capture the flag, and such as that.

H: Did you think at this early age that you wanted to become a soldier?

LH: Good God, no.

H: And your experience in the Sea Cadets confirmed that idea.

LH: Yes, but I think when I got into the Sea Cadets, I was more interested in the cool uniforms.

H: While you were growing up at home, did your family spend time at dinner discussing books, politics, or world events?

LH: Not that I can remember. My father told bus driver stories—when he was there. Otherwise, it was "clear the table." My mother had this babysitting brokerage and worked from the dining room table. People on the North Shore would join this service, and she hired working-class women trying to make a little money on the side. We ate and left so she could conduct her business on the dining room table. My mother was always working the phone.

H: Was religion an important part of your upbringing?

LH: I'd have to say no. I was raised Lutheran, and my father was one of those people who said, "You will go to church." It was a small congregation. I was even an altar boy, of all things. I didn't volunteer; my father said, "You are the altar boy." So, I did Sunday mornings until it was coming out my ears, and then went through catechism. I wasn't that much of a motivated student anyway; I struggled along with Cs and Ds all the way through. So catechism was one more thing to all but fail at. When it came for the time of the actual confirmation, there were six of us in the first confirmation class. The whole congregation came to see us, and the custom was that any jackass in church could stand up and ask a question. I swear to God I failed the test; I didn't know any of the answers. So, I've always said that I am a failed Lutheran.

H: Did your father go to church with you?

LH: The whole family went. We were driven to church. Go to church, or else. For me it was an agony.

H: You have mentioned a little bit about your father. Describe your relationship with him during these years of growing up? Were there any particular tensions?

LH: My father was one of those people who were not comfortable with their own body. It took him five years to finish high school, and he flunked out of college twice. I have a sneaking hunch that he also had an extraordinary learning disability. It took me a long time to learn to read and write. It took my brothers a long time. One of my uncles had brain tumors and finally died in his late twenties. Another uncle has had a stutter all his life. So for the men in my family, learning was never easy. (How the hell did I ever become a writer?) My father wasn't athletic. He was not handy; I don't think I ever saw him mow the grass. He never took us fishing, or ballgames. He had a job driving a bus that required him to be out of the house from dawn until long after dark. When we were in our teens, he finally had enough seniority so he could pick bus runs that got him out of the house at five o'clock in the morning. He'd work what's called a "split"—two round trips in the morning and two round trips in the afternoon for the rush hours. And often he wasn't home until eight or nine o'clock at night. So, we'd have dinner without him. He was not a communicative man. I don't remember the two of us sitting down and talking about anything. I don't think parenthood was fun for him. There was a point at which my parents stopped talking to each other. They were not warm people, in any case. I never saw his parents, my grandparents, touch. I think that one of the frictions between my parents was the fact that my mother was making more money than my father. If he was handy with anything, it was his belt.

H: Was your father in any way a model or a guide for you?

LH: God, no! I didn't have one. Well, there was Grampa Denton [maternal grandfather], but he was not exactly the hero that moms and dads want for their kids. He was one of those guys who thought nothing good could come of a day that didn't begin with a double shot of bourbon—but look, he'd run a farm and raised eleven kids with just the one arm, so by the time I knew him he was more than entitled.

H: Given the sometimes difficult relationship you had with your father, what was his response in later years to your writing career?

LH: I didn't find out until the last year of his life (in '77) that when he was in school he wanted to be a journalist, and his father wanted him to study law. And they had a large falling out. That was amazing to me. When I first started writing (I was working on Close Quarters) and Edie and I would go out to my folks' place on a Sunday for dinner, my father would meet us at the door and take one look at me and say absolute classic "get a haircut, get a job." In no uncertain terms, he let me know that writing a book was not a good idea. But when the book was finally published the week he died, he got to see it, and he thought that was really cool. The one large regret I have is that my dad and I never got to sit down as grown-up adults and settle up. For my part there is a large hole there.

H: What do you remember about your time in high school?

LH: High school was an agony. I wasn't interested in much of anything. I'm not a math person, so I took one semester of algebra and let it go at that. I learned geometry shooting pool. I don't know anything about physics or chemistry, except that water is one part oxygen and two parts hydrogen. I took the shop courses—wood shop, metal shop. And mechanical drawing, drawing machine parts. I took two years of architectural drawing. I was utterly intrigued and got the idea to be an architect. Houses, *homes*. You had to design a house from the bottom up and do all the plans: the electric, the plumbing, the landscape. And I had just come back from those two weeks in Japan, so I designed a house that looked something like a pagoda. So I thought, "Architect, I could dig that," but I could not do the math.

H: Describe your relationship with your three brothers during this time.

LH: There was Jim, the oldest. He was awkward, like our father. When Jim was a kid he'd been whacked in the head a couple times. One winter he ran his sled into a tree, and then a couple years later a neighbor kid slammed him with a shovel in an argument over a snow-shoveling job. His head injuries were never dealt with beyond first aid, that is, and he was just plain odd. I am the second. Then there is Richard, brother number three, and he and I flat-out didn't like each other.

H: How much older was Jim than you?

LH: We were all about two-and-a-half years apart. The brother I was closest with was Philip, the youngest, who dropped out of high school to join the Marine Corps. That broke my heart. I didn't know how much it would break my heart, but it did. He got out of the Marine Corps in the early '70s after two Vietnam tours, and he and I did not exchange a word for ten years.

H: And he later disappeared from the family, right?

LH: Yes, literally one of those guys who went out for a pack of smokes and never came back. . . . My brothers and I were not that close. I think part of it had to do with a very strict German upbringing and the fact that my father would just get into these rages. I remember Jimmy would run away from home and hop a freight. And the next thing you know he's in Duckbutter, Iowa—or some such place. The cops would call, and my father would have to take off two days of work, drive out to get him, and drive back. Two days off work, mind you. I can only imagine what those car rides were like because nothing would happen until father and Jimmy got back to the house. My dad would take his bus driver belt (you know those great big thick black leather belts) and just beat him within an inch of his life. I remember Richard and me downstairs in the bedroom holding our ears, and you could hear my brother screaming, shrieking while our father was giving him a beating. He had scars on his back. So we were terrified of our father. And when my father wasn't around, my mother had a bundle of willow switches.

H: Is that the type of upbringing that contributes to people becoming writers?

LH: Well, you couldn't prove it by me—a shitty childhood isn't a prerequisite for anything—but as far as I'm concerned it certainly does give you a point of view about what makes the world go around—being on the receiving end of a belt whipping is like nothing else in the world. "This is going to hurt me more than it's going to hurt you." Wanna bet?

H: So this family situation wasn't the motivation for you becoming a writer; the war was the motivation for you becoming a writer.

LH: Yes, the story that would not die, the story that wouldn't fuckin' go away.

H: After graduating from high school, you attended nearby Kendall College in Evanston, Illinois. What was your reason?

LH: It was right there. It was affordable, more or less, and it was a draft deferment. This was back in the days of Selective Service, and students were automatically given a deferment. I did not want to go into the army.

H: You're attending Kendall College right across the street from Northwestern with all these rich kids going to this four-year, very prestigious school—any resentment of them?

LH: No, we never got over to that side of the street.

H: Other side of the world?

LH: Yeah. Not even to walk around to see what it looked like. No, I was still sort of fumbling around, still not doing well as a student.

H: Working part-time still?

LH: Oh, yeah. A lot of kids were. . . . I worked in a record store. I'll never forget it, in downtown Evanston, Lashon Records on Sherman. I learned a lot about music. Oh, and then one summer I got this job at a summer-stock theater in Lock Haven, Pennsylvania. And that's when it was shown to me with great demonstration that a life as an actor wasn't going to work. I simply could not memorize dialogue. I embarrassed myself more than once. So that was it.

H: With no background in the theater and the arts, what led you to pursue summer stock?

LH: Well, it looked like fun. I had tried out for the high school senior play. We did *Guys and Dolls*, and the guy who was the theater department was very kind to let me and three other guys try out way at the end and then put us on the crew, which we thought was pretty cool because you got out of class. And this looked like fun, so "let's see where this goes." But, of course, it went nowhere.

H: Were you writing at this time?

LH: No. Well, I did take a writing course because I was coming to the end of my time at Kendall, and needed the hours. But the guy who taught the class was a little "off bubble" as they say, and I don't remember doing any writing or anything he had to say about the craft. I heard a couple years later that he would hang around the fountain in downtown Evanston and talk to God. My first writing teacher—stone fucking crazy.

H: Not much help in your development as a writer.

LH: Absolutely not. Are you kidding? How can you learn anything from a fool? But I still had this vague notion about theater, and when I graduated from Kendall in January, the plan was to work for six months and then transfer to San Francisco State, which had a good reputation for theater. But the notion was extremely vague, and that whole notion became academic when I was drafted in May.

H: While you were at Kendall in 1962 through 1965, did the subject of American involvement in Vietnam ever come up?

LH: No, that is how clueless we were.

H: You mentioned that one of the reasons why you attended Kendall was for the deferment. Obviously, you were conscious that getting drafted was a definite possibility for people your age.

LH: Yes, but that was also early '65 and there were only a handful of Americans there. The big news was Laos. I don't recall ever talking about Vietnam with anybody.

H: Finally, in this "Son" section focusing on your life prior to entering the military, are there any other details from your life that might help people understand you better as a writer and as a person?

LH: I can't recall that it was especially unhappy, but maybe we didn't know how unhappy we were. We didn't know that beating your kid wasn't the way to raise kids. There was plenty to do. We were given a lot of time by ourselves. The word in the house was "go find something to do." And in a small town like Northbrook, it turned out that there was plenty of what is referred to nowadays as "imaginative play." If you couldn't find anything else to do, you could go up to the Milwaukee Road Station and hang out with the station agent, and he was a hoot. There was a telegraph key (this was back in the days when they still sent telegrams, I think), and he had a spare. So he would sit you at the desk and teach you a sort of play Morse Code. Or you could help with the boxes and stuff like that. He was sort of a cranky, harmless old guy. Every once in a while, of course, a train would come through, and we would go out and stand at the edge of the platform. These huge greasy, ugly machines would come roaring into town, and that was daring and scary—and great fun. This had something to do with my becoming a train buff, I expect.

We didn't get an allowance, so I went to work when I was twelve. The word was "whatever money you make during the summer, that's it." And we all worked and floated along. Actually, I think a lot of writers, a lot of artists, came to adulthood by floating along. It may well be that a lot of writers were not particularly successful in school. Mark Twain dropped out early and taught himself his letters by working as a printer's devil. So he basically learned his "letters" upside down and backwards.

SOLDIER _____

H: Just after you and your brother received your draft notices, did you seek counseling about ways to evade the draft?

LH: No. Years later I had a sit-down conversation with Studs Terkel's wife, Ida. She wanted to know what it would have taken to get me out of the draft. And I told her that she would have had to come into the house and sit down at the dining room table with the six of us—mother, father, and the four sons—and explain it. No one told us we could go to Canada; no one told us we could become conscientious objectors. We knew about joining the National Guard, but everybody knew that you had to be somebody's kid. Plus, look at the numbers—six years in the National Guard or Army Reserve. I wasn't interested in six years, any more than I was interested in two years. Being an NG turned out to be a suck-ass job. Lots of professional athletes were NGs, and there was a certain resentment attached to that. A lot of current politicians were NGs and didn't have to really show up—guys exactly like President Bush. I mean that's a source of some bitterness, especially when he makes such big deal of his war in Iraq. But to answer your question, no. No one told us we didn't have to go.

H: Describe your and your brother's feelings when you received draft notices in the same mail.

LH: We just looked at each other and just said "Ah, fuck. Okay, you gotta do this, and if you don't, they send the cops after you."

H: What was your father's response to the draft notice?

LH: My dad said, "Go ahead and do it. It'll be good for you." My mother said, "It'll make a man out of you." That's what she said a year later when my youngest brother, Philip, dropped out of high school to join the Marine Corps. She had to sign his papers because he was a minor. Well, it didn't make a man of him. From my point of view, about the only thing the marines give you is what James Jones called a "pointless pride."

H: What were your initial impressions of basic training at Fort Polk, Louisiana?

LH: Everybody else was seventeen and eighteen. Richard was twenty, and I was twenty-two. The first couple of weeks there was this great skepticism. We had a young drill sergeant fresh out of drill sergeant's school, and he and I had this very clear, unstated agreement: "You know this is bullshit. I know this is bullshit. We both know I have to get through this in one piece. I'll run your magic little mile in the morning. I'll do your little push-ups. I'll scream my bloody head off in the bayonet pit. I'll go out to the range, and zero my rifle. I'll sit through the chaplain's nitwit 'character lectures.' But please don't bullshit me with 'drop and give me ten.'" And we basically kept to that. He got the gag. He knew exactly where we were going, and he was very compassionate in that way—not a lot of yelling. Our other drill sergeant was perhaps the dumbest person I have ever met, as well as a sadistic prick. He thought Richard and I were twins, and try as we might we couldn't talk him out of it. He would yell at us, and run us around, and give us a hard time the way those guys were supposed to, but we just laughed at him. There were a couple other NCOs in the company who were just pricks and couldn't wait to fuck with you, even on payday. I come from a working class family where the word was, "It's payday. They owe you the money."

H: So you didn't have a macho image of yourself or romantic illusions about the military?

LH: There is nothing macho or romantic about learning what it is to be a piece of meat. Richard and I were about as close as we had ever been and talked about this a good deal. The best way to do this is to do everything we can to get into shape. We did a lot of physical training: "We've gotta take this seriously because this is serious business. God only knows where we're gonna wind up." I don't remember much talk about "you guys are going to the ''Nam' and we're gonna teach you how to kill gooks." But getting into good physical condition was important; oh, and let's pay attention on the rifle range. You never know.

H: Since your basic training was in mid-1966, there weren't a lot of drill sergeants who had come back from Vietnam.

LH: No, they didn't talk about it if they did. But Fort Knox [advanced individual
training] was different. A couple of the NCOs had stories, but very little
actual information. The training I got at Fort Knox was utterly irrelevant for
Vietnam. We trained for classic garrison duty in Germany. If I hadn't been
sent to Vietnam, I probably would have wound up in an armored cavalry
outfit on the Czechoslovakian border and spent my time watching my little
two hundred meters of Iron Curtain for eight hours a day.

H: Did you feel basic training was a humiliating experience?

LH: You were reminded everyday that you were nothing more than a piece of
meat. Also, basic training was supposed to be ten weeks, so they were shov-
ing people through as quickly as they could. This was the middle of '66, and
they needed bodies now. Robert McNamara decided to lower the physical
and intelligence standards, and the famous "Project 100,000" [a Pentagon
program to draft low-aptitude recruits] was born. And we had some of those
guys; I'm sure. And it was clear that those guys were not equipped for military life. At one level you simply have to regard the training as work, and all
you have to do is pay attention. And if you can't hack it—regardless of the
reason—well, you're screwed. Ninety percent of being a rifle soldier is physical, and if you can't even carry a pack, you are simply not going to last.

H: How did you manage to survive the experience of basic?

LH: No one has asked me that question ever, and I don't have a ready answer.
It was always just "okay, whatever the next day brings," just like everybody
else. I'll learn to stand at attention. I'll learn to pack a footlocker. I'll learn
to spit-shine my boots. I'll learn to "sir" any nitwit who comes down the
pike, and whip a salute on the son of a bitch. Whatever it takes.

H: Was your time in advanced individual training [AIT] at Fort Knox in
armored cavalry reconnaissance any different, any better?

LH: AIT was like butter on a hot skillet. Our officers and NCOs definitely got
the gag: "This is bullshit. We know this training is pointless. We know
you're never going to see this equipment again" (which was obsolete in the
first place); "but the training manual says we do it this way, so this is the
way we're going to do it."

H: It seems from your unflattering descriptions of basic training and AIT, the
only valuable part in preparing you for Vietnam was the physical training.

LH: Yeah, it was the physical training, everyday, all the time, and the week at
the rifle range. I had never handled a weapon in my life, but became a very
good shot, even if I do say so myself.

H: After AIT, you were transferred to a permanent post at Fort Knox with an armor unit training officers for armored cavalry units. What were your responsibilities?

LH: The officer training school guys were on the fast track to an officer's commission, and they "trained" on our equipment. We drove. They told us where to go.

H: What were they learning?

LH: How to be officers, platoon leaders. If there's one thing I think a lieutenant should be obliged to understand, particularly if he's in a combat job, it is to read a fucking map and use a compass. The other thing that an officer should know is know is how to lead. "You're in charge, bub, so lead." A lot of those ninety-day wonders [commissioned after abbreviated ninety-day OCS program] looked as if they didn't know their ass from a hole in the ground. Lieutenant Calley of My Lai Massacre fame was a ninety-day wonder.

H: Were you doing any reading at this time?

LH: I vividly recall reading *Catch-22*. And I did not think it was all that funny.

H: As you're reading *Catch-22*, is it confirming everything you're already thinking about the military system and lifers?

LH: In spades. Right down to the funny names, the bullshit missions, and the institutional stupidity and arrogance of every ticket-punching lifer I ever met. When my orders for Vietnam came through around Thanksgiving, I just collapsed. "Oh, fuck." That fall more and more guys were transferring into the company from Vietnam. And these guys did not look well at all. A little scary, actually. In the memoir, *Black Virgin Mountain*, I say it wasn't like they had an attitude. They had no attitude at all. And my memory of these guys is they were 100 percent fed up with the lifers and their garrison bullshit to the very eyeballs. The best example I recall is a young staff sergeant who drank all the time. And he went from E-6 to nothing in about six weeks—bang, bang, bang.

H: Tell me more about First Sergeant Alva, who was the ranking NCO in this training company and about whom you write favorably in your memoir.

LH: A very cool guy. He's the one who took me aside the day I signed out of the company on my way overseas. "Vietnam," he said, "is not a white man's war." I'd never heard him talk like that before, and he was very blunt. He was built like the Pillsbury Doughboy, a fireplug-looking guy just as sharp as they come, and I'm thinking, "What on earth is he doing in the army?" After I read *From Here to Eternity*—Sergeant Warden—I'm thinking, "Oh, there are people like that [insightful] in the army." One of the very few lifers I met then or since, that I had any regard for. Wherever you are, First Sergeant Alva, my sincere regards to you.

H: Did your brother Richard, who was with you in basic and later went to AIT with an artillery unit, have a similar attitude toward his training and the military before being sent to Germany?

LH: His experience was even worse.

H: This situation is later confirmed when he is given an early discharge from the army.

LH: I have to tell you I didn't see it coming, but it made perfect sense. He was sent to Germany, and like any sensible person simply would not put up with the bullshit. He started telling people off. Told off the officers, told off the NCOs, told off a couple chaplains, told off a couple shrinks. That takes stones, as they say. "This is bullshit. You're a fool, and I'm not going to go along with anything you say." He kept it up and kept it up, so finally they let him out. I was home on leave before I went overseas. He calls from the airport out of the blue and comes home. Definitely a surprise. He and I sat down in the kitchen for two hours, just the two of us, and that was maybe the bluntest conversation I've ever had with anyone in my life.

H: How did you feel about his comments? Was he saying that you were a fool for going to Vietnam?

LH: No. He felt terrible about my going. Just terrible. But I told him, "Richard, you did the thing that everybody wants to do: 'fuck you, colonel; fuck you, sergeant, fuck you. You want someone to paint your jeep trailer? You fuckin' paint it. It looks fine to me.'" I felt glad for him. He had done the thing—telling off the lifers—that everyone wanted to do. Good for you, Richard.

H: Did you think that you should do the same thing and not go to Vietnam?

LH: Well, I just didn't. I wasn't looking forward to it, but not showing up looked like a lot more trouble than it was going to be worth. Prison is prison, you know, but military prison is something altogether different. Ask anyone who's done serious time at Leavenworth [military prison at Fort Leavenworth, Kansas] breaking rocks for twenty years [laughs].

H: Your brother got an honorable discharge, right?

LH: Under general conditions. They had a couple of phrases for various types of discharges that were really blaming and shaming. One of the phrases was "unsuitable for military service," as if it's your fault the army is so fucked up. As if being in the military is the be-all and end-all of everything, which is another reason I have it in for lifers. One of the great things lifers don't get is that (this is one of the great gags of being a writer) writers always get the last word.

H: Larry, are you saying that one of your motivations for writing is to get even and to get that last word?

LH: Yeah, why resist the temptation? Unsuitable for military service? Well, fuck you. Why not? Who was it said "Don't get mad, get even"? Liferism [sic] seems to be taking over American culture by leaps and bounds. The serious anxiety about the way of the world, the real prospect of endless, serial wars, spills over into all kinds of behaviors that have to do with "sit down and shut up and let me tell you the way it's going to go down." There are more cops; there's more cop behavior. I mean, it seems as if everybody's a cop. Not long ago I made a trip to Boston on Amtrak. This is a train. I'm minding my own business. All of a sudden this guy dressed in black from head to toe came up to me to get my ticket. He was definitely not the conductor. He would not look at me in the face, which tells you something right away. People who will not engage you one-on-one are up to something. He checked my ticket and said, "You got identification?" "Yes." "Can I see it?" "Of course." Showed him my driver's license. "When were you born? Your birthday?" I looked at him finally and said, "Are you the conductor? When were you born?" Why is he fucking with me? Chicken shit, we used to call it. Pissed off? You bet. Why does it seem as if the government is making war on its own people? Get even? You bet.

H: After your home leave, you flew to Oakland, California, and then flew out of Travis Air Force Base for Vietnam. What were you anticipating about your approaching tour in Vietnam?

LH: I had the image in my head that the plane would land, pull up to a spot on the tarmac, they'd roll the stairs up to the door, we would be issued rifles, and then low-crawl down the stairs straight into a ditch and off to the war.

H: So you were scared?

LH: Yes, of course. Any reasonable person would be. We had absolutely no idea what was going to happen next. As far as we knew American soldiers were dropping like flies.

H: What were your first few days like in country?

LH: At the 90th Replacement Detachment at Bien Hoa, there was absolutely nothing to do while we waited for our orders, and there were a million of us, so we were divvied up into chickenshit details of one kind or another. And swear to God, that first day I pulled the detail that burned shit. So, my first job in Vietnam was burning shit. Welcome to Vietnam, bub. And, of course, it only went downhill from there.

H: What were your initial impressions of the land and the Vietnamese people when you arrived in country?

LH: God, this is hot. And it's hot twenty-four hours a day. How is anybody going to be able to do anything in this heat? Just like every other fucking new guy I was seriously disoriented by so simple a thing as the weather. Altogether, it took about three months to get used to it. The other thing that impressed me is, this is chaos. And, finally, the countryside around Saigon and Cu Chi is not what old timers would call "handsome." Still isn't.

H: What were your impressions of your fellow soldiers?

LH: The first time I saw the company, they rolled in from the field, Operation Junction City—up to that time the largest operation of the war. They'd been up along the Cambodian border, and they looked like they had had it—much worse than the guys who were showing up at Fort Knox. At least those guys had been hosed off a little. These guys just looked like they didn't have anything left, thousand-meter-stared to death—like you see in a prizefight at the end of the round where the guy who's really taken a whupping is just sitting there beat to a pulp and staring off into oblivion. He can barely keep track of the colors—that kind of numbness, and I really didn't get to understand that for about eight months. Nowadays, psychologists have a perfect word for it, "combat psychosis." But now it's also called PTSD. They should find a better word for that. After the Civil War, it was called "soldier's heart." There's that famous photograph of the '68 Tet Offensive in Hue where the Marine is sitting with his back to a wall, and he's holding his rifle in front of him and his helmet canted back on his head. There is just, whooo, nothing in his face. That was that: "Oh fuck, this is going to be a long year." The other thing that was clear, and it became clearer as I went along: whatever it takes, cousin, whatever I have to do to get out of here in one piece. It's just that you never realize exactly what that means, because you wind up giving up almost every good thing you ever thought about yourself. And you don't give it up; it's taken from you: it's boiled off; yanked out; ripped. And the hard part of that process is that, afterward, you don't always get it back.

H: Your humanity?

LH: Your emotional and spiritual connection with anything that came before. All kinds of fellow feelings, all kinds of physical feeling. Your senses are blunted. I'm sure it was different in the so-called elite units, but for garden-variety, slug-it-out, ground-pounding grunts, you just grind it out until there's nothing left to grind—that's the soldier's work. And that's the thing about what's going on in Iraq that makes my heart sore.

H: Describe a typical day for you in the war, when you were out in the bush and away from base camp.

LH: The recon platoon sat a lot of perimeters for the artillery. We had ten tracks [armored personnel carriers], thirty machine guns, and forty guys. When the battalion went to the field, we would always take a battery of howitzers for close-in tactical support, and recon was perfect. Everybody was a machine gunner, and if you weren't a machine gunner, you were driving. So we sat a lot of perimeters for the artillery. The line companies would work the bushes, and every once in a while they'd call in for artillery support, fire missions. Recon would sit. Did that a lot. We became the artillery's responsibility, so we ate with the artillery guys, used their showers, and drank their beer. Well, for every 105-mm howitzer there was an ammo truck, an equipment truck, and, it seemed, a beer truck. To make a long story short, all I ever saw the artillery do was strip to the waist, fill sandbags, hump rounds, and drink beer. We sat on our asses a lot, but every night we put out an ambush, and those were never fun. But at least we weren't pounding ground with the straight-leg infantry. Anything but that.

And every once in a while recon would go on an actual operation. Search and destroy missions, S&Ds we called them. We'd drive down a road, and then at the word we would turn into the woods, busting jungle, looking for bunkers and camps and out-of-the-way villages. Busting jungle goes like this: you drive up to a tree in the wood line and gun the engine. The treads dig in, the front of the track "climbs" the tree, and you knock it over. Then you go on to the next tree, and the next, and the next. Slow going. Basically, you were making your own road. Then we would come to a village, say, and pound it into the ground.

The other thing we did was escort the Dau Tieng–Tay Ninh convoy because our ten tracks were absolutely armed to the teeth. We got up around five o'clock in the morning, and had breakfast. Then two or three tracks would escort the engineers with minesweepers to clear the road of mines. Halfway to Tay Ninh, we'd meet the engineers coming the other way. We'd turn around, and go back to pick up the convoy. So you did basically a round trip and a half to Tay Ninh, and that was a day's work. The tracks had Chrysler V-8 engines, a four-barrel carburetor, straight-pipe mufflers that came right off the manifolds, so the tracks made a very large sound. It was great fun driving these large, ugly machines. Great kicks. The same kicks that helicopter pilots talk about. The tracks would only do thirty miles per hour top end, but we drove those things as fast as we could possibly drive them. I can't remember ever changing the oil or the spark plugs.

I cannot recall if there was a spark plug wrench in the whole platoon. We didn't have a lot of stuff we were supposed to have.

H: For each track, you had a driver and three people manning the mounted machine guns.

LH: We had one 50-caliber machine gun and two M-60s. If I could have gotten hold of a 20-mm or a 40-mm anti-aircraft cannon, I would have had one of those. Plus a hundred pounds of C-4 [explosives], a couple dozen grenades, couple dozen claymores, thousands of rounds of ammunition— we were armed to the teeth. We could keep at it all day if we had to.

H: Did you think about the political aspects of the war while you were there?

LH: Not even once that I recall. Once you're in the field, the argument has passed clean through the "politics" of the discussion. You were standing in the middle of an awful nightmare. Politics had nothing to do with it. First things first, cousin. No, we were completely focused on making it through the night. A ghetto mentality.

H: Did you know about the growing war protests in the U.S.?

LH: Well, we did, but who cared? All of that was irrelevant to us. My ass wasn't in a sling; it was in a hammock. The war was fucked up, that was clear. We were not very sophisticated about the rightness or the wrongness of the war, but everybody did know that it was bullshit. The lieutenants knew, the captains knew. When our new platoon leader, the one lieutenant I had any regard for, came into the platoon in the fall of '67, he had the NCOs, the track commanders, meet. He looked at us and said, "Gentlemen, our job is to make sure everybody goes home in one piece." And we looked at him and said, "Lieutenant, this is an excellent plan; how can we help you?" And just like that we stopped doing ambushes; we stopped doing a lot of crazy, just-looking-for-shit-to-do stuff. There was a lot of just hanging back, lots of convoys. Meanwhile, we were, of course, headed straight for the Tet Offensive of 1968. Not fun. I should have come home in a bag.

H: Okay, at this point in late 1967, why did you know this war was a disaster?

LH: The gag was we were there to "win their hearts and minds." That was the propaganda excuse, anyway. But there weren't any hearts and minds won that I ever saw, and I'm sure that we radicalized more Vietnamese than you can shake a stick at. No one was ever able to show us the good of it. We can't be doing this, going through this, for so little. The Vietnamese didn't look like they were prospering, not around the Iron Triangle, Cu Chi, or Tay Ninh, anyway. It was clear that a lot of the Vietnamese didn't like us or want us to be there, and the rest just sort of put up with us because we were good for business. We were nothing more fancy than an occupation army, and the Vietnamese went along with it because we were easy money. I'm sure a lot of expatriate southern Vietnamese would dispute that, but from an American point of view, that's what we saw. All we're doing is wrecking people's lives, wrecking the countryside. What is the famous quote? "We had to destroy the village in order to save it." And everybody felt, "I'm going to put in my year the best way I know how, go home, and that will be that." If we had been there for the duration, there would have been a fucking mutiny. It would have amounted to something like, "Let's drive these mother fuckers [the tracks] to the Brigade CP and shoot up a bunch of lifers; we've got nothing to lose." We were not fun to be around and took it out on the Vietnamese, I must say, to my great shame. And I don't know if the lifers understood just how precarious their situation was.

H: Were there any instances of fragging in your unit?

LH: Well, not a fragging, but. . . . Bravo Company was almost all black guys with white officers and NCOs. Out in the field one night, three guys were on an LP, a listening post out in the woods, and the first sergeant went out to check on them. They shot him dead. The story we heard was that he didn't give the call sign. Well, nobody paid any attention to the call sign because we knew each other's voices, even in whispers. So this guy went checking on the LPs, and these three black guys had had enough of first sergeant whatever his name was. So, they shot him.

H: Did you use this incident in *Close Quarters*?

LH: How could I not? And, *snap*, just that quickly, they pulled Bravo Company out of the field and sent them back to camp. A provost marshal came down and investigated around, but nothing could be proved. There were two credible witnesses, after all. Very shortly after that, the next day or the day after that, all the white officers and NCOs were gone, and an entirely different cadre of officers and NCOs was brought in.

Then, in our platoon we had a guy who came in from some garrison outfit in Germany, this E-6 staff sergeant. And he starts right in with his lifer chicken shit. Now, we know what we're doing; we know how to clean our weapons; we know how to top off a gas tank; we know how to set out our claymores at night; we know how to keep quiet at night; we know how to walk an ambush. We got it down, okay? But the guy would go around and it's "do this, do that, do the other," and blah blah—like he's really in charge. From our point of view he's just another fucking new guy. Some of us started to talk, "Let's just shoot the mother fucker." But I said, "Let me talk to him." Now, we're in a laager out in the woods somewhere, a million miles from nowhere, and I take him aside. We sit down on a log. I say, "This is just between you and me. Look around, what do you see?" "Well, I see a bunch of slack troopers who need to get whipped into shape," or some bullshit like that. I said, "Well you know what I see. I see a platoon full of guys with guns. And there are a couple of people in this laager who don't like you. So from one human being to another, cut it out." But he just wouldn't, so then they started taking up a pot, and it quickly came to serious money. One guy said he'd do it because he was coming up on his R&R.

I said that I'd talk to the clown one more time. Same laager, same log, I said, "Look, pal, cut it out. Just between you and me, we don't give a shit what your rank is. You're the fucking new guy. Cut the chicken shit. Shut up, sit down, watch." Then he goes into this tirade. I said, "No. No. You don't understand. There are some guys in this laager who simply do not like you. It's the easiest thing in the world to fake a firefight at two o'clock in the morning, and somebody with a shotgun or an AK-47 is going to come up behind you and blow your head off. So, cut the chicken shit." After that, he snapped out of it.

H: One term that keeps emerging throughout our conversation is "lifer." Obviously lifer refers to different types of people and attitudes both within and outside the military. What exactly is a "lifer"?

LH: Well, the first level of meaning is that a lifer is a person with a career, but a lot of people have a career, and don't behave like lifers. Paul Fussell [World War II veteran, professor and literary scholar, author of *The Great War and Modern Memory*] is a good example of someone with a very successful career who works for a large organization and maintains his integrity. Lifers are the guys who go along with the program for the sake of their precious little careers, "punching their tickets" along the way. They want Airborne-Rangers, because that's a punch on the ticket; they want to be a rifle company CO; they want a purple heart and a bronze star; they want to put in time at the War College. On and on. After a while, there's an active resentment for people like that because they don't really care about anything else but the punches on their tickets.

H: Lifers, in a sense, no matter what career they have, are basically using other people as a means to advancing in the organization.

LH: It often works out that lifers are simply incompetent. It wasn't until I met John Clark Pratt in 1983 [Air Force Vietnam veteran, professor, and author of several books including *The Laotian Fragments*] that I met a colonel who had actually read a book. Of course, he had because he used to teach literature at the Air Force Academy.

H: Returning to the daily life of a soldier in your unit, was there widespread drug use?

LH: Heavens to Betsy, yes!

H: What was the purpose—recreation, escape, boredom killing?

LH: All three categories, and more besides, I suppose. The only guys who didn't smoke grass were the guys who couldn't—for some reason it didn't agree with them. So, they drank.

H: Were soldiers using heroin?

LH: No. My understanding is that heroin didn't become a big thing until 1969 when the American generals finally figured out that the enlisted men were smoking grass and they went to the ARVNs and said, "Cut it out; no more marijuana." It was a common understanding of the corruption in Vietnam that nothing moved unless the ARVN [Army of Vietnam] generals moved it. Anyway, that's when marijuana became more expensive than heroin. If I'd been there in '69, I'm certain that I would have become a heroin junkie.

H: Were you and other members of your unit smoking the marijuana on missions?

LH: Oh, yeah. We'd get up at five o'clock in the morning and smoke a joint by the time we finished breakfast, and we were good for the day. It certainly wasn't a physical addiction, but it did become a serious habit—and let me say that I never heard the word marijuana until I went overseas. That numbness became more and more cherished the further into your tour you got. I was always astonished by marines up-country who would tell me that they never saw any marijuana. Well, the kids in our neck of the woods would bring the stuff out to us from the villages: Cokes, beer, marijuana, hookers, or anything else we asked for. For five bucks you could get a pack of tailor-made opium-soaked marijuana cigarettes, still sealed in the cellophane—and it was very good grass. And the further you got into your tour, the more you're drinking, too. We drank anything we could get our hands on, PX beer, Vietnamese beer by the liter, and Vietnamese cognac by the fifth, which was just this god-awful stuff. There's a letter from me to Edie, maybe a month and a half before I came home, and without any mention of it in any of my other letters, I told her that I had stopped smoking so much marijuana and was down to a quart of cognac per day. So we were drinking a lot. Soldiers have always been heavy drinkers. Ask the guys from World War II.

H: Did you ever have a sense you were putting your life and others' lives in jeopardy by being high and drinking?

LH: The goal was to be numb, and the further you got into your tour the more earnest was that desire. This has everything to do with the growing sense in you that you just didn't care anymore. We even said it out loud to each other, "I don't fucking care." There were all kinds of self-destructive behavior. Being stoned in a firefight was pretty bizarre, but we weren't incapacitated. Just stoned.

H: How many guys in your platoon of forty were smoking marijuana?

LH: Well, there were never forty guys in the platoon. We were always short bodies. Smoking marijuana? Maybe two-thirds. The stuff was practically growing up out of the sandbags; it was everywhere. You could get opium tabs, which are like aspirin; the medic could get Darvon, mild painkillers. And you'd take the capsules apart, throw away the aspirin, and save the little dots of serious stuff. You'd get twenty of those and throw those back, and wash it down with a slug of beer.

H: Were your officers using marijuana?

LH: Not that I knew.

H: And for the lifers, alcohol was their drug of choice?

LH: Yes. Officers could get beer and hard liquor from supply. Our hard liquor came from the Vietnamese.

H: After your one-year tour, what impressions did you take with you about the Vietnamese people and the land?

LH: Well, it certainly wasn't complimentary. When I left, I had the clear sense that I had turned my back on a nightmare, and those people and that place were part of it. It wasn't for years, not years, that any of that changed.

H: Is the particular Vietnamese place that remains with your from your tour the Black Virgin Mountain [Nui Ba Den] so prominently featured in your memoir? Or is there another place that you think about?

LH: No, I'd have to say the mountain. There was one stretch of fifty-one days or so in the summer that we stayed in laager with the artillery near the village of Suoi Dau about two miles south of the mountain. My track was pointed right at it. Then in December, we were at a place called Fire Base Grant not far from Suoi Dau, and the mountain was right there. So, we got to see the mountain close-up morning, noon, and night, and in all weathers. Certainly undeniable, all but overwhelming. When I started working on the memoir, I came to understand that Nui Ba Den gave us something right then and there that we didn't even know we needed. No one I know who served in that neck of the woods had any idea what the story of the mountain was or what the mountain meant to the Vietnamese; didn't care, actually. All I can tell you is that I was always glad to see the mountain, especially at first light, and that it has always been an image in my imagination, but I'm not exactly sure what that amounts to or what to make of it. Come back in a couple of years.

H: Later, we're going to come back to this notion of the mountain's meaning in your life, because on the final page of the memoir, you write . . .

LH: [Heinemann interrupting] About going home?

H: Yes, because finding a home seems to be an important theme in all of your works. Philip Dosier in Close Quarters is, in a sense, looking for a home, and obviously Paco in Paco's Story is looking for a home and holds on to this romantic image of a place and a home: "He [Paco] wants to discover a livable peace—as if he's come up a path in a vast evergreen woods, come upon a comfortable cabin as solid as a castle keep . . . " (Paco's Story, New York: Farrar, Straus and Giroux, 1986, 174).

LH: What? That's a surprise [Heinemann exhibiting mock surprise].

H: Another theme that appears in many excellent pieces of war literature involves an individual's heart-of-darkness experience, in particular, episodes of soldiers losing control and in a primitive fashion revealing the dark, evil side that resides in us all. Did you experience or observe any of this during your Vietnam tour?

LH: Well, none of us were much fun to be around, but there was one man in the platoon who scared everybody; one of those guys who liked it, and he was self-destructive from the day I met him. He was the model for the character Quinn in Close Quarters. He was an extraordinary man and one of those guys you could see giving himself up to it, almost embracing death, and as curious as anyone about how it is going to come to him. He was the guy who wanted to kill the NCO [incident mentioned earlier], and he was not kidding. He just didn't give a shit. He was the guy who faked a firefight one night and with his 50-caliber machine gun chopped a tree down, and the trunk was about eight inches thick. He is pounding out rounds right at this tree, and then we hear this crack. The thing falls over, and the top of the tree falls over right in front of us. He's laughing, laughing, laughing. If there was a killer in the platoon, he was it, but he wasn't going along with anybody. He was definitely on his own, too. The morning after this big firefight in January [Suoi Cut, 1968], he was in base camp. He didn't even leave the base camp when we went to the field; he had talked himself into some housecat job. So they call to bring all these replacements in, and none of the other TCs wanted him on their tracks because he was so much trouble. But he was a dead shot and a great mechanic. I thought, "Yes, I'll take him absolutely. At a time in our lives when we needed killers, yeah, I'll take him. He's not perfect, but. . ." Touching evil is a very peculiar sensation.

H: Joseph Conrad in *Heart of Darkness* also comments on the inexplicable "fascination of the abomination." Although repelled by evil, death, and horror, participants in the horror also find something attractive, exhilarating, fascinating about the whole dark experience. Did you experience or observe any these phenomena?

LH: Oh absolutely, yes. The Bible refers to it as (it's a wonderful phrase) "lust of the eye." Lust of the eye, it's in the Gospel of John somewhere. That happened after you'd been there awhile, and it's part of the process. The excitement of it, the adrenaline, the momentum, the movement of the event takes you up, and yeah, "kill 'em all." That's the thing that makes my heart sore about what's going on in Iraq, because you know that's part of the process these guys are going through—"Kill 'em all."

H: What did you learn about love in Vietnam? Or was that an emotion that you never experienced during your tour?

LH: The love among brothers, and (I don't want to make this up) I think the part about love that I learned was that it's not necessarily a two-way street. Because I love you does not necessarily mean that you have to reciprocate. And it [love] comes out of a trust. Because I love you, I will trust you with my life—no small thing—and when push comes to shove, I trust you to hold up your end, because I'm sure going to hold up my end. Something like that is hard to come by. Love is hard to come by in whatever form it comes to you.

H: What did you learn about courage during your tour?

LH: Wow. Hard to come by. I suppose there is a kind of banal courage. It's the sort of everyday, ordinary, garden-variety, get-up-with-the-chickens-and-do-what-you-got-to-do kind of courage, but we never called it that. Then there are those extraordinary moments, and you don't even know you have it in you until you get to that moment. The curious thing is that young soldiers, if they ever get to that moment, get to it when they're eighteen or nineteen or twenty years old, and learn something unique about themselves. Some people never get to it; they never understand that about themselves. And it is always an extraordinary moment, which is what bothers me about war propaganda. You're not a hero just because you fucking show up. To be a hero, in the old sense of the word, means you have to do something extraordinary. No one ever caught me being courageous enough [for that person] to turn around to someone and say, "That's one brave mother fucker. That's an act of courage." It doesn't happen that way, but when it happens, it is as if a jolt goes through you. On the other hand, anyone who stands on his hind legs and says, "I'm a hero," is just an asshole.

H: Upon leaving Vietnam, how were you a different person from the one who entered Vietnam one year earlier?

LH: I was twenty-five pounds lighter. Lean and solid, the one-thousand-meter stare, and wrapped pretty tight. That's what soldier's work will do for you.

H: Bitter?

LH: Absolutely. Actually, I didn't know how radicalized I was until I went back to school. Much changed. I don't know anyone who does a combat tour and isn't changed. You are changed. It is irresistible. There are changes in your body, and the physical things don't change back, like the nervous system. If you don't change, the event itself will simply squeeze you out. And I saw that happen, too. You come home physically and spiritually changed. That's what's happening to the guys coming back from Iraq. People back here, they just don't get it.

H: How were you radicalized?

LH: Radicalized against the war.

H: How about against your government?

LH: Yeah. I wanted to get even with somebody. I mean *even*. The war was not needful; this was an evil thing done to a lot of people, me included.

H: One of the clichés of the Vietnam veteran's return is the story of people spitting on the returning soldier and making negative comments; did you experience any of that?

LH: No, nothing was ever said to my face, not at Columbia, not on the street or anywhere else. The only time anybody ever said anything was at this reading I did on a university campus in the '90s. After I read, I usually say to the audience that "we can close the doors, and we can talk about anything you want to talk about." So this history professor, who was later described to me as the faculty pill, says, "If I had been in the airport, I would have spit on you." And he said it with a keen invective in his voice. This was the one and only time I have ever lost my temper at a reading. I came around from behind the podium, and I walked up the middle aisle, right to where he was sitting. I said, "Let me straighten you out, pal. First of all, spitting on somebody and shooting them with a rifle come from the same place in the heart, and don't you forget it. And second, if you had come up to me at the San Francisco airport or O'Hare and spit on me, I would have given you the beating of your life."

H: Did you experience what you would consider PTSD symptoms upon your return?

LH: Lots of sitting up long, long nights. I don't remember being plagued with nightmares because, I suppose, all my imaginative energy was going into my writing. I remember every couple of months hopping into the car and just driving for two or three days, driving out until I got really exhausted and then stopping and driving back. That went on for, oh, I don't know, years. And I still have what I can only describe as an exaggerated startle response, a kind of tick. A VA shrink once told me that it was a kind of flashback, and he called it something-something seizure. I got back in March of 1968, and by December I was just not having a good time at all. I went to the Veterans Administration, and that's when I started taking valium. I was on my ass for about four months, and finally I had to go off the medication because I went back to driving a bus that summer. You're not supposed to take medication while you handle heavy machinery. Driving a bus was very intense, but then I was an intense person. (It is one of the strengths of my writing, the intensity of the storytelling.)

H: An intensity created by the language you use and the situations?

LH: Yeah, all of those things. I really can't recall just how intense I was overseas. Perhaps I was smoking a lot of grass and drinking a lot of booze just so I wouldn't explode. But I remember the time after my homecoming being very intense. Edie often describes it as being tight as spring wire. I don't think it was a good time for her either. She didn't really know what to do, and I think that's common with a lot of spouses—"What the fuck is this?" The last time she had seen you, you were this other person. Letters don't prepare you for what walks through the door. I was pretty intense, also just really didn't give a shit, but I was taking the writing courses and that was the focus of my intensity. One of the things my writing teacher made sure of is the same thing I tell my students: "Flat out, I don't care about the language or subject matter or point of view. All I care about is the quality of the writing. I'm not here to teach political correctness." And as far as my own writing back then, well, no one ever said anything to my face, but every once in a while I got the feeling other writers in the class wanted to say: "How dare you tell these stories, how dare you use this language, and how dare you represent this point of view." My attitude was "fuck off." I knew I had a story nobody else had, and I was going to tell it whether they wanted to hear it or not.

H: If you had not gone to Vietnam as a soldier, would you have had a story to tell and have become a writer?

LH: I would have ended up driving a bus. Bruce Weigl [Vietnam soldier-poet] would have ended up working in a mill somewhere. Tim O'Brien would probably have become a teacher. I think Robert Olen Butler would have become a writer, anyway, because that's where he was headed. Philip Caputo would have become a journalist.

H: It's ironic that so many writing careers were started by serving in the Vietnam War.

LH: By now, it's an irony that we understand. If it hadn't have been for the war, I would be driving a bus. That's not true; I'd be retired by now. It really is a remarkable irony. The Vietnamese writers I know say the same thing. Guys like Bao Ninh, he'd be on some farm somewhere, grinding out a living with his back. I mean, he's lucky he's not dead, first of all. The Vietnamese writers that I know all came up the hard way.

AUTHOR

H: Did you know when you arrived home from Vietnam, radicalized against the war and your government, that you were going to write about the war and your anger regarding it?

LH: No. Anger seems too small a word to describe it. Pissed-off is more to the point. The whole impulse began when I bumped into a superb writing teacher who understood what I was trying to do, and ended with the simple desire to tell the story. But being pissed-off certainly helped.

H: Were you writing for therapy?

LH: At first, yes. But then you get into the process of craft, and telling the story became anything but therapy. . . . I had the clear sense of getting the "story" straight in my own head.

H: This leads to an interesting question: as I think of your youngest brother, who came back from the war and would not talk about his experiences, at least to you, and the history of your family—of your brothers disappearing or committing suicide—was it your writing that enabled you to survive after your return from Vietnam?

LH: I resist thinking it's that simple. I think I outlasted my brothers because I don't own a gun. It's that simple, and there's no other way to say it. I got married right away, and Edie, my wife, saved my life more than once. Writing, learning the storyteller's craft, was important because it focused my intensity outward, not in. Writing was therapy, catharsis, for about twenty minutes. After I'd done a rewrite or two of Close Quarters I came to vividly understand that the writing craft was much more difficult than I had first supposed.

H: Was this first novel Philip Dosier's story, or was it your story?

LH: Well, it started out as my story, but when I discovered Dosier, the story really took off. I know a good deal about Philip Dosier, but he doesn't know a thing about me. In his book *The Great War and Modern Memory*, Paul Fussell says that war stories are usually first novels, and the fictionized memoir—first person, past tense—is the form and structure most easily accessible to rookies.

H: Did you read any of James Jones's war writing?

LH: Almost from the beginning when I went back to school. Reading *From Here to Eternity* really snapped my head back. Don't quote me, but I think that Jones is the first American writer to insist on using the word "fuck"—and he used it plenty. He and the lawyers must have had a fine time getting through that. My point is that Jones really nailed prewar, old-army barracks life. The life and language. Lifers with a capitol "L." Virtually set it in amber.

H: What about Jones's *The Thin Red Line*?

LH: A masterpiece among war stories, and ground zero of the large, long World War II combat novel.

H: Compare Jones's war writing with Mailer's, specifically Mailer's *The Naked and the Dead*.

LH: Mailer will tell you this. Jones had a knack for ordinary barracks language and getting to the nut of the story. Jones was self-educated. Mailer went to Harvard. Jones's writing is visceral. Mailer's more literary.

H: Did Jones become a literary model as you began writing your first novel?

LH: Absolutely, you bet. It turned out that we had many things in common. Came from the same neck of the woods, both served as ordinary soldiers in the 25th Division, both pissed-off, both became writers.

H: And is the James to whom the ghost narrators tell their story in *Paco's Story* James Jones?

LH: And all of the other Jameses. I wrote the first chapter in two furious weeks, and I sent it to my editor, Pat Strachan. She said, "Who is this 'James'? It wouldn't be James Jones, would it?" Well, he wasn't, but the irony was too remarkable a coincidence to ignore. "James" comes from a joke I do not recall, but the punch line is "Home, James." A pick-up on the home-theme in my work: home, comma, James. I always had the notion that Paco's story was the sort of story that you'd hear at the kitchen table late of an evening, or on the porch stoop, or under the deep shade of a picnic.

H: With your story [*Close Quarters*], what was that fine line between making up the story and writing down what actually happened? For your first book, why didn't you just write a war memoir?

LH: I could never have done it that way. My war year, my personal experience, was simply not dramatically interesting, as a story, I mean. Like everyone else, I began writing autobiographical stories, but there was more to the story of the war than just what happened to me. I was more concerned with teasing out the emotional truth of the event. I began stealing other guys' war stories, stealing from other novels. As I worked through the many, many rewrites, it became a reliving of the event, whether it happened or not. Your body is reliving it, too, but it's also akin to an imagined reminiscence, a consideration, a ciphering out of what the hell all that means, but without saying what the story means. Or being obvious about a moral.

H: Is that one error that many inexperienced writers make; they want to make sure the readers get that point by telling them what the story means? They don't rely on the storytelling to get the meaning across?

LH: Yes. Story is not essay. A storyteller doesn't have to explain anything. Let the story speak for itself. Just tell the story as straight as you can, without the bullshit. Sometime in the late nineteenth century, when the army was trying to corral the Apache in the Southwest once and for all, the army gathered a bunch of Indians to a palaver. Before anybody said anything, Cochise, one of the great chiefs of the Chiricahua, stood up, and before anybody said boo, he said, "You must speak straight to us so that your words will go like sunlight to our hearts." A very elegant way to put it, and, in a nutshell, that should be every writer's ambition. Cut the bullshit, and tell the story.

H: And bullshit goes to the head, or the ears, and talented writers write for the heart?

LH: And any inference, if there is an inference to be had, I will give to you. I am just arrogant enough about my understanding of craft to tell you that you will not get an inference that is unintended, "home" notwithstanding. Nothing in *Paco's Story* is a mistake or unintended. There's a reason why the book took eight years.

H: When did you decide to devote full time to your writing?

LH: Probably the end of the first semester at Columbia College. I'd finally bumped into something to match the intensity of the energy that I had. I was looking for something, and I got lucky right away.

H: When did you think you could make a living with your writing?

LH: Not for years, and it still isn't a get-rich-quick scheme. I started writing when I was twenty-four, but didn't publish anything until I was thirty.

H: What was your first published piece of writing?

LH: It was the "Coming Home High" chapter of *Close Quarters* for *Penthouse* magazine in 1974. That's the last year I had to work a summer. It is an odd place for a war story, but there will always be a warm place in my heart for *Penthouse*, somewhere.

H: Was your wife supportive of your writing career?

LH: Oh, absolutely. I know this sounds so dumb and such a cliché and obligatory, but I am positive that if Edie and I hadn't married, I would have wound up either in prison or a nuthouse. She worked full time. I was a full-time student, writing and reading and all those other things that young writers do. Twain called it "putting in time." Vonnegut referred to it as "messing around." Everybody else calls it "fucking off," a kind of purposeful adult play. The first piece I wrote for class that fall in '68, well, she took one look at it just as I was about to leave for class, and she said something like, "You're not handing this in, are you?" I am not a typist, and the story was, well, messy. She sat down and retyped it—zip-zap. Perfect. So, was my wife supportive of my writing? You bet, and thanks. Edie typed her way through both my first novels, revision after revision, on and on, and she became a very good editor and someone I depended on with my whole heart.

H: As a student at Columbia, what did you read and talk about in your writing classes?

LH: We would read out loud. Did a lot of that. Excerpts from novels, short stories, nonfiction. Russian. French. German. English. American. Eighteenth, nineteenth, twentieth century. Literature of all kinds. We might read a chapter from *Moby-Dick*, *Naked Lunch*, and Orwell's "At a Hanging." Brothers Grimm's "Master Thief," William Carlos Williams's "Knife of the Times," and Kafka's "Jackals and Arabs." There were endless combinations of genre and style. We'd talk about similarities and differences, form and structure, language, and the impact of the stories—and what they reminded us of. What I picked up on was that story seems to be a connection of the most intimate kind, like in a really good letter. That it's kin to sharing a secret. Rhetorically, you get to look the other person in the eye while you tell the story, and that is crucial. Wasn't it Whitman who said, "I won't tell everybody, but I will tell you." Who on earth is he talking to? I learned to use the whole dictionary, including the seven famous words you cannot say on television. Those particularly, and more besides. Language really is neutral, but depends for its impact on how it is received. Mark Twain said that the difference between the right word and the almost right word is the difference between lightning and the lightning bug. I learned precision. The other thing I discovered is that story doesn't just happen from the neck up. That a story has a physical, visceral impact, both for the teller as well as the listener, and for war stories that's half the game. If a story is given in the spirit in which Cochise means, the story must "go like sunlight." And, if you don't mind my saying so, I think I had a knack for it from the start.

H: One of your chief assets and distinguishing features as a writer is your use of graphic detail and frank language.

LH: People started calling me "the grunt's grunt" and "a working-class writer" a long time ago, but I never thought of myself in that way. I'm just a story-teller. When I first began in the writing trade all I had was war stories, as alien a topic in the 1960s and '70s as Melville's story about the white whale was to people in the middle of the nineteenth century. And how do you make an alien experience clear? There's no reason not to use simple bar-racks language, grunt patois, I guess we could call it. There's no reason not to be graphic. There's no reason to leave anything out. Language, bloody murder, or the blunt state of mind. Otherwise the story doesn't have the ring of authenticity, doesn't land on its feet, so to speak.

H: What's the key to writing an effective combat scene?

LH: The reader must be able to "imaginatively participate." You have to tell the story so that the person who's reading or listening can see it and experience the story in the way that everybody experiences a vivid dream. With that kind of immediacy, impact, and physical feeling. Writing a firefight scene or a battle scene is like writing any scene that's compact and intense—what is going on from one moment to the next, but in this much heightened way so that the reader can see it, and without any looking-the-other-way ambi-guities or fuzziness. Still and all, the overall story's the thing. A battle scene is just another turn of the screw. Look at *Johnny Got His Gun* [Dalton Trumbo].

H: What are your writing habits?

LH: I'm a morning person. I get up with the chickens, and work every day. You've got to look at it like a job. I have a studio in the attic, the biggest room in the house, and painted the ceiling white, so it's like being on the inside of a sugar cube. I work at a seven-foot-long dining room table. And, of course, I use a computer, marvelous invention. And, of course, I use a journal. Who doesn't? I work until the middle of the afternoon, and then it's Miller time.

H: How do you begin a writing project—with a character, a story idea, a moral or emotional conflict?

LH: *Close Quarters* began with a story about an ambush. *Paco's Story* began with the ghosts telling James about all the war stories no one wanted to hear. *Cooler by the Lake* began with the impulse to write a Chicago story. Edie told me, challenged me, to write a funny story, and years later my daughter Sarah told me that while I was working on it, it was the first time she'd ever heard laughter coming from the attic. *Black Virgin Mountain* began with the ambition to write a train travel book. There are plenty of train buffs in the United States who would pay good money to go there [Vietnam] and ride the rails. I was finally going to scoop Paul Theroux. With the current murder mystery, I started with the idea of modeling the main character, Isham Pepper, after my toothless, one-armed, retired farmer grandfather I have spoken of. He would button the cuff of his empty sleeve and tuck it into his pocket. He walked with a cane because he had a bad hip. Every night at dinner he'd sit down, stick the stump of his arm out, hang the cane on it, and then eat. And when you're six, that cane swinging back and forth makes a powerful impression. I laugh and tell myself I'm doing the murder mystery for the money.

H: What do you see as your legacy as a writer who happens to write about war in general and the Vietnam experience in particular?

LH: Go ahead and tell the stories that get the hair up on the back of your neck, and the hell with what anybody thinks. You've got to be honest with yourself, and that's not easy, cousin. You can't pull any punches. Good writing will always find an audience, regardless. It's the same as when you talk to kids about birth control or other such things. Teenagers want a serious, grown-up no-shit answer. It's their bodies, after all. In a democracy you must be able to talk about things in a meaningful way. That's the whole point, isn't it? Democracy is a great blessing and a remarkable invention, if sloppy. Let's talk about Vietnam and the war unsullied by sentimentality, what it is to be an ordinary soldier in a democratic army and what it means to a democracy when a war comes along that is based on a lie.

H: And by the latter you mean our country's actions in Vietnam and now in Iraq?

LH: Yes. There are similarities between our war in Vietnam and our war in Iraq and Afghanistan, but also unique differences. Political and military stupidities aside, both events have one thing in common. Any enterprise that begins with a lie is doomed to fail, whether it is the Gulf of Tonkin incident or the imagined Weapons of Mass Destruction. That is the very least you can say. Our involvement in Vietnam dragged on and on and on, accompanied by a social catastrophe both for us and the Vietnamese. It's anybody's guess how long we'll have troops in the Middle East, arguing, basically, over who is going to get the last barrel of oil. Goddamn the fools who got into this mess.

H: And you see your books contributing to such discussions from a perspective and in a manner that may be more brutally honest than some of the other perspectives?

LH: If there is an ambition to it, yes, I think that's it, or close. I think my style of telling a story comes out of the impulse to be utterly clear, wrinkles and all. And to be honest with the story. Well, sometimes you wind up being brutal about what it's like down where the rubber meets the road, so to speak. The other part of it is a kind of challenge, a matter of passing the story along. "I'm going to tell you this story. Now the story becomes your responsibility. What do you do with it?" That doesn't mean that you can't be eloquent; you try. If my writing means anything to anyone, I hope it means they can trust me to skip the bullshit. I'm not going to tell you something that isn't right, and with a vividness that you won't soon forget. That's the ambition, anyway.

H: You have read some Vietnamese soldier-authors, Bao Ninh in particular. Do their writings about the American War differ from those of American soldier-authors writing about the Vietnam War?

LH: Actually, not that much, and that was a surprise to me. When I met Bao Ninh, who wrote *The Sorrow of War*, he said the hardest part of the war was burying all his friends. I wouldn't want *his* nightmares. He fought right up to the last day. He is one of the few Vietnamese I've met who actually looks his age. He's one of those guys who carry the war around with them wherever they go. What I've noticed about the war fiction, both American and Vietnamese, is that there's a very tight little subgenre of ghost stories. As far as I'm concerned, that says a lot more about the character of the war itself and the human response to our shared experience than some conscious decision that a couple of us made to write a ghost story. *The Sorrow of War* is a ghost story; Le Minh Khue has written ghost stories; *Paco's Story* was always a ghost story; *Meditations in Green* by Stephen Wright is a ghost story; *The Short-Timers* by Gustav Hasford is a ghost story. In Fussell's book, he quotes a German ex-soldier of World War I: "We are the war." The participants are the ones who embody the spirit of the war, just as Tolstoy says in *War and Peace*. It is the spirit of the army that matters, and not what the generals think or say, or the king. It would be interesting to find out what the spirit of the American army in Iraq is, aside from just being scared shitless or profoundly unhappy. What's going on underneath all that; what's that dynamic?

H: I want to end our conversation by discussing in more detail three of your Vietnam-related books—*Close Quarters, Paco's Story,* and your recent memoir *Black Virgin Mountain.* What is the underlying connection between *Close Quarters* and *Paco's Story?*

LH: Both are stories about the downward path to wisdom. Both stories have to do with what you look like when there's nothing left in you. Both stories carry the strong impulse that amounts to: if I don't tell you this story I am going to burst. Both stories just might scare the shit out of you, because they certainly did scare the shit out of me. Both stories carry a strong sense of irony. I'm one of those folks who think that everything contains its own irony, and in the same way that Melville said that there is aesthetics in all things. I used to be chagrined that the war was all I had to write about, but now it is an irony that I deeply appreciate. Some stories are put into your hand, and you have to do the best with them that you know how. Some stories simply don't go away. Writing about the war was a way for me to learn my craft. Trust me, if you can write about war, you can write about anything. In the last decade of Mark Twain's life he said that when he was younger he could remember two kinds of things: the things that happened and the things that never happened, but now in his mellow old age he could only remember the things that never happened. In other words, if you can see it, you can make it live. So, the writing doesn't get simpler, but certainly the stories do.

H: Related to Twain's observation, how do you respond to the following comment by Tim O'Brien in our 1995 interview: "Everything that I am doing flows out of the life I have led. And the life I have led is a life of finding it hard to distinguish within myself and without about what's true and what's not"? Do you care if the two things—the actual and the imagined—get mixed together?

LH: Absolutely not, that's the short answer. In terms of story, it doesn't matter, because what any writer cherishes is the emotional truth. Story is not document. That's for historians. Whether this, that, or the other actually happened or not, who fucking cares? Always the test is, when you read a story or hear someone tell a story, does it [the detail] help the story along and what is your response to it?

H: Okay, you've just said that in the service of the story, it doesn't matter whether the story elements are real or imaginary. The story's impact is the principle concern. However, when you are writing a memoir, does your writing approach change because you have an obligation to both the genre and the audience to not invent the material, even if fictional events would drive home the emotional point?

LH: Yes, you've got to keep to the rule.

H: What's the rule, for you?

LH: When I was working on the memoir, my editor Jerry Howard said, "Larry, the only thing about a memoir that you have to keep in mind is that everything had to have happened." So that became the fucking rule. Then the challenge became how to render the actual events in a way that makes a good story. Not easy, as it turns out. Take dialogue, for instance. Apparently, you are required for the sake of the lawyers to verify conversations. And I didn't want to insult my brothers' memory, any of the three of them. We were not especially close as a family. One of my brothers did blow his brains out with a nine millimeter, and another did go to Vietnam twice and came back, as far as I'm concerned, a basket case. My father did beat my older brother with the buckle end of the belt within an inch of his life more than once, and Drill Sergeant S. *was* the dumbest person I have ever met. Hanoi is a very funky town. The Citadel in Hue is formidable. The Cao Temple in Tay Ninh *does* look like the inside of a banana split. Humping the Cu Chi Tunnels on my hands and knees *was* an agony.

Going back to Vietnam the first time in 1990 was much looked forward to. It's interesting that the trip takes the form of a J, the train trip from Hanoi to Saigon, with this sort of side road trip at the end. At the end of the trip is Black Virgin Mountain, and I understood from the first that I was telling the story of going to the center of my own dread. To travel to the center of this thing that you have tried to avoid in all the ways a person can avoid it. You travel the long way and climb the mountain, and what a hell of a climb it was, to the very center of it. And here is almost literally home—sweet home. But I don't mean it to sound so simple. It was a very particular moment, but I would have to give it a good long thought before I called it an epiphany. A much-overused word. Rather, it was an astonishing revelation, because I had never thought of the mountain that way before. On the other hand, there were those parts of the story which we could call stretchers. Like the Cu Chi tunnel rat riff toward the end of the story that I could not leave out.

H: But the tunnel story was true. It happened.

LH: Well, yeah, but not to me. I wrote that piece of the story in the month after 9/11, when I had a residency at Heinrich Böll's cottage in Ireland. Böll was a German veteran of WWII, wounded four times, and being in his house was, well, special.

H: You have this strict rule for the content, but the freedom in writing memoir comes from creating the narrative structure and voice. When did the "J" narrative structure of Black Virgin Mountain come to you?

LH: Not until my trip back in 1997. I'd been to the mountain many times, but never up to the temple. We got to the temple, and I had this enormous flashback of my war year. The things that other people had told me about that part of the county and the stories about Ba Den waiting for her soldier's return. And it was undeniable, an almost physical feeling of being home—oh, home. And I think this is one of the things about the memoir that my wife, Edie, had a hard time with. I'm supposed to be home, here, at the house where we live. She's supposed to be home. But I don't think there's a distinction. I am home, here, in Chicago, and this is a real place. And I'm home, here, on the Black Virgin Mountain, and this is a real place. Never mind that they're almost exactly half way around the world from each other. How can you be home at both places at once? You tell me. All I know is what I know.

H: And the narrative structure then naturally followed that J.

LH: Yeah, that's the literal gesture of the trip. We traveled from Hanoi to Hue to Da Nang and China Beach to Saigon, and then a day trip up to Tay Ninh for the Cao Dai Temple and Nui Ba Den.

H: Think about two of your books, Close Quarters at the beginning of your career and Black Virgin Mountain as your most recent book. Together, what do they represent in terms of your development as a writer?

LH: Well, Black Virgin Mountain is my last word on the subject of Vietnam. The irony, however, is that I know I will always be able to reach around behind me, touch that time in my life, and find story, whether it has anything to do with the war or not. The war, and the god-awful aftermath, will always exert a pull, as well as a push, on my imagination. That is to be cherished. It may well be the grandest irony of all. That's one of the things that Tim is talking about. The fuzzy distinction between memory and imagination.

H: But did you think the war was always going to be there when you were writing Close Quarters?

LH: It never occurred to me.

H: You simply had a story to tell, and you were writing it down?

LH: Yes, first things first.

H: So, in a sense, during your development as a writer, you have discovered how much you haven't fully explored within yourself or in your imagination?

LH: Yes, for a writer, how can it be otherwise? You are always pushing the envelope, so to speak, challenging yourself to explore the depth of your imagination, the use of language, the form and structure of story, and, most importantly, what makes the world turn among the ordinary horrors of everyday life.

H: It's interesting to compare your first and latest book, because a lot of inexperienced writers would have written the memoir first and then moved into the fiction, right?

LH: No, I wasn't that sophisticated in 1968. Then again, Close Quarters began as a memoir, but then transformed into something much more interesting.

H: Wouldn't it have been easier simply to write down your real war story?

LH: Sure! Just sit down, cousin, and type it up. I was too wound up to do a memoir.

H: But were you doing some of this with Close Quarters?

LH: Yes. The novel began as a memoir, but after I started doing my homework, reading other war stories, as well as literature in general, the story transformed into something much more interesting.

H: You mentioned at one point you were borrowing stories from other people?

LH: Oh yeah. Other Vietnam veterans didn't much want to tell the stories, but I said no, no, I want to hear the stories. Tell me the stories. And I was reading all the war literature I could get my hands on. And stealing from everybody.

H: Are all good war stories antiwar stories?

LH: I think so. Certainly those stories that mine the deep and thorough humanness of it. There's a quote by Renoir the filmmaker who says that all war movies are prowar and all war novels are antiwar. I thought it was a pretty canny insight.

H: Movies are prowar because they give a visual glamour to war?

LH: I think the great shortcoming of film is that you never get past the visual glamour of what is basically pornographic violence. And I don't want anyone to mistake the phrase the "glamour of violence." What I'm talking about is the rich, blunt image of ugliness. We can sit in the theater, be appalled and frightened, and at the same time be utterly safe. It is a kind of lust of the eye that I mentioned earlier.

H: In thinking about the narrative voices in your first book and the memoir, what's the relationship between these voices? And I guess I'd even include the ghost voice of Paco's Story because, at times, I hear the ghost narrator of Paco's Story surfacing in Black Virgin Mountain.

LH: I won't deny it. It's an acceptable form of cheating. I'll put it that way. I think the only difference in the voices is the age. I can't think of anything else. The narrator in *Black Virgin Mountain* is an older voice, and he's saying, "You know that's what this is; this is what it means to me."

H: And you said earlier he's speaking to the current generation and trying to educate them in some way.

LH: Educate is an awfully big word. I'm just telling stories. Every dad gets to this point. The kid is finally old enough. He knows that you're not a complete asshole and that, yes, you have been around the block a couple times. "Ok, now, this is the real deal. You're finally old enough to sit and listen and not call me names or throw a dish or tell me I'm an old fuck-up."

H: And a younger Philip Dosier in *Close Quarters* is telling his story to his peers?

LH: Yes.

H: He's not trying to impart wisdom, just saying, "here's my story; do with it what you want."

LH: This is what I saw, this is what I did, and this is what I became. And, now that you've heard the story, it is part of who you are. I don't know anything more about what it means than you do.

H: Now, however, the narrator in *Black Virgin Mountain* does know a little bit more about what the story means.

LH: And thirty-some years later, I know what home is. And that's no small thing.

H: But you don't articulate for your audience what home means to you. It's left up to us as readers to infer what the various meanings of home might be.

LH: Yes, and help yourself. The concept of "home" is universal. In baseball, for instance, you get to go home, and they even give you a run for that. The story is never just one thing. *Paco's Story* taught me that everything is contained in its own irony. Its own opposite. I've heard people speak of it as the "shadow," and when they say the "shadow," they do not speak of it as a kind and wonderful thing. So, yes, it's all of that.

H: Obviously the subject of war dominates most of your published writing. Writers who focus so much on telling war stories sometimes bristle at that label "war writers" because they feel their stories transcend the battlefield. Are you uncomfortable with the label war writer?

LH: Well, I used to be chagrined that all I had to write about was the war, but not anymore. Sometimes you're given a story and you just have to do the best with it you are able. Subject matter is the hook that you hang all these other things on. It's in the nature of critics and the culture to pigeonhole everything, and keep it simple. And of course the stories are about all these other things. . . . But it's hard to get past the pigeonholes. If people want to call them war stories, fine, but the thing I object to is when they say "war stories" and then spit. Well, fuck you! Years ago Rita Mae Brown spoke for many writers. She had written *Ruby Fruit Jungle*. She was one of the first lesbians to write a decent novel on the topic. And she took a lot of shit for it. So, she begins her second novel, *Southern Discomfort*, with a brief foreword. Something like, "If you don't like my novels, go write your own; and if you can't, that should tell you something. Meanwhile, go find something you do like to read. Life is too short." Thank you, Ms. Brown. I know that I will always be able to reach around behind me, touch the war, and find story, whether the story has anything to do with the war or not. Even the murder mystery I'm working on has the Civil War in the background. The detective is a one-armed veteran, and many of the other characters are veterans, and there are casual references to the war, a catastrophe if there ever was one. So it goes, as the poet once said.

H: In an earlier published interview, Philip Caputo says, "One thing that tends to drive people to become writers or to need to be writers—Hemingway talks about this—is some sort of wound. Really happy, well-adjusted people don't become writers. At least they don't become what we think of as literary writers." How do you respond to Phil's observation in terms of your own writing career?

LH: I can speak only for myself, here. I have heard it said that when you are young you receive a wound, self-inflicted or not, intentional or not, and often from your father. But the wound is also a great blessing because it leads you to discover your great gift. Now if that's not an irony, I don't know what is, because I certainly do regard storytelling as my gift. There are many stories in the folk literature of the world that speak of this phenomenon, so the irony is appreciated around the world.

H: You noted in another interview that when you returned from Vietnam and arrived home, you took the army dress-green uniform off and "balled it up, hauled it to the garbage, and threw it away" ("Larry Heinemann in Conversation with Kurt Jacobson," *Logos* 2.1 (2003): 145). Why did you do this? Have you kept any artifacts from your tour of duty in Vietnam?

LH: By the time I got back to the house where I grew up, I was so fucking furious that I could hardly spit. This was March 1968, remember. I was pissed off for sure. Irked to distraction, my grampa would have said. I didn't want anything to do with the uniform, didn't want it around, didn't want to save it for a souvenir. Fuck the army. I wore it once. I didn't want to look at it anymore. When I went back to school a lot of folks were wearing army surplus clothes, field jackets and such, but I would have rather taken a poke in the eye with a sharp stick than wear anything that had to do with the army and the war. Fuck that. And I didn't get my actual medals until the late '80s. Then, I took them to Vietnam and left them at the Truong Son Cemetery near the old DMZ, where something like ten thousand Vietnamese war dead are buried. Even my Combat Infantryman's Badge, the only medal I actually worked for. I did, however, keep Edie's letters to me when I was overseas, all 226 of them. Somebody knew I wasn't dead.

WORKS BY & INTERVIEWS WITH LARRY HEINEMANN

Black Virgin Mountain: A Return to Vietnam. New York: Doubleday, 2005.

Close Quarters. New York: Farrar, Straus and Giroux, 1977.

Cooler by the Lake. New York: Farrar, Straus and Giroux, 1992.

"Fragging." *Atlantic Monthly,* June 1997: 68+.

"'Just Don't Fit': Stalking the Elusive 'Tripwire' Veteran." *Harper's,* April 1985: 55–63.

"Larry Heinemann." In *Contemporary Authors: Autobiographical Series,* ed. Joyce Nakamur, 21: 75–98. Detroit: Gale, 1995.

"Larry Heinemann in Coversation with Kurt Jacobsen." *Logos* 2.1 (2003): 141–60.

Paco's Story. New York: Farrar, Straus and Giroux, 1986.

conversation with
TIM O'BRIEN

In this chapter, I do not distinguish between O'Brien's comments in 1995 and those in 2005. Prior to my arrival in Austin in 2005, O'Brien reviewed an edited transcript of the 1995 interview (material I planned to use in this interview) and felt that the material could be included in this book without updating. O'Brien also decided that he did not want to review an edited transcript of this combined 1995 and 2005 interview before its publication, stating in an email that "I'll trust your judgments. Just don't have time to read and edit, however minor my changes might have been."

This composite interview emerges from my three sessions with O'Brien in two different cities, ten years apart. As noted in the introduction, Tim and I first met for two three-hour afternoon sessions on July 9 and 10, 1995, in his apartment in Cambridge, Massachusetts, about ten blocks from the Harvard campus. Our third meeting, one four-hour afternoon session, took place on August 13, 2005, in O'Brien's home (a small 1990s neoclassical villa), which he shares with his wife and two sons and sits adjacent to a fairway of a prestigious golf course in a residential complex outside Austin, Texas. I used the son-soldier-author structure for questions in both the 1995 and 2005 interviews. The 1995 interview focused on the son and soldier portions of O'Brien's life and an in-depth discussion of his most recent book at the time, In the Lake of the Woods. In the 2005 interview, we updated life information since 1995, explored his military experience in more detail, and then moved into more general questions about his writing and his teaching. The major differences in the two interviews were the settings and the overall atmosphere. The 1995 sessions took place in a sparsely furnished and decorated two-bedroom apartment during a particularly difficult time in O'Brien's life—a period described in a 1994 article for the New York Times Magazine ("The Vietnam in Me," New York Times Magazine, October 2, 1994). Then, O'Brien, dressed in T-shirt, work-out shorts, and baseball cap, chain-smoked his way through the two sessions, and the two of us drank wine, as O'Brien candidly and introspectively discussed his life and writing career. At that time, O'Brien was reluctant to be interviewed ("I'm near the end [granting interviews]. If this isn't the end, it's damn close") and expressed frustration with his writing ("I pretty much have quit. . . . I'm still trying. But I'm only trying whenever the mood hits me now, which is once a week for an hour"). Ten years later, O'Brien met me at the door of his expansive and well-furnished home with a big smile and his one-month-old son cradled in his arms. He apologized that we would have to delay the interview for a few minutes while he took care of his sons (the awake Tad in his arms and a napping two-year-old Timmy in another room) until a babysitter arrived. Some things hadn't changed—the shorts, T-shirt, ever-present baseball cap, and cigarettes (now, however, accompanied by a personal air-purifier). Other things had. Over coffee, we talked in his family room surrounded by books, children's toys, and a TV set occasionally turned on to check the progress of the 2005 PGA Championship golf tournament. His comments about his life, war, and writing were consistent in tone and substance with remarks made in our 1995 interview, and he presented them in the same lyrical, image-laden voice found in his books. Throughout this afternoon, O'Brien exhibited a joy and contentment with his complex life as father, husband, writer, and even homeowner dealing with the frustrations of a remodeling project. Still expressed on this day, however, were O'Brien's continuing guilt over his military service in a war he opposed and his anger about government deceit—past and present.

SON _____

H: Describe growing up in Worthington, Minnesota, and the town's impact on your development as a person and a writer?

TO: I had and still have mixed feelings about the place. Not just the town itself, but what it represents: all the towns like it, or the values across America that the town embodies—a kind of "know-nothingness" and "not-caringness" about big, important issues. Who's Ho Chi Minh? And why are we going to Vietnam? Or who cares if there were no weapons of mass destruction? A sort of willingness to go along with whatever the prevailing political and social tenor of the country might be. It's what Sinclair Lewis [Main Street] wrote about all those years ago, and it's still present in middle America. We are a product of that era. The town, like other towns, had many great virtues. I had a terrific education in a public school and a safe place to grow up. Bad influences were few; booze, drugs, and that sort of stuff weren't strictly policed by parents and schools. All said and done, it's not a place I was happy with or would want to go back to, nor would I want to go back to a place like it.

H: In some of your writings, you use the term "polyester" in referring to this town. What's the symbolism of this term?

TO: It's a symbol for a mindset. I don't mean it just in a JC Penney way; I mean a JC Penney of the brain, where to get along means to go along and there's virtually no limit to it. You don't complain about your president or your country and why people are getting shot. If you, in Worthington, were to show any sympathy, for example, for the Iraqis now or the Vietnamese back then, they'd look at you in a funny way because our troops and our boys are dying. It's a kind of place where you erase the other side's casualties, orphans, and widows. It's the kind of mindset that says it's okay to be in Iraq; they attacked us—forgetting that they didn't attack us; they had nothing to do with 9/11. So it's not just Worthington; it's the whole country that sort of ticks me off. I go after Worthington only because I know the place well enough to make it particular in the details of it, but it's representative to me of a whole mindset in this country, the mindset that elected Bush.

H: I read that your father, who was with the navy on a destroyer in the South Pacific during WWII, had written articles about his war experiences that were later published in the *New York Times*. Did you read these when you were growing up?

TO: Yes, maybe six or seven of these little vignettes. They were all very short. . . . My mom just went back, in the last four months [2005], to Norfolk, Virginia, where she had met my father during World War II. And while she was there, somebody dug up for her one of the many pieces that I had read when I was a kid. But it wasn't in the *New York Times*; it was in some navy magazine.

H: Did reading these vignettes at an early age pique your interest in becoming a writer?

TO: Yes, it was probably the first glimmering of a possibility for my life: to see rendered in words by someone you know well, your dad, an experience that you can feel, see, and hear through language, dialogue. They were nicely written, peppy pieces. They had the flavor of World War II in their [references] and the kind of talk. I can't say I decided I'm going to be a writer, but some of those stuck with me. I never forgot those pieces.

H: Did you and your father talk about these pieces at the time, or did he just give them to you to read?

TO: He didn't give them to me; my mother did. He told me stories about Iwo Jima, and he talked about the kamikaze attacks and how terrified he was, and he didn't make the war seem glorious. He just said that he was scared to death, and yet he had a sense of humor about things that happened aboard the ship. One of my regrets is that, now that he's gone, I didn't press him more for detail. But he was a private guy in some ways, and I knew I wasn't going to get very far. We'd talk about the surface of an event, very glibly almost. But to go much deeper, I was really scared. . . . I never got very far with him, and it might be partly my own fault that I didn't want to press him.

H: Did you play games of war as a child?

TO: I played war games out on the golf course as a kid. Sort of war games based on war stories I heard from my dad and stories I heard from adults who had served as foot soldiers in Germany or the Pacific, games based on comic books and on movies. Audie Murphy's *To Hell and Back* was a movie that impressed me a lot. *Pork Chop Hill* was another movie that impressed me a lot. And as a kid I played these games. I was the American hero, and there were Germans and Japanese out there to be killed, out on that golf course. There was an army surplus store in Worthington that sold relics from WWII and Korea—ammunition belts, helmet liners, canteens, and the like. I would buy these things and strap them on. In that way, the history of earlier wars influenced the games I played as a kid. Also, the games I played as a kid in some respects reflected my self-image: "Tim the Hero" just like the Lone Ranger—"Tim the Lone Ranger." That whole constellation of imagination and history, those heroes from both sources, combined in my head to form a self-portrait of sorts that suggested when the time came I would be physically and morally brave.

H: What were some of the books that you read as a child?

TO: As a very young person I was big on *Grimm's Fairy Tales*. I read *Tom Sawyer* when I was very young. I read *Huckleberry Finn* when I was very young, not reading it the way that you read it in college, but just reading it as a story. I remember reading little Wonder Books, those tiny books for kids, from the time I was six to about nine. *Timmy Is a Big Boy Now* was my favorite Wonder Book. The book is still around. I saw it in a friend's house; his son's name is Tim. *Larry of the Little League* was influential. I played Little League as a kid in Worthington, Minnesota, and that book really caught my attention. Made me try my hand at my first work of fiction called "Timmy of the Little League." I think I was ten or eleven when I wrote this little thirty-page piece, what I called a novel.

H: In various places, you have talked about your interest in magic as a youngster. How did this interest develop?

TO: Books again, through the library. I remember checking out a number of books on magic from the Worthington Public Library. I don't remember the titles of any of these books, but I can picture the covers. When I was ten or eleven years old, I began practicing the hobby fairly rigorously, every day. On trips to New York City that we took periodically for my dad, insurance conventions, I visited Lou Tannon's Magic Store in New York City, which was a mecca for big-time magicians where real illusions were sold, expensive illusions. And I would always end up getting a twenty- or thirty-dollar trick. My father would buy it for me.

Magic for me was a way of escaping the world at that time. It was a terrible time at home—my sense of not being loved, my father's alcoholism, my feeling lonely. So I think that it was a form of escape, of trying to change that world, that mad world, a little bit—making miracles happen, a way of earning applause.

H: During your childhood and teenage years, did you have any particular heroes?

TO: Oh, sure. There were all sorts of heroes—heroes out of the imaginary world. Huck Finn getting on that raft was a hero, escaping the social conventions of small town Missouri. And I wanted to get the hell out of small town Minnesota. There were no rivers to float away on, so I imagined other means. But, nevertheless, Huck was a hero of mine. As a youngster, I had imaginary heroes like every young kid: Roy Rogers, Gene Autry, the Lone Ranger—cowboy heroes. They were the kind of hero who knew right from wrong and was willing to act on this knowledge to the point of risking his life. I also had real-life heroes. Those were sporting types. Ted Williams was a big hero of mine, also a first baseman for the New York Yankees named Bill "Moose" Skowron, because he played once for the Austin, Minnesota, Packers and I was born in Austin, Minnesota.

H: Any political figures as heroes?

TO: President Kennedy was a hero of mine as a high school student. I actually went to Minneapolis to listen to a speech he gave. So I wasn't just a long-distance worshiper. I really admired his politics, but I'm not so sure that I'd be such a fan today. Back then, notions like the Peace Corps meant a lot to me. His seeming elegance of style meant a lot to me, the way that he carried himself, his wit, his intelligence. All those qualities impressed me and still do. I'm not so sure some of his politics impress me as much now as they did back then.

H: Did your family spend time discussing books, politics, ideas, religion, values?

TO: Yes, those things came up constantly at the dinner table. Their reference points usually were such things as movies, TV programs, articles in magazines, books, and so on. And then the discussion would move from the particular to the general: from an article on the hydrogen bomb to a discussion of whether we were up against a nuclear war or whether Worthington would be hit and what the consequences might be from fallout. I remember this issue being a continuing one at fourteen, fifteen, sixteen years old. Politics was discussed a lot, especially during the Kennedy and early Johnson years. Religion was discussed in a fully heated way. My father was a lapsed Catholic. My mother was a Methodist. My father certainly scoffed at religions of all sorts—especially Catholicism. My mother was a staunch defender of "meat and potatoes" Midwestern religion. You go to church every Sunday.

H: Did you and your brother and sister go to church?

TO: We went to church [Methodist] up until the time of going away to college. My father would sometimes go, but most often not. If he did go, it would be kicking and screaming.

H: Describe your relationship with your father during these years of growing up at home. What were the particular tensions? Was he a model or a guide for you?

TO: It was a difficult relationship, like everything, complicated. On one hand he was a model—his intelligence, his wit, his grace in public, an extremely stylish guy. A charming man. His capacity to devour books and to understand what he was reading impressed me and does to this day. His judgments about literature impressed me then and to this day still do. His judgments were ordinarily pretty black and white, but they were firm; they were heartfelt, not wishy washy. They were not complicated, but firm. And he had good reasons for them. Those things impressed me.

We had a lot of problems, too. I was picked on a lot as a kid. For reasons that I still don't understand teased relentlessly, at least it seemed to me, from the time I was nine years old until I left for college. I felt that I was never good enough for him, could never please him no matter what I had accomplished. And to this day, I still don't understand what it was that didn't please him. I wanted desperately to win his love, affection, and esteem but never seemed to be able to do it, no matter what I did in the world. He was an alcoholic, bad alcoholic, institutionalized a couple of times. His alcoholism hurt me deeply. That is, it changed his personality so radically that it made him very hard to be with. That had a lot to do with his taunting of me and his nonstop teasing. He could detect how much I despised the change in personality that he would go through, and because he could detect it, he would call me on it.

Dinner would be especially difficult because he would sometimes begin drinking after work, and by the time dinner came around, he would be sullen and way inside himself. And the man that I loved and adored, the charming and stylish guy, had vanished. That was a horrible, horrible time in my life, all through junior high and high school. He would vanish into institutions, and I would wonder when he was coming back—if he was coming back and in what condition. I was always hoping for some radical change that never came about.

H: What were some of the things he teased you about?

TO: Weight was one thing. He would taunt me about my response to his alcoholism in a sense. He could feel my disgust at his drinking and would turn it on me in a funny way: "What's wrong? What's wrong with you?"

I want to say a couple of things, though. I hope you downplay some of this information as much as you can. I don't mind you using this stuff, but I don't want to make it appear as if this guy was all foul. He had many, many virtues. And I want to make sure that those virtues balance the negative aspects of my dad's problem. Among his virtues was his intelligence; he was also well-read. He was extremely supportive of me in things like Little League and managing the team. Played ball with me all the time. Taught me to golf. Took me golfing with him all the time. Took me on trips with him when he would go out and sell insurance. A lot of times when he was sober he was a terrific father. And I want to make it real clear that his influence on me was probably dominantly affirmative as opposed to dominantly negative, but coming across in our conversation, because we are spending so much time on it, is the dominantly negative. It was the opposite. It was a dominantly positive influence.

H: Your father died in August 2004; what was your relationship with him like the last ten years?

TO: It improved, substantially. In his old age he became more loving and open. He stopped drinking in large part because he couldn't anymore; he was so sick. He had all kinds of things wrong with him. But it became much more loving over the last ten years, openly so. It was always loving; it became more demonstrative.

H: Related to your growing up, one of the historical events that becomes important in two of your books (*Northern Lights* and *The Nuclear Age*) has to do with the Cuban Missile Crisis (October 1962). Do you remember what you were thinking at the time when this event occurred?

TO: Very much so. I was in a play. I think it was called the *Curious Savage*. The play was about a bunch of inmates in a mental institution and all their odd dreams. I was a character who wished to be a violinist, but couldn't play the violin. And there was a woman who wanted a baby desperately, but couldn't have a baby, and so on. I remember doing the dress rehearsals for this play, and the crisis kept escalating throughout the dress rehearsals until the night the play was to be given for the first time to the public. That combination of the mental instability, which was in the play, with the instabilities in the world at the time—the fragilities in the world and the fragilities in these personalities we were depicting—will never go away. That combination will be in my memory forever. The two are locked forever. And it's an interesting lock. It's not as if one were playing hopscotch at the time. It's a meaningful, important association.

H: Any additional details about your family important in understanding your development as a writer?

TO: I think the fact that my mom was a schoolteacher, an elementary school teacher, had a lot to do with my interest in books, reading, grammar, and things like that. That she cared about where the commas, apostrophes, and dashes go, things that in the long run make a huge difference to a writer. Without a command of English, you cannot fulfill yourself as a writer. You can't make full use of the English repertoire. I think, too, that my father, who was on the library board and an avid reader, was a huge influence, bringing books into the house—stacks of them—from the time I was very young until the time I left home to go to college. There were always books around, and I would pick them up and read them.

H: Did this period of your life contribute to your development as an author in other ways?

TO: In myriad ways, so many ways that it's impossible to articulate anything more important than another. The threads are not only numerous, but they are also incredibly important in my work: the father theme, the theme of heroism, the theme of history and war. There's the theme of loneliness and alienation. There's the theme of the importance of imagination in our lives as a way to escape and to change the world. There's also the theme of magic that runs through all of my work, even the most realistic of my work like *If I Die*. That is to say, artistry is a kind of trickery or a kind of illusion building. Those are just big chunks of my books that have their sources in childhood.

H: After graduating from high school, why did you choose to attend Macalester College?

TO: Macalester turned out to be a terrific college for me to go to. I would have been killed by the University of Chicago [first choice], especially after seeing the place physically. Macalester is a place where I feel I blossomed intellectually. Studied hard. Learned a lot. Took it extremely seriously. Got great grades. In high school I was a cut below the best in my class. However, at Macalester, I blossomed as if my IQ improved for some odd reason. Partly it was the sense of freedom, being away from that crummy little town of Worthington. Partly, it was a sense of freedom from any sense of parental—especially my dad's—pressures. It was a real awakening.

H: At Macalester, in addition to the novel you wrote in 1967 while on an exchange program, did you do any other writing at this time—college newspaper, literary magazines?

TO: I wrote for the newspaper, about what I can't recall, and wrote a couple of poems.

H: At this time, were you planning to be a writer?

TO: That's a good question. I'm not sure. I know I'd always wanted to be one. It was in the back of my head from the time I saw those pieces by my dad and read that book *Larry of the Little League*. It never went away. I was conscious of it. But it seemed to be an impossible, almost fantastical, vision of myself that couldn't ever really happen. Why I felt that way I'm not sure. I liked writing, and I was reasonably good at it, even as a kid. I wasn't good, but I was better than most. But it just seemed that some things were done in Philadelphia, New York, L.A., and Chicago by people from those places and not by a kid from the Turkey Capital of the World, as ridiculous as that is. So I wasn't planning on being a writer, but I always wanted to be.

H: Describe attitudes (yours and your fellow students') about the Vietnam War.

TO: I was opposed to it. There were active campus debates. Macalester wasn't a radical school. That is to say, it wasn't full of Communists and SDS [Students for a Democratic Society] types. But it was an extremely politically conscious school, partly because of the [Walter] Mondale and [Hubert H.] Humphrey connections to the school and partly because some of the professors at the school were well known in Minnesota politics. A fellow named Ted Mitau had written numerous textbooks that were and still are well known. He later became chancellor of the Minnesota State University system. It was a highly politicized school, and the war was debated in campus forums. I personally took part in many of these debates, stood in peace vigils, and rang doorbells for Gene McCarthy when he ran for president.

H: Why did you become so actively involved in the Eugene McCarthy campaign?

TO: I can't say that I was all that active. I wasn't an everydayer. I was a week-ender. Why involved? I guess because the war seemed ill-conceived and wrong. At the time, McCarthy was the only candidate who had taken a po-litical stand against the war. I remember right after he announced for the presidency, he spoke in Macalester's field house, and it was jammed with supporters. It was a heady occasion. I was full of hope. I was a children's crusader in my soul. I wanted that war ended so badly. But I wanted it ended through legitimate political means, a view that separated me in that year, 1968, from the years that followed '69, '70, '71, when more and more vio-lent means were both advocated and used by students and by the Rubins [Jerry] and the Hoffmans [Abbie] and the Yippie movement, whom I had no sympathy for and had no relationship with. My attitude was an old-fashioned liberal attitude: change is effected though legitimate political means—caucuses, elections, and so on.

H: How did this period of your life in college—people, events—influence who you are and contribute to your development as a writer?

TO: In a couple of traditional ways. One that we haven't touched on was that I took some terrific courses in English [although a political science major] at Macalester, taught by wonderful professors: Roy Swanson, Harley Henry, Roger Blakley. Courses in the modern novel and American colonial literature. I remember going through *Ulysses* in a study group indexing the book, bit by bit by bit, mapping that book out. I had my first exposure to Faulkner and *The Sound and the Fury*, to Hemingway and *The Sun Also Rises*, to Dos Passos, and to Fitzgerald. I also read a lot of Hawthorne and the Amer-ican colonial period writers. I was excited about literature in a way that I hadn't been prior to taking these courses. I had read a lot as a kid, was in-terested in books in general, but I had liked them for story and for what they would do to me emotionally. But the technical aspects of fiction excited me in college for the first time. I have a feeling that had I not taken those courses and not had those great professors, I wouldn't be a novelist today.

SOLDIER _____

H: In the early and mid-1960s, what was the general attitude of the people in Worthington about the Vietnam War? Did these attitudes influence your own thinking about the war and the draft?

TO: Well, I've written about this extensively in *The Things They Carried*. It was the sense of the town watching me that made me go to the war—the fear of embarrassment. I didn't want to feel embarrassed in front of not just the town but maybe Minnesota as a whole or maybe beyond that the whole country. The [Worthington] mindset was one of saying, "Well, you're supposed to serve your country, and you're supposed to obey the laws of your country, including the Selective Service laws, and go to the war." Civil disobedience, for example, wasn't big in Worthington, and it's not big in that mindset. It would be inexplicable in that mindset. So in a negative way, Worthington sent me off and made me a writer. It sent me to the war and made me do things I should not have done: to not listen to my own conscience but rather listen to the conscience of this [judgmental] organism and obey it.

H: At home, did your parents talk about the war?

TO: I'm sure that it was talked about. But I sure don't recall anything that was said, not a word. I know that in general both my mom and dad were skeptical of the war. But that's all I recall. The degree of their skepticism I just don't know. I know that once I was drafted, they were damn skeptical of the war. Once I was over there, they wanted that war over.

H: Did you think about securing draft counseling about options to avoid the draft?

TO: No, my thoughts were thoughts of the imagination and fantasy. I would fantasize that I was going to Canada, crossing the Rainy River. I'd fantasize getting in my car and just driving away. They were fantasy kinds of thoughts. They were elaborate fantasies. They were waking fantasies. I would imagine what I would have to pack, what documents I would have to bring, what clothes I would bring along, where I would leave the car, and the note I would leave for my parents. I mean they were elaborate heuristic exercises.

H: Both of your parents were WWII veterans, and you spent so much of your young life playing war games on the golf course and reading about war and acts of heroism. But when you came face to face with the Vietnam War, you were against the war. Was your opposition strictly political?

TO: From a political, humanistic ground, not just politics. It seemed a barbarous, inhuman war, a war fought for uncertain reasons. War, in my opinion, having read a lot of Aquinas, requires some sort of just cause, like WWII. . . . My thoughts were that Vietnam did not have a clear, just cause behind it. It was a war containing a myriad of ambiguities: legal, philosophical, moral, historical, and ambiguities of fact, pure fact. What happened in the Gulf of Tonkin [August 1964] on those two separate nights? What really happened? There was so much ambiguity reflected in the national response to that war. There was ambiguity of support for the war.

That ambiguity grew more and more gray as time went on to the point where it became really conspicuous that there wasn't a lot of political support for the war. My thought then, and it remains to this day, is that you don't kill people and you don't die when everything is so ambiguous. There wasn't some sense of consensus on the side of rectitude for that war.

H: Paul Fussell in *The Great War and Modern Memory* analyzes WWI memoirs and comments on their basic three-part structure of prewar innocence, battlefield experience and disillusionment, and then a post-battlefield consideration stage. In your war memoir, *If I Die in a Combat Zone*, you definitely portray the experience stage, and you obviously have a consideration stage. But the innocence stage (the romantic notions of war) is missing.

TO: There's not an innocent stage. I didn't go to war as an innocent. I went to war knowing, at least convinced, that the Vietnam War was ill-conceived and morally wrong. That was my conviction. I didn't go to war an innocent. I went to war a "guilt," that is to say "guilt" being a sort of weird noun. I was not an innocent, I was a "guilt." I knew that the war was wrong. I wasn't a Henry Fleming [*The Red Badge of Courage*]. I wasn't a Caputo or a Kovic [*Born on the Fourth of July*]. I wasn't a Paul Baumer [*All Quiet on the Western Front*]. My situation was different, and it separates me from a lot of veterans to this day. It doesn't make me better or worse, but different, in the sense that I believed that the war was wrong and I went to it anyway. I didn't go to the war with a sense that I was going to prove my own courage, for reasons of glory, for reasons of adventure, for patriotic reasons—a lot of the variables that send men off to war that are so conspicuous in most literature about Vietnam and other wars. In my case, these didn't apply.

H: Once you entered the military, what was basic training like?

TO: It wasn't the Boy Scouts for me; it was god-awful. In some ways, my memories of basic training are more horrific than my memories of Vietnam. The principal way was the humiliation, the constant ridicule that everyone in basic training went through. You are debased in all sorts of ways. It drove me crazy. That's the intent, obviously, to make you a little bit less than human, to take away your individual characteristics so as to mold you into a group. I understood the process intellectually, but I still despised it. I despised the individuals who did it, that is to say, the drill sergeants. I hated their guts. I really despised them. I thought they were evil creatures. I mean genuinely *evil*. And to this day, one in particular, I still think he is evil. This man, his name is Guyton. I wish I knew his first name. I'd tell you. Drill Sergeant G-U-Y-T-O-N. I called him Blyton in *If I Die*. That sense of being debased and humiliated day after day after day after day I found to be absolutely despicable, and I thought it was taken way beyond what was required. The physical pain of basic training exceeded the physical pain of Vietnam: the sleeplessness of basic, the long marches, the night marches in particular, the forced marches in general, and the craving for food. We'd just die for a decent meal, instead being hustled through that mess hall—two bites and you're out. Always hungry. The regimentation of it all I hated. When it comes to regimentation of behavior, regimentation of attitude, regimentation of all sorts of ways, basic training exceeded anything I experienced in Vietnam, and I despised it. Those aspects of basic training I really hated to the point where I felt increasing depression that went beyond the norm. And it's possible that my basic training unit was a bit out of the ordinary. Having talked to people who have also gone through basic, I found their experience wasn't as bad as mine. There was a certain kind of camaraderie that they felt and a certain jovial attitude that they felt toward it all that our unit didn't feel.

H: In terms of the humiliation and horror, was your AIT at Fort Lewis any different from your experiences in basic training?

TO: It was worse in some ways. Easier in the sense that the humiliation stuff was over. Even the physical aspect got easier, probably because you're in such good shape after basic. Spiritually it was probably worse than basic because once I was assigned an infantry MOS and was in AIT, I knew that 'Nam was a certainty. In basic I had modest hopes that they would make me a clerk, truck driver, typist, or something. So spiritually I plodded through AIT in kind of a daze, even worse than in basic. My best friend Eric [mentioned in If I Die], for example, wasn't around to talk to, so I was with a bunch of guys I didn't know, didn't much like, and with this stone hard knowledge that I'd be a foot soldier in Vietnam.

H: How did you manage to survive, psychologically, both basic training and AIT?

TO: I imagine in the same way that people survive concentration camps, people at GITMO [Guantánamo Detainment Camp] do now. You hold onto the slenderest bit of hope, the slenderest bit of ambition for yourself. Even though at times it feels you're just holding onto a little cobweb, you hold on for all you're worth. It's kind of a literary explanation, but it's as close to the truth as I can get. You find some little strand inside you of strength, the way a cobweb is small but it's strong. In my case it's sort of your "Tim O'Brienness," the person that you value. There's just a little bit of it left, but it's strong and you just hold onto it—making promises to yourself, "I'll try to comport myself with some dignity."

H: What did you learn about yourself during these first two stages of training?

TO: Well, I learned a lot of bad things about myself that I would do—go to a war I shouldn't go to, a pretty big thing. When I was a kid, I imagined I'd always do the right thing, the thing that I believed was right. That I would have the courage to say no if I were asked to do something I considered dishonorable or evil. And to learn that my sense of personal self wasn't strong enough to show that kind of courage was a rude awakening.

I learned a few good things about myself. One was that I could endure—hold onto that little thread I was talking about. I'm not a big guy. I'm not an outdoorsy guy, and I learned that I could do it if I had to do it. I could physically handle it, and that's something you learn about yourself. I know it sounds trivial, but it's something that you do learn. It takes a kind of courage just to make your legs move, especially when you're walking through minefields and getting shot at. The temptation to fall is always there, and I think probably for almost everyone. And by fall I mean quite literally just stop walking.

H: In *If I Die* you have that chapter about endurance as a type of courage.

TO: It really is something that's overlooked, and that's why I mention it again. It was a kind of learning for me. I didn't know it was a kind of courage, and if I had known, I wouldn't have known that I was capable of doing it. I would have suspected, "Well, if it's that bad, why don't you just fall down and not move and let a helicopter take you away and there's the end of it. Let them do to you what they want."

H: In contrast, the Audie Murphy and John Wayne war movies present a different type of courage: the unthinking courage that you talk about in *If I Die*, a courage without wisdom or understanding—the "charge-up-the-hill" courage.

TO: Yes. And I despise that. That is to say I learned it as a kid and practiced it on the golf course. It was a childhood value that changed through junior high, into high school, and into college. I thought [in college] it was ridiculous and stupid to die for glory, to die for honor, to die for reasons that seemed to me less than fully human.

H: What did you learn about the military during these first two stages of training?

TO: I learned that all the novels I'd ever read about it were right on the money, and all the nonfiction as well. It's racist, straightlaced, thoughtless, mindless; I can't think of enough adjectives to pile on, holier-than-thou, presumptuous, complacent. I wish I could think of enough derogatory adjectives, but I gave you a few of them. I really learned to hate it.

H: Did these periods of training prepare you in any way for Vietnam?

TO: I suppose in a way. I'm not sure in what way. It's hard to believe that it wouldn't in some way, but not in any important, life-saving way. More in a behavioral way.

H: Describe the first few days in country—people, procedures; did you go through in-country training? What were you feeling at this point?

TO: I went from Cam Ranh Bay to Chu Lai, and at Chu Lai I went through seven days of what they called the "now or never training," which was nothing. Walking through make-believe minefields with no ordinance around. . . . Mostly, I remember feeling incredibly lonely and displaced in the sense that "God, this is real."

H: What were your initial impressions of the land, Vietnamese people, fellow soldiers, overall atmosphere of the place?

TO: The overall atmosphere I tried to capture in the chapters in *Cacciato*, which are rendered fully realistic. The smell of the place. The faint smell of mildew and mustiness. I remember that. I remember the sense of dawn breaking, which I wasn't used to. I'm a late sleeper, at least I had been. Seeing every dawn break and that mildewy smell, I had a sense of imminent doom with me at all times. Even at Chu Lai, a big safe American base, I wondered if my next step would be my last or if they really swept the place for mines. I remember at night watching from a distance the gunships off the Batangan Peninsula, maybe ten miles away, putting down sheets of red flame and thinking, "My God, I'm going to be out there at some point soon." I remember the nonstop sound of artillery, booming constantly, supporting the companies and the platoons out in the field. After seven days I and maybe ten other guys got on a truck, and the truck took us down Highway 1 to my final firebase, which was LZ Gator south of Chu Lai about seven miles.

H: Did you begin your tour as an RTO [radio-telephone operator]?

TO: No, I was a rifleman for February, March, and April [1969]. Sometime in April I carried the radio for the lieutenant of the 3rd Platoon. Not much later Captain Anderson enlisted me to carry one of the company radios. There were two. There's the battalion radio where you're in contact with battalion headquarters. Another guy carries a radio that is in contact with the various platoons. I carried the battalion radio.

H: I would think that for someone interested in storytelling, this would be the perfect job. In a sense, weren't you listening to stories over the radio and also telling stories?

TO: We were telling stories, too, a lot of them. That is to say, real made-up stories as if we were out on ambush.

H: When the unit didn't go out, even though ordered to do so?

TO: When the unit didn't go out, acting a little bit.

H: Did you have to make up those reports, or did the captain feed you the information?

TO: No, I knew we weren't out on ambush. It was assumed that I would call back and pretend that we were.

H: You would have to call in situation reports?

TO: Situation reports every hour. It's over in a second. You make your voice real quiet: "This is blah, blah, blah. Sit rep negative." Very quiet, matter of fact. Every hour you do that. I should qualify this by saying we were in dangerous positions anyway. We were out in either company- or platoon-sized units, out in real hideous country. Quang Ngai Province was really a shit-kicker of a province. I didn't know this then, but all my reading since then (including Jonathan Schell's work on the province [The Military Half]) indicates that Quang Ngai was a heavily, ardently VC province from way, way back—back to the Vietminh era. Seventy percent of the land and structures in Quang Ngai had been destroyed by '67 through bombing and displacement. It was really a horrible, fucking place. So when we were faking ambushes, we were still in the shit. We just weren't quite as much in the shit as if we were out in a squad on ambush. It wasn't that often. It was once every three weeks we would fake an ambush.

H: Describe the people in your frontline unit—highly motivated, apathetic, scared?

TO: God, it's really impossible to generalize. They were all the things you said at different times. The same person would be scared, then macho, then playful, then nasty, much of it as in life I suppose—but heightened. The nastiness was nastier, and the playfulness was more playful, and the nostalgia was more nostalgic. Everything was magnified because of the stakes involved, death all around and maybe I'll die, and the horrors of taking lives. The contradictions in personality magnified by the stakes and by the kind of open-door policy toward moral behavior that anything goes. Torture, burning people's houses, and acts of generosity, too, were magnified. Guys giving up lives for Coca-Cola, for the pickiest things.

H: Larry Heinemann talks about widespread drug use among the enlisted men in his unit. Did you encounter drug use in your unit?

TO: Damn little. I think it really depended on partly when you were there but also partly on your unit. [Heinemann] was in a track unit, and there's a certain safety you don't have when you're out in the bush day after day that you may have in a track. I think most of us were just so terrified. We were so close to the ground all the time, so terrified of losing someone, where's my buddy? It's hard to lose a track, a big armored vehicle. But it's easy to lose a guy, especially at night, the guy next to you. And you're so afraid of getting lost, physically lost and separated from your fellow soldiers. There was some drug use. I don't mean to say there was none, but it was all dope. That I know. There were no hard drugs, as far as I know, in my unit.

H: Were fraggings ever discussed?

TO: Well there was one that I wrote about [*If I Die*]. It wasn't a hand grenade, but it was an M-79 grenade where a black guy had blooped a first sergeant who had come out to the field. The first sergeant was white, and the first sergeant was giving all of the rear jobs to the white guys and none to black guys. [The black soldier] didn't kill him. He ended up hurting him badly.

H: After seven months in the field, you were assigned to a job in the rear at battalion headquarters as a clerk. How did you get this assignment?

TO: I don't know quite how I got it. I know my company commander, who's called Johansson in *If I Die*, thought highly of me, and he may well have, after he left the field, put in a good word. That would be my guess. I didn't want to ask. I should clarify, though, this base [LZ Gator] was just a little hill. It was a forward-fire support base. And in some ways, I was more afraid of that place because in the field there's credible field discipline. You know it's dangerous, but in LZ Gator, where there are maybe three hundred guys at a time, people took comfort in numbers and in some barbed wire strung around you. But when we were attacked, maybe eight times, it was much worse than in the field. Guys shooting every which way, I mean across the hill at one another. There was an attack, and I can't remember how many of our guys were killed, but it was many, including our lieutenant colonel, who ran our battalion. So it [this job] wasn't like being in Saigon or Long Binh. It was in some ways scarier because you'd see this lackadaisical attitude and guys walking around with weapons. In the field, you'd put your weapon on safety and have your thumb on it so you could get it off in a hurry. But here they'd just leave the weapon on, and they wouldn't even know it was on. In some ways it was scarier than the field because of the absence of discipline. It was like being in a bad high school, where the monitors and the principals left, all the bullies have taken over, and there's horseplay with lethal stuff. That was the feel of LZ Gator.

H: The hamlet of My Lai and its surrounding area called "Pinkville" by American soldiers (due to the color on military maps), as well as the My Lai Massacre (which occurred almost a year prior to your arrival in Vietnam), obviously have had considerable impact on you personally, as well as on your writing. Why?

TO: Probably the physical place of Pinkville, how beat up it was and scarred and mangled. How hostile the remaining villagers were. There weren't many left, but those who did remain in those villages, My Khe and My Lai, were hostile. You could smell it and taste it in the air. As a company, we were terrified whenever we were sent into this area. It was full of land mines, just littered with land mines. The odds were very high that somebody would hit a mine when we were out there. You prayed to God it wouldn't be you. There was no strong enemy to fight. That is to say, we never faced any battalion, even though we were searching for the mythical 48th Mekong Battalion. We never found them, never even saw them as far as I know. We never had any fire from them. We were getting a lot of sniper fire, a lot of short little firefights. Mostly it was just mine after mine after mine after mine after mine after mine after mine after mine after mine. The land just blew us to smithereens. We were afraid of the physical place the way kids are afraid of closets or darkness under the bed. The "bogeyman" feel of that place still haunts me. I still dream about the physical place. I don't dream about events that occurred, but I dream stories that happened in that hell—devastation and ghosts, the ghosts being the ghosts of My Lai. But they are not just from My Lai. The ghosts are from what happened prior to my getting there in terms of the bombing of the place, the wreckage of this area, the dislocation of all the villagers. They were taken out of the villages and put into little tin huts, concentration-camp villages. My Lai was a place where evil had occurred, conspicuously had occurred. You could tell by the wreckage all around you, even prior to the My Lai story breaking in the news.

H: One theme that links soldier-author James Jones's novels and nonfiction books about war is his focus on a "soldier's evolution": "this psychic process culminates when soldiers accept their own insignificance in the larger scheme of things and thus subordinate personality, repress civilian habits of mind, and accept anonymity in death" (James Jones, WWII, New York: Grosset and Dunlap, 1975, 54). Did you observe such an evolution take place among your own men and you?

TO: I certainly didn't experience it. If I had bet, I would have bet I would have died. So I would have said, the day I arrived in country, "Tim, a hundred dollars, are you going to make it or not?" I would have bet, no; I'm not going to make it. Probably because I didn't know what the hell I was doing. I wasn't a Boy Scout and all that stuff. I didn't like guns. I hadn't paid much attention during basic training and AIT. I just learned the basics, and that was it, always hoping somehow I'd be rescued and I wouldn't have to go. But I never resigned myself [to death]. That's what I meant by that little slender cord I was hanging onto, my "Tim O'Brien-ness," that somehow I would not just make it through physically and come home, but that I would salvage something from it. That was my main resolve in basic, AIT, and in Vietnam. I didn't know there'd be writing. If I'd have guessed, I would have said probably, but I didn't know. . . . So almost the opposite of resignation, I was determined that somehow I would not just survive, but I would take all this terror and criminality and murderous stuff, and I would find some way to salvage something from it. That's what got me through, not just the war but also through the earlier stages and maybe got me through the stages when I came home too. I came home disconnected and not knowing what I would do with respect to what I'd been through, but knowing I'd do something with it to try to make something good out of this horror called Vietnam.

H: And making something good out of it turned out to be writing about it.

TO: Turned out to be that way. I didn't know that for sure at the time. But that's what it turned out to be, fairly quickly.

H: Many excellent pieces of war literature focus on the heart-of-darkness experience of soldiers—in particular, episodes of soldiers losing control and in a primitive fashion revealing the evil side that resides in us all. You seem to describe such experiences in *If I Die* and *In the Lake of the Woods*; were these experiences similar to Conrad's descriptions of Kurtz's experiences in his novella *Heart of Darkness*?

TO: Well, *Heart of Darkness* isn't even the equivalent of this. *Heart of Darkness* has to do with kind of natural savagery, kind of primitive. This was an imposed savagery, not indigenous, but imposed by years and years of bombs, napalm, artillery fire, physical dislocation, and massacre. These acts caused, among the populace that we were trying to save, not just anger, but incredible sorrow and grief that was palpable as you walked around this place. And the response to all the savagery on the part of the enemy was to litter the place with land mines and blow the shit out of us. The place was blown to shit anyway, so why not blow some more?

H: I was also thinking of soldiers in your unit having a heart-of-darkness experience in suddenly understanding the depths of evil residing within them. Or is such a description simplifying the experience too much?

TO: I think it is. I don't think we felt that. I think that by and large we felt incredible terror mixed with a kind of ignorance. How did this place become the way it is? All we saw was devastation. We knew nothing about what had caused it. We didn't know that Americans had done it all. We thought, "Maybe this is how people have lived here forever, poverty and wreckage." We knew nothing of the My Lai business. One has to remember that My Lai was not just one event. It was two events on the same day. There were two separate massacres in two separate places done by elements of the same unit on the same day. About all this we were ignorant. All we did know was that the place was incredibly hostile, incredibly dangerous, and incredibly spooky. I don't think we felt any evil inside us. We felt mostly terror and ignorance rather than the capacity to commit evil.

H: Conrad in *Heart of Darkness* also comments on the inexplicable "fascination of the abomination" (the attraction of evil). Did you experience or observe any of this phenomenon while in Vietnam? Does this fascination ever emerge as a theme in any of your writing?

TO: Regarding the attractive qualities of war, I've acknowledged them [in my stories] . . . but in the final analysis one must come down—decisively and hard—on one side or the other. And I come down hard on the antiwar side. . . . Most of the so-called virtues of combat . . . take on their primary value in hindsight, after the horrid fact, and often have the artificially sweetened taste of nostalgia. Those virtues do not cross one's mind when a landmine explodes, or when a friend dies, or when one is engaged in a firefight. At such moments it is all undiluted horror. And in any moral sense, when the virtues and horrors are put on the scale, there is no question that the horrors weigh much, much, much more heavily. [O'Brien's response to this question about a soldier's attraction to combat came in an email to me dated July 8, 2000. I had written to him about a public lecture I was presenting, "Good Soldiers Fighting Unholy Wars: Siegfried Sassoon and Tim O'Brien."]

H: Crazy question: What did you learn about love in Vietnam?

TO: Plenty. It's not a crazy question; it's a very important question. Love of virtue and how difficult it is to be virtuous. I learned to love acts of virtue. Because I realized in part how difficult they are to do, to be brave in a moral sense and in a physical sense. Love of peace. Peace, as I wrote in *Cacciato*, is a shy thing. It does not brag about itself. . . . Love of peace is something that war gave me. . . . Love of things that you take for granted in ordinary life, which one doesn't acknowledge unless these things are not present. Clean air and the absence of noise. That is, no artillery around all the time. The sense that you can walk down the street without worrying about hitting a land mine. You learn to love sidewalks that aren't booby-trapped. Love of family that you take for granted in ordinary life. They'll always be there.

Well, they won't always be there. Love of one's own possibilities. A human being has a shining Silver Star [medal for bravery], each of us, inside of us. I wrote about it. You are not aware that the possibility is there until it is actualized by circumstance that requires its presence. There's a passage where Paul Berlin is going to war and he looks at his own hands, "my hands; my hands." Love of one's limbs. Love their presence because in war there's always the proximate danger of their absence. No hands. No legs. No feet. No testicles. No head. That passage in *Cacciato* was written with a real purpose in mind: "my hands." Those are things that we take for granted. We don't look at our hands and take a shower and say "my hands." But war teaches you to value those hands.

H: What about love for fellow soldiers?

TO: Cuts both ways, love for some and real hate for others. A real hatred for those who commit atrocities on a small scale—the "Mad Mark syndrome" [character in *If I Die*]: shooting at peasants, cutting off ears. Also, hatred for guys who fall asleep on guard. I mean real hatred, because they're fucking with your life. Hatred for bullies. War is a place where bullies are allowed to really strut their stuff and really be bullies in a way they can't on the streets of Cambridge. You can be a bully in Cambridge, or at Wabash, or in Minneapolis, but you can't be a bully to the extent where you're knocking people around with absolute impunity with the butt of an M-16 rifle. Or when you're slicing up people under interrogation with a bayonet. You can't be a bully that way; you'll get arrested. In war you don't get arrested. You get applauded, or at least your actions are implicitly sanctioned. So there's a lot of hatred for my fellow soldiers. There is this incredible myth that fills the literature of war about fraternity and brotherhood. I say myth because it's just not, in my experience, true. It's much more of a mixture. There's a lot of love, but there's also a lot of real hatred that goes along with it. I didn't love all my comrades. Some of them I despised. Many I was indifferent to.

H: What did you learn about individual courage and cowardice during your time in Vietnam?

TO: Well, I learned the word [courage] itself is a multilayered concept and there are varieties of it. I don't just mean moral courage versus physical courage; I mean varieties and layers of, say, moral courage. That it comes, like everything else, in degrees. I guess Vietnam made me less of an absolutist than I had been prior to going. I had been a kind of black-and-white guy: "It's just bad and that's it. Courage is courage and that's it." My experience made me more of a relativist in my approach to my own life and the world around me.

H: Speaking of courage, when you were visiting a class at Wabash College in November 1994, you reluctantly talked about receiving a Purple Heart for wounds you received two months after arriving in Vietnam and being awarded a Bronze Star (Valor) for rescuing a fellow soldier. Tell me more about this last event.

TO: It was just a common thing; it was nothing. I think I told the class that it was nothing that wasn't done every day by somebody. A guy was wounded, and I ran out and pulled him back. That's all there was to it.

H: An unthinking act?

TO: No, thinking. I was scared shitless, but also thinking, "The guy's hurt." Partly, I was calculating the odds. What are the odds that I'm going to get shot? It wasn't a huge firefight. The odds of getting shot were not that great. I think that if it had been a full-scale sort of Okinawa battle, you know just grease [weapons fire] all over the place, I would have calculated my odds of being hit, and they would have been a lot more severe, maybe on the side of just waiting ten minutes. There was a slight calculation, but the odds seemed pretty slim that I was going to get hurt. It was over in twenty seconds.

H: Tell me a little bit more about your writing activities while you were in Vietnam.

TO: Just little vignettes.

H: What was the reason for writing the vignettes?

TO: I don't know why, preferable to writing letters in some ways. A letter seems so personal that you cannot get the full truth out. Writing vignettes instead of letters, I could be more objective, a slight distance. My letters home tended to be full of self-pity and terror.

H: Did you eventually publish some of these vignettes?

TO: I published a couple of them when I was in Vietnam; two pieces were in the *Minneapolis Star Tribune*, and one or two appeared in my hometown newspaper, the *Worthington Daily Globe*. All of these were rewritten for *If I Die*. And then I sent a piece into *Playboy* that was accepted after I got back from Vietnam and appeared July of 1970, called "Step Lightly," about land mines [also rewritten for *If I Die*].

H: From your tour of duty, what are your lasting impressions of the Vietnamese people and the land?

TO: A great and abiding mystery is the best I can say—great and abiding. To this day, abiding, partly because if you don't speak the language, you know little about the culture, the history. You're twenty-one years old; you're thrown into this thing; you come home. You don't have much opportunity, unless you're a linguist, to speak to the Vietnamese, to learn anything about their hopes and ambitions, on an individual or collective basis. A mystery in the way it's not a mystery if you go to France or Germany. You may not know the language, but you know enough in terms of your reading and cultural history that you absorb things about the European world, our antecedents. A mystery—and it remains that way. How could [the Vietnamese] summon the fortitude and faith to persevere against, in the case of the American War, such long technological odds? This eighth-rate military power persevering under such a storm of technology and weaponry and to somehow persevere by pushing bicycles up hills and crawling into tunnels with a little sack of rice and five rounds of ammunition and a beaten-up, old AK. Yet they did. How they did it is a mystery to me.

H: Upon leaving Vietnam in March 1970, how were you a different person from the one who entered Vietnam thirteen months earlier?

TO: Well, I mentioned one big way: I'm less of an absolutist about the world. It's not as black and white as I used to think. I'm a much more cynical person than I was. It's not that I didn't think that politicians would lie; I knew they would and did. I just didn't know the scope of it until the Vietnam experience—the breath-taking, stupefying, ballsy way in which deceit is carried out. I don't like getting lied to. I never have. And I didn't like it then, and I like it even less now. . . . Our country doesn't like to admit errors. Who do you hear storming the White House now about no weapons of mass destruction? Either it was a lie, or it was incompetence. It was one of the two. . . . Either way, you ought to be outraged. We're going off killing people and having our own sons die. But I don't see much outrage about it. I just see George Bush getting elected *again*, and I don't understand it. You can say, well, we got rid of a bad guy, but that's not the reason we went to war. Colin Powell didn't stand up in front of the United Nations and say, "Hey, join us to get rid of a bad guy." It was a systematic case of terrifying the American public over weapons of mass destruction, nukes, and biological warfare in the aftermath of 9/11. We were terrorized into a war, and nobody seems to care much. They're incompetents or lying, and I don't understand it. I didn't get outraged the way I am now, back then [before Vietnam]. The second time around outrage is there. And it's not directed just at the politicians; it's directed also at a nation of sheep willing to say, "Well, that's okay. We went to war for one reason, but we changed reasons in the middle of the war. Let's get rid of a bad guy as a new reason." You don't do that. . . . It's a question of democracy, goodness, and value that, after having seen the corpses pile up, really gets to me. Sorry to go on like that, but that's just one place where I really get tied up.

H: In *If I Die*, you mention that one of the things that emerged from your Vietnam experiences was the vow you made to yourself to return to the United States and crusade against the Vietnam War.

TO: That I've done, haven't I? I haven't kept many promises. That one I did keep.

H: But obviously yours is not a crusade against all wars. It was more a crusade against the Vietnam War.

TO: This war and wars that are analogous, which there are some. . . . My crusade is against an ignorant imposition of one nation's will on the aspirations and desires of another nation. I guess I should say the legitimate aspirations and desires of another nation. That excludes, for example, Hitler's aspirations and desires. I can't say this is a true crusade, but a literary expression of disgust and anger about what can happen when a nation goes to war out of ignorance and inflated will.

H: From the late '6os on, veterans' protests were occurring in Washington, DC, including those coordinated by the Vietnam Veterans Against the War [VVAW] led by John Kerry and others. Did you consider joining that organization?

TO: I was in absolute sympathy, but I wasn't a joiner, and in a way regret it. That is, I wish I had taken a stand then in a way that was political—gone to Washington and thrown my medals at the White House or at the Capitol steps, wherever they were demonstrating. On the other hand, I'm pretty sure I was doing the same thing through my writing. I took my writing seriously. At that point, I really did want to get a book out—*If I Die*—about the realities of the war. It seemed that a lot of the literature about Vietnam coming out at that time, which was 1972 and '73, was of the patriotic grunt experience— sort of the "we did our best. Came home disillusioned, but disillusioned only because we couldn't win the war." I wanted to write a book about the infantryman's experience through the eyes of a soldier who acknowledged the obvious: we were killing civilians more than we were killing the enemy. The war was aimless in the most basic ways, that is, aimless in the sense of nothing to aim at, no enemy to shoot, no target to kill. The enemy was among the people. Consequently, the weapons fire put out was put out in massive quantities against whole villages, whole populations. I wanted to write a book that got at that. So I felt that I was doing something.

H: In your fiction, you portray several characters suffering from PTSD related to their war experiences. David Todd and Billy McMann in *July, July* and John Wade in *In the Lake of the Woods* immediately come to mind. Did you experience PTSD symptoms upon your return?

TO: In the way they [Wade, Todd, McMann] did. Not a crippling, debilitating suffering where you have to check yourself into a VA hospital, but more a life-suffering, the kind you just witnessed, in a way. That little tirade I gave earlier about government lying—what you just heard was a kind of post-traumatic stress syndrome resulting from witnessing the consequences of deceit, incompetence, and blundering. The consequences are your friends dying and your watching Vietnamese die and houses burned down. And it stays with you, and it affects you in ways that aren't all terrible. They're not all terrible. It's good to have a little post-traumatic stress syndrome, so you won't get stressed again, so you won't get traumatized again. It's like putting your hand in a fire. You do it enough times and you're going to be careful of fire. So although there are negative things associated with post-traumatic stress syndrome, there are positives, too, that are very rarely written about. You learn to survive, and you learn what moral behavior is. And maybe you can do a little better yourself in summoning it. So in the ways that David Todd, Billy, and John Wade suffered, I suffer in some of those ways, too. Like John Wade, I don't like talking about the past. I'd really prefer to bury it for my psychological well being. And yet as a writer, because I've chosen to write about it, I can't. I've made a choice, and so I've got to stick with it. Like John Wade, I'm trapped in that I can't forget it, nor could he.

H: Have you ever thought why you adjusted relatively well when other Vietnam veterans were and are having more serious psychological and behavioral problems?

TO: I think it is because I acknowledged from the beginning, even before going, that I was a coward, *guilty*. I have never changed this opinion of myself. I've been urged to, billions of times by billions of people at billions of readings: "Oh, you weren't a coward. You did the right thing. You did what you had to do." All of which is bullshit. None of which I believe about myself. To believe that about oneself is to forgive oneself for the unforgivable. Or to lie about oneself, or both. And I'll be damned if I'm going to lie about myself. I did the wrong thing. I shouldn't have taken part in the war, given what I believed. That is to say, others can do what they want to do, follow their own conscience. In my case, I committed an act of unpardonable cowardice and evil. I went to a war that I believed was wrong, and I actively participated in it. I pulled the trigger. I was there. And by being there I am guilty. And the issue then becomes what do you do afterward? To me, acknowledging the guilt helped me, from the start, helped me adjust, as opposed to kidding myself and finding out later.

H: After your return from Vietnam and a summer spent in Minneapolis, you enrolled in the Ph.D. program in government at Harvard and continued all the way through to finishing fifty pages of your dissertation ("Case Studies in American Military Interventions"). Along the way you read a lot of political philosophers. How did these graduate school experiences contribute to your writing career?

TO: They informed it in the same way the Macalester experience had, but in a deeper sense. I came to my studies at Harvard with Vietnam behind me. In the process of taking classes, I developed an interest in Aquinas and just causes for war and Marsilius of Padua, who wrote about issues of domestic tranquility being the chief virtue of a state. These issues took on a new significance at a higher pitch because of my war experiences and found their way into my writing in conspicuous ways. For example, the chapter in *Cacciato* is very important with the Paris Peace Table sequence with Sarkin Aung Wan. A lot of the philosophy comes from my study at Harvard, the writings of Michael Walzer, Aquinas, Marsilius, and Aristotle. The dialogue between Paul Berlin and Sarkin, whether to fight or to flee, is grounded in both my experience and in my subsequent readings.

H: While at Harvard you had two summer internships (1971 and 1972) and then a year-long leave of absence (1973–1974) working as a journalist for the *Washington Post*. Did these experiences help your development as a literary writer?

TO: Very much so. They taught me all kinds of great things, chief among them discipline, keeping my butt behind a typewriter 'til the thing was done. Taught me important things about the composition of stories. Newspaper stories are called "stories" for a reason. What a lead is and what efficiency and economy in language are. When to use "that" as opposed to "which." The use of active verbs. Stay away from "was," "were," "is," "seems." Taught me the value of pronouns. Make sure you pay attention to your pronouns. It was a great writing course, better than going to an MFA program. I kind of view it that way. In the final analysis my time at the *Washington Post* was my substitute for an MFA program.

H: Early in your writing career, you described a writing routine characterized by writing seven days a week for seven to eight hours a day. Has that routine changed over the years, especially now that you are a husband and father?

TO: I'm afraid it has. I kept it up until the birth of my first son, probably even more than seven hours a day. But once he came along, I'd say if I can get in four hours, five, or something like that, I'm really lucky, and I'd say most often it's three. . . . I try to write in the mornings, if I can. It doesn't always work that way. But I keep the door open [*writing office in the house*], so when Timmy comes in, I play with him.

H: Do you find this starting and stopping difficult?

TO: Very difficult. For me as a writer, I have to be in the dream of it. And that used to mean going into the room and turning on the computer, or looking at the typewriter, and seeing where I was—entering the dream, and then staying in the dream of the story until I quit work. That for me was essential, and it's hard now to keep the dream alive when I'm going in to change a diaper. But somehow I'm muddling through; it's still working, knock on wood.

H: How do you begin a writing project? Do you outline the project?

TO: I don't. Language comes to me almost always, a first sentence that's interesting and worth pursuing. I don't have any notion beyond that. I never have any notion beyond that, until I'm sixty, eighty, or a hundred pages into a book, when the thematic material begins to coalesce. At this point, the story is far enough along to where I know, generally, the direction it's going—not where it's going, just the direction: Cacciato, going away from a war. *The Things they Carried* was coalescing around issues of reality and truth.

H: Do you have a moral, thematic, or character center as a starting point for the language?

TO: No. It's always linguistic: "It was a bad time" [*Cacciato*]. That line comes to you. Then almost instantly I think of *A Tale of Two Cities*. That sort of intrigues me: "It was the best of times. It was the worst of times." "It was a bad time. Frenchie Tucker was dead." It's just a series of words leading to a page, a situation, a scene. "First Lieutenant Jimmy Cross carried letters from a girl named Martha, a junior at Mount Sebastian College in New Jersey" [chapter—"The Things They Carried"]. The language comes to me. I don't have any idea if the story is going to be about the things they carried or that the book is going to be about the things we carry. It starts with a bit of language, always, every time. And I follow the words. If the page is interesting, then I go on to the next page. And by the time I get sixty pages, the words have accumulated into a flow of story that includes plot, characters, and what I call an "aboutness." This aboutness is memory and imagination in *Cacciato*, framed around a surreal, imagined, daydreamed journey to Paris. Or *The Things They Carried* is framed around the burdens we carry, not just in war, not just physically, but spiritually as well. The general aboutness includes issues of truth and what is truth and layers of truth.

All my books began with bits of language. I've learned over time not to do anything but trust the language, nothing but that. Not to force a theme into a book or to force a story into a book. Not to force characters into a book. Simply let the words carry me along as if the words are a river. If the river is strong enough and has a sense of direction to it, I will follow it.

H: I am intrigued by these comments about your sense of uncertainty and mystery as you begin a writing project. Many readers assume that authors have everything figured out related to their plots and characters before they begin a project and certainly by the time they finish the book. But you suggest that questions readers have, particularly about your characters, are questions that you as a writer have.

TO: I think if Melville knew what made Ahab tick, he wouldn't have bothered to give us all of *Moby-Dick*. It leaves so much of the man's soul unexplained, the same with any other major figure in literature. Hamlet's question "to be or not to be" is a question of the soul, not just a question of die, don't die; suicide, not suicide. It's a question that goes to "Who am I? What do I want? What are my values?" That conflict goes on inside all of us. Characters that don't work, I believe, are ones explained away by the author. They are cardboard figures. You know precisely what makes that character tick and that gives the character a melodramatic, stereotypical, cardboard feel. It's one of, I think, the chief determinants of whether a character will survive as a character, or die the death of Simon Legree.

H: From your writer's perspective, what else contributes to a good story?

TO: There's a moral gravity and certainly moral choice where characters choose, make hard choices. Should I marry him or him? Should I walk away from this war, or not? The character pays a price for that choice and then has to make new ones. The stories I don't much like are those in which things occur to a character. The character is not initiating that choice but is sort of responding to things as they come. There's a frenetic cleverness to it all that doesn't have gravity for me in the end because it's just these things have happened [to the character]. Huck Finn *chooses* to get on the raft to go down the river, and Ahab *chooses* to chase the whale. Those stories appeal to me more. They have less of a happenstance feel to them, so I probably will always write that way.

H: Would you use the same criteria to describe what makes a good war story?

TO: I think the same principles apply. A bad war story is one in which things just happen to characters.

H: Are all good war stories antiwar?

TO: I never read a prowar story. Maybe there is one, but I have never read it. . . .
I can't imagine a book that would say, "Well, war is not so bad really." It
would be written by a lunatic.

H: Should a writer consciously set out to write an antiwar book?

TO: I don't think so. I don't think consciously that would be your purpose.
Your purpose would be to have the characters just deciding something.
Even Donald Rumsfeld knows war is not fun and good, and he'd prefer not
to have it. (I think he does. I'm not sure of that, but I think so.) So I don't
think even he, Nixon, or Bush, if they were novelists, would set out to write
a prowar or antiwar book. Catch-22 [Joseph Heller] is a good example. I'm
sure even Heller thought, "Well, you've got to stop Hitler." Yet certainly,
you couldn't call it a prowar book. Its final impact is this war is god-awful
and hideous. For all its humor and everything else, that's the final impact
of it.

H: In various interviews, you have mentioned several prominent writers who
have influenced your own writing. Let me mention a few of these authors,
and you tell me something that, through their works, they have contributed
to your development as an author. First, Ernest Hemingway.

TO: Kind of a love/hate relationship. I love the lucidity and clarity of his sentences, but I find him simplistic in his moral philosophy.

H: William Faulkner.

TO: I love the ambiguity, complexity, and mystery at the heart of his stories and
his characters, Joe Christmas, for example, or Quentin. Why did he jump
off that bridge, really? There is a beautiful ambiguity of character and theme
in his stories also reflected in the stories' structure.

H: John Fowles.

TO: I love the moral significance of his themes. He goes after big game. I'm
thinking of Daniel Martin and The Magus, thinking of The French Lieutenant's
Woman, thinking of one of the best stories ever written, The Ebony Tower.

H: Joseph Conrad.

TO: For me, one of the two or three greatest writers who ever lived. Despite the
awkwardness of a number of his sentences, there is a mixture of sublime
artistic integrity—simple, blunt, direct, clear storytelling that makes me
read and reread his works. You can look right up there [points to a shelf of
books] and see a shelf of Conrad. I still to this day reread him, probably once
a year.

H: Why?

TO: The density of his prose, which among most writers would be off-putting
to me. Conrad is like watching a photograph develop in paragraphs with

the accretion of details that goes on. It has a weight to it; that's part of it. Also, there's a corresponding moral gravity in his work, moral tension in his work. One could think of Lord Jim, for example, the tension: abandon ship, ship doesn't sink. Jim spends the rest of his life partly running from this event and partly trying to atone for it. That moral tension you don't often find in fiction, at least you don't often enough. Too much fiction that I dislike suffers from an absence of moral gravity where there's something both human and philosophical at stake. Lord Jim is an example where there's a sense of self that's been violated by that momentary lapse of courage, which influences the rest of a man's life. . . . That appeals to me. [Among current writers] Cormac McCarthy has that quality; it's not utterly abandoned. Other names come to mind, Robert Stone and some of John Irving's work. I don't mean to say [the moral gravity] is absent in all modern fiction, but I'm thinking of a wave of clever, humorous books by the David Sedarises and the Dave Eggerses of this world that are the new big sellers. I find them fun to read, but ultimately I feel like I've eaten Sun Chips.

H: You have noted on several occasions that ultimately you hope your writing will aid in understanding the "war of the living." What exactly do you mean by this statement?

TO: We all, in our daily domestic lives, are at war as we live. We are at war with issues of conscience. We are at war with temptation. We are at war with the evils all around us. We are at war with our own despair—anyone who is going through a rocky marriage or lost a father. We tend to think of war as this foreign experience involving bombs, bullets, and aliens, when in fact, war doesn't involve any of those three. It involves people right next to us in bed at night. The bombs can be words. The bullets can be misdeeds. We're all at war, all of us, all the time. For me the use of Vietnam and war in general is a way of getting at what all of us face all of the time, every moment of life.

H: This idea reinforces your view that you cannot be categorized as a war writer because you write about issues and feelings that people encounter in their everyday lives.

TO: It's like calling Toni Morrison a "black writer," Shakespeare a "king writer," Conrad an "ocean writer," or Updike a "suburb writer." Those are easy categorizations based on surface, and the issue is whether a story's underpinnings and a story's moral compass go beyond plot or not. The stories that don't go beyond plot alone, war alone, to me aren't art. Art goes beyond a kid on a raft going down a river. Art is what a kid on a raft going down a river encompasses.

H: Are your books about war and life political or apolitical?

TO: As a student of politics, to me everything is political in one way and not political in another. The characters in all my stories and novels are characters set in situations where the world at large impinges in a real way. In life, the outside world also suddenly asserts itself, requiring a response. I have a short story called "Loon Point" [in *Esquire* and a chapter in *July, July*], and on the surface it is not a political story at all. It is about a married woman who runs off and has an affair with a guy, and on page 2 the guy drowns. She is required to respond to his death, and she is worried about being found out by her husband. But she is also worried about not being found out. She is worried about having to live with the death being kept secret throughout her whole life. This little section also appears briefly in *In the Lake of the Woods* [character of Kathy Wade]. I stuck it in the novel. These are still political issues in a funny way, though, because politics has to do with the adjudication of competing values. For example, you need money for this or for that. And what do you value: budgetary discipline or feeding your kids? Adjudicating competing values is political. That's what I call politics. "Loon Point" is a domestic story, removed from the global world impinging. Nonetheless, it is political in my opinion because it involves adjudicating values: on one hand, I wish I could be open about this. On the other hand, if I am open, I'm a known adulteress. On the other hand, I wish my husband cared enough to ask a question or two about what happened on my little journey.

H: Is the term "autobiographical fiction" ever an appropriate label for some of your writing?

TO: No, because it's so transformed by imagination. It is inappropriate, I think. It's appropriate only insofar as I'm a human being. I've lived a life, I was in Vietnam, I did not want to go. But so much of what I've written is made up. Or there's a stem of truth, and then the rest of the story is invented. "Sweetheart of the Song Tra Bong" [*The Things They Carried*] grows out of an anecdote that I heard while I was in Vietnam about a girl being in Vietnam. Well, I never saw her, but I heard it from enough places to sort of believe it. So that little stem of a story comes out of my autobiography: I heard this. But Mary Anne Bell and her seduction by the war, all that's invented. And so to say it's autobiographical is to be in error, worse yet, is to undermine art.

H: You said in our 1995 interview that "everything that I am doing flows out of the life I have led. And the life I have led is a life of finding it hard to distinguish within myself and without about what's true and what's not." This link between memory and imagination in your approach to writing also becomes a recurring theme in many of your books as characters use imagination as a heuristic process. Talk more about this memory-imagination link in your works, as well as in your life and in your creative process.

TO: That's right. It works several ways. The memory-imagination link is used thematically in probably all my work, especially in *The Things They Carried*, in *Cacciato*, and in *In the Lake of the Woods*. But it also has to do with why I'm a novelist, why I write fiction. I generally believe that imagination, like daydreams and maybe like dreams themselves, is a way of modeling the world. For example, if one were in college and trying to decide, "what should I do with my life? what kind of career should I follow?" one ordinarily doesn't sit down and say well, "I'm going to be a doctor," and then draw up a list of pros and cons.... Human beings don't just work on purely a rational basis. We work also in emotional ways. That is, we lead our lives partly based on reason, but also based on daydream and on emotion. If the imagined event doesn't have a felicitous conclusion of some sort, the odds are—no matter how much reason would say you should be a doctor—the imagination, the imagined event, the imagined doctoring, will, if it's unhappy, send you off to business school or send you off to consider another occupation. We tend, generally in our lives, to underestimate the power of imagination in determining how we behave, the people we marry, the phone calls we make, the decision to write a book or not.... Often we will pursue what appears to be an irrational course in our life because imagination somehow will dominate....

H: Memory, then, provides the raw material, the data for the imagination to work with?

TO: I think that is exactly right. You can't daydream in a vacuum without some sort of images to work with, or some condition of emotional memory, even if it's just raw terror, eyes-closed raw terror. There has to be some condition of history for the imagination to play with, shape, rearrange.

H: A perfect example of this process at work would seem to be in *In the Lake of the Woods* where you used your own war experiences in the village of My Lai and in surrounding areas, along with the historical events of the My Lai Massacre, and then let your imagination shape your creative presentation of that event.

TO: As a writer that is exactly what I did. I researched [at the National Archives] what happened that day until I knew that village inside and out. I studied maps until I was blue in the face. In fact, when I visited My Lai [1994], I knew the place so well that a couple of the villagers, by my comments, would say, "No, things didn't happen here; it didn't happen here. Were you here?" They knew that I was there. They showed me the site of the ditch massacre, and I knew it wasn't right. They were showing me the right ditch, but the place the massacre had occurred was outside the village. I said, "It didn't happen here. I know it didn't happen here." A villager asked me, "Were you here that day?" Most tourists would accept that that is the ditch. The villagers don't want to take them out into the paddy where it really happened.

I used that raw material to write the My Lai chapters in *In the Lake of the Woods*, but rearranged a lot of it. That is to say, I changed some events. I had the American soldiers return to the village when in fact they didn't. Also invented is the fly imagery. I gave dialogue to [Lieutenant William] Calley; I made it up for him. I put characters in the company who weren't in the company, rearranged a couple of the actual incidents of atrocity, had things happen out of order. I did it knowingly and did it for novelistic purposes.

H: One of the issues emerging from this relationship between memory and imagination is the tension between fact and fiction, truth and lies, which you address with the terms "story truth" and "happening truth." Talk more about these two forms of truth.

TO: You have to understand about life itself. There is a truth as we live it; there is a truth as we tell it. Those two are not compatible all the time. There are times when the story truth can be truer, I think, than a happening truth. This is an example I have used a thousand times, but it is familiar for readers to respond to. It has to do with a fish story. You go fishing and pull in a twenty-pound walleye—big, big, big walleye. Well, you go tell the story, and to make it feel for the reader as big as it felt when you reeled that fish in, you make it twenty-four pounds—a twenty-four pounder. In one sense it wasn't a twenty-four-pound walleye. It's a lie; it was a twenty-pound walleye. In another sense, the extra four pounds that you tacked on, while a lie, gives a little added heft that's "true" to the feeling of bringing that fish in, and maybe when the story is told again the fish is a twenty-eight pounder. It really feels heavy. And in those ways, in our lives, we will make up things in order to get at the truth. That is, lies aren't always told just to lie. Lies are sometimes told, and always told by fiction writers (good ones) to get at the truth. So I make up a character like Azar [*The Things They Carried*] or Stink Harris [*Cacciato*], and I make up an event, Curt Lemon playing catch with a smoke grenade before he is blown into the tree [*The Things They Carried*]. There was no smoke grenade. There was no Curt Lemon, in a way. There was a real guy who I used to model Curt Lemon after. But the thoughts that

I put into Curt Lemon's mind I invented: "Was it the sunlight killing me? must have been Lemon's final thought." I invented that. It was imaginary. It never happened as far as I know, as far as anybody will ever know. Yet it is a way of getting at things that factual truth just can't get at. The truth is, a friend of mine was blown into a bunch of bamboo. And I wasn't even present [see "Ambush" in *If I Die*]. I was maybe a hundred yards away. And all I saw was the aftermath. I saw Chip's body in the tree. But I didn't see him step from the shade into sunlight. All of that is invented. The singing of "Lemon Tree" is invented, because, of course, the guy's name wasn't Lemon; it was Merricks. That is a way the invention gets at a kind of truth, the truth in that case is the way the macabre response, which will often link humor to tragedy, can diffuse horror or at least make it endurable.

H: What would you say is your chief asset as a writer?

TO: Oddly enough, I'd say lyricism of a sort: passages of *The Things They Carried*, *Cacciato*, *In the Lake of the Woods*, *July, July*. That's my strong suit: a kind of odd lyricism in the midst of a horror. I don't mean lyricism in a Byronic sense; I mean it in my sense. That's my strength; that's, I think, when I'm writing best. The passages that are most often quoted from my works have a lyrical quality to them. It's an odd word to use in the context of Vietnam.

H: Compare your writing to that of other American soldier-authors writing about the Vietnam experience, specifically Robert Olen Butler, Philip Caputo, and Larry Heinemann.

TO: That's a hard thing to discuss, but there's a tonal difference among the four people you've chosen to do your book on. I think tone probably is a function of personal temperament in large part. Larry writes kind of the way he talks, and so do Phil and Butler. . . . I don't know if you've ever talked with Michael Herr at all, but *Dispatches* sounds like Herr. There's a voice coming at you from each of these people, and if there's one thing that matters in good writing, that's going to be it—the voice that's coming to you. Conrad's is grave and somber, serious. There are very few belly laughs in Joseph Conrad. I doubt if in life you'd be swapping dirty jokes with that guy; however, with Larry you couldn't go ten minutes without a good loud laugh. In the midst of his bitterness, even, there'll be a moment of laughter.

H: How does a young writer tap into that voice?

TO: You pay attention to the way you talk. I don't know how you teach it. It's a reminder that I've given to myself and to my students, but mostly to myself, which is be Tim O'Brien. Don't try to be Conrad, Shakespeare, Larry, or anybody. Try so far as you can to pay heed to your own voice. And by voice I don't just mean language; I mean the values that are under the language, which in my case are small-town values in some ways and in other ways the values of a guy who's been to the war and seen the criminality and horror of it.

H: Do you think Vietnamese soldier-authors write about the American War differently than American soldier-authors write about the Vietnam War?

TO: Yes, I do. It's a literary tradition that's hard for an American to, at least for this American, fully appreciate, which is a kind of epic mythological distance. There's a distance, and I mean a psychological distance from event and character. Especially in contemporary American fiction, you're inside the head of a character in the way that there's a strict point of view you adhere to. With the Vietnamese, the camera's going all over the place. But there's a distance to it, a formality that can be off-putting. I think one reason Bao Ninh's [*The Sorrow of War*] work has, among probably all the Vietnamese writers, most succeeded here is that there's less of it in his work than in most others. It's, I guess, a question of literary and cultural tradition more than anything.

H: And is the Vietnamese writer's extensive use of folklore part of the difference?

TO: Oh, a huge part of it. That's what I meant by distancing. There's a reliance on traditional structure, folklore, and history that contemporary American literature doesn't have much to do with.

H: Did your return to Vietnam in 1994 alter in any way your perspective on the country and influence your subsequent writing?

TO: Not on an intellectual level, probably on a subconscious level. My impressions [prior to the trip] of Vietnam were the impressions of a twenty-two-year-old kid coming home scarred, full of bitterness and disgust and cynicism, and the returning softened some of that. It softened some of the ragged edges of it all. I don't mean all of them, but some of them. The old memories live and will always live in that terrible time in my life, but alongside those horrible memories there are now some lovely, utterly different memories of the same pieces of ground. There's a paddy that was bubbling with machine gun fire and will always bubble, but now it's the same paddy that's at peace and a little boy on a water buffalo waving at me. You could multiply that by many other examples, so that's why softened isn't the right word. The past will always loom for me, as it does for all of us. You remember your hometown and your dad, and they remain, those images, but there are new ones you accumulate through life that then live side by side.

H: Why is the American public still so fascinated with literature emerging from the Vietnam experience?

TO: I'm not sure they are, number one. When I look at the books from Vietnam that have survived the scars of syllabi, reviews, and time (the few books that sort of managed to keep bobbing on the surface of consciousness), there aren't many. For every one that survived, maybe thirty or fifty utterly vanished. I don't think those that have lasted have survived wholly for cultural or war reasons. I think the ones that have survived have survived for artistic reasons. . . . I think that *Dispatches* probably has survived because of its incredible prose. We've all known about Khe Sanh. We've all read a million things about it, but there's something about Herr's Khe Sanh that's alive and with us. It's still happening in a way that comes from the sentences that Michael wrote. Look at Larry's new book [Heinemann's *Black Virgin Mountain*], and I think that's what's going to survive for its relentless, unforgiving bitterness, yet an earned outrage softened in the end by the conclusion to the book. He doesn't say no more outrage and no more bitterness; that's going to be there forever. But there's something else that comes from that mountain at the end.

H: A feeling of being at home?

TO: Yes, that "home-ness"; [the book is] art and it's not 'Nam. The book isn't about 'Nam per se; it's really about outrage per se and hurt, and finally a kind of salvation that could apply to WWI, the Civil War, Hastings, or Thermopylae. So I'm not sure that Vietnam matters much to people when it comes to those books. I think it's the book that matters more than anything else.

H: How has twice becoming a father later in your life changed your perspective on life and your writing?

TO: It's given me good material to write about. As you know, and probably every parent learns, you have an incredible fear for the well-being and safety of your child. You imagine terrible things happening that you hope to prevent. It could be anything: getting hit by a car, falling and breaking a leg, or getting kidnapped. I'm using this fear as material for my new book. In my other books, characters had been concerned largely for their own well-being, moral and physical; it's now shifted a little bit. The well-being of another is prompting a character in the book I'm writing now to take drastic steps in his life, and that's a plot thing in part, but it's also, it seems, a slight moral shift.

H: You have also experienced another major change in your career—your current teaching position at Texas State University as a writer in residence. What are the joys and frustrations of working with students in a creative writing program?

TO: Teaching is harder than I imagined. Reading bad prose is my idea of hell. That's one thing for sure, and it's tough. I'm a guy who can't let an indefinite article pass by, every little detail. So you get these big novels to read, and they're full of mistakes of all kinds. It's overwhelming. I find myself teaching grammar a lot of the time, sentence structure, not to mention all of the big stuff that I have to teach along with that: form, structure, and characterization. A lot of it is teaching sentence-making. It's hard enough to make my own sentences decent. A lot of the stuff is hard to articulate: this thing I was mentioning earlier about how hard it is to articulate the why-ness of choices. Why is it [manuscript] then too slow? Why is it melodramatic? Why is it boring? Why is it unconvincing? You can say it's unconvincing, but to explain why is not easy because for each little thing you may say, there's a counterargument to it that you also have to address. So it's a joy when you get through to the student, not to convince the student but to articulate [the problems]. For example, I might feel I have articulated as best I can why it's melodramatic. The frustration is having to do this in the first place. "It's so transparently obvious; you've got a guy tying a woman to a railroad track twirling his mustache with a train coming. You haven't seen that in an old 1920s movie?" That's an exaggerated example, but not that much exaggerated. So the frustration and the joy are sort of the same thing. The joy is when you feel like, "oh yeah, now he or she has gotten what I meant" and let them go away and do what they have to do. Teaching is a frustrating thing to do, because most of what you [a writer] do in your head, you don't articulate to yourself. You've just got to know that scene's not working.

H: Which is your whole point in The Things They Carried about what makes a good war story: it's in the gut; it's not in the head. So it's very difficult to articulate what's in the gut.

TO: Yes, that's true. That's a really good example. I don't need to say any more because I think you're right.

H: I want to end our conversation by discussing three of your books in more detail—your first book and two of your more recent books: If I Die in a Combat Zone (1973), The Things They Carried (1990), and July, July (2002). How do these works reflect this relationship between memory and imagination/story truth and happening truth that you talk about so frequently?

TO: So many similarities. . . . The past is always with us; it's part of our "now-ness." We tend to think of history as "then-ness": then I was young, then I was in love, then I was in 'Nam. But those things are part of our now-ness. They form the way we speak, what we speak about, what we care about, what we bring to our graves with us; and the three books you mentioned, they seem exactly the same.

H: In *If I Die*, however, which is memoir, you're drawing more closely on your own memory, and in the other two you're moving away from that memory and letting the imagination take over.

TO: You're right in terms of absolute time proximity. *If I Die* is closer to it, and even a couple of chapters were written in Vietnam, or partially written there. But the book as a whole was written from six months to two years after the fact. So even then, there's a slight gap. And what one also has to bear in mind about *If I Die* is that the book is scrambled in terms of chronology; it's not in chronological order. It's also selective, a very short book about a year and a half of my life, counting basic training. So much is left out. It's selective in a way that fiction is, where you leave out a lot. Much is omitted, and that's true of what a memoir is, in essence. Even a memoir is necessarily selective.

H: So even in memoir, imagination comes into play?

TO: Oh, of course it does. It comes into structuring things and selecting what goes in. Who remembers, for example, the exact dialogue that occurred five minutes ago, much less a month ago, or a year ago, or eight years ago? But from five minutes ago, I couldn't repeat any of the sentences I just said, but you pretend to do it. In *If I Die*, I had quotation marks indicating Captain Johansson said "blah, blah, blah, blah." The idea is to replicate as best you can the feel, the intent, the meaning of what was said, what was witnessed [story truth]. But to pretend that it's an absolute faithful rendering of a prior event [happening truth] is its own fiction. That's why this dichotomy between fact and fiction is always intriguing, because it seems to be meaningless in the end. . . . They're both part and parcel of the human effort to explain the world to others and to ourselves. The differences are there [fact and fiction], but they seem so modest in comparison to the intent of a good memoir or a good novel, which is to render as well as you can the truth of something, the best you know it.

H: Are these three works representative of the overarching content and style of your writing? Specifically, all three, in interesting ways, appear to examine the dominant theme in your writing—"the things we do for love." Is that an accurate assessment?

TO: Very accurate. It goes back to my childhood, I'm sure, and my dad, and 'Nam, but primarily to childhood. It's of personal interest to me, but it's become more of a thematic interest the older I get and the more I write. At first, it was associated purely with Vietnam, but now it's associated with life in general—the things we will do for love. And I don't think it's uncommon. I think it's one of the fundamental binding elements in human nature that we share to one degree or another. To a greater or lesser degree, we make our choices partly based on the desire to be loved, not only by others, but by ourselves as well. There's a tension between those two because sometimes they're in opposition. . . . There's a perverted side to it that interests me as much as an affirmative wonderful side to it, the good things we'll do for love: protect our kids and make great sacrifices for noble, good things. And it's that tension between the terrible things we will do in the name of so-called love and the wonderful things—how you adjudicate that in life. If I were to say there is a central theme in my work, I would say that's it. I've said this before: I view all of my stories and novels as about that fundamental question. Courage comes up and all this other stuff, but the other themes serve this central theme, which has to do with loving: finding a love for oneself and others and behaving honorably in that service. It's so easy in life to compromise and forget, erase the values you truly find important for self-love and the love of other people, and not just in political ways, in small, personal ways as well. That I think is my theme as a writer, and it's not just an afterthought. I began writing out of this hatred for myself, as a coward for going to Vietnam and not saying no. And the whole thing with my dad and winning his love is embedded in my life. So it's not an afterthought that I'm putting on top of my work. It's where I began as a writer, and it's something I have of necessity been faithful to. I can't write about anything else. It's not an intentional faithfulness; it's the only subject that really interests me.

H: Another recurring pattern in these three books involves characters choosing to confront or to avoid complicated situations—to flee or to fight, so to speak. Is such a choice important because, as one character says in *July, July* regarding choices in life, "what we choose is what we are"?

TO: They do, they really do. It's that old John Mitchell thing where he said during Watergate, "Don't judge us by what we say; judge us by what we do." And we did. We did judge him by what he did. He went to jail, based *not* on what he said: "Let's have a systematic program of break-ins and eavesdropping and using the power of the presidency to get back at newspapers through the FCC." We judged him by what he did, not by whimsical thought, and that's what that quote refers to. That quote from *July, July* isn't in a political context, but in life itself. It's what the Hindus would call karma, our behaviors in the world.

H: All three works also have a similar structure—the series of vignettes carefully linked together. Does the structure have something to do with your notion that "the angle shapes reality" and your narrative technique of exploring similar incidents from different perspectives?

TO: It's the only way I know how to tell a story, and as writers we all have our, I want to say, preferences, but I mean it in a stronger way than that—our gifts or how we go about getting at material. I can only do it through sets of fairly short stories because life comes at me that way. It doesn't come at me in a whole. It comes at me, and then there's an interlude of forgetfulness, and then the next thing happens. What I'm left with as a human being are chunks of memory, and I tend to write all my books that way. I think John Irving has a sense of the wholeness of things. When he writes a book, he begins with an epilogue, and he has a whole sense of the arc of the story. But my life isn't that way; hence, I can't write that way. I think most of us are that way, too. All that you'll remember thirty years later if you were in college are a few images and events, and even those events you won't remember much of. Our lives have a way of boiling themselves down to chunks of just really discrete memories that we call a life. And I think what's memorable to us are those chunks in which we've made moral choices and have gone through hard struggles and somehow seen our way through, maybe not happily and maybe not even successfully.

H: And for each of us, those memorable chunks often emerge from who we are and what has driven us: the quest for love, the choices that we've made.

TO: That's right. The reason you will remember those chunks is they have to do with that underlying craving you may have for this or for that.

H: And is that what links all your books—those underlying cravings?

TO: As different as Tomcat and July, July are in comparison to my so-called Vietnam books, they're not that different to me. They're just a domestic side of another kind of war for me.

H: Interesting, I was going to say I see July, July as the domestic version of The Things They Carried in which you explore the "war of the living."

TO: It is in many respects. It's a book that, you know, got horrible reviews. But it's a book that, I think, has incredible merit and which I am proud of. That's not true of all of my books, but it's true of that book. I didn't really read many of the reviews and was told about a couple of them. But it's a book that I can pick up, unlike some of my other books, and say, "Wow, I really like it." It addresses the issues I care about, and the stories I find interesting. Maybe, some day, I'll read the reviews and see what they didn't like, but I'm not going to do it until I'm like ninety years old.

H: Together, do these three books (first, middle, and latest) represent an evolution in your writing?

TO: I don't think they're an evolution. I think it's just a path of repetition. As different as the books are, their central concern remains the same: this battle for I call it love, though it involves self-respect, moral integrity, the difficulty of doing the right thing. Only it's in different contexts. It's like Conrad. One of his stories is aboard a ship; the next is in South America; and the next is in darkest Africa. On the surface, they may seem different, but the moral about-ness of the books is the same. His stories are largely about, not entirely, but largely about fear causing a blunder that must be overcome somehow. *Lord Jim* is a conspicuous example, but it's certainly true in *Heart of Darkness*. The wail at the end [*Heart of Darkness*], "The horror! The horror!" is not just about brutalities witnessed. That cry [Kurtz's] is about himself, I think. "What have I done; what have I become?" Lord Jim could make the same cry, and Nostromo could make the same cry.

H: Could you make the same cry?

TO: Well, mine's somewhat different. Mine's not what have I done, but how hard it is to salvage something from the waste. . . . I just sort of know I made mistakes in my life, with 'Nam being paramount on the list, but others as well. It's a question of how do I make something better out of it, and that's what these characters in all of my books are trying to do. John Wade [*In the Lake of the Woods*] tried to make a life after My Lai through lies and deceit, but he's still made a life that has come crumbling down on him. How do you go forward having been discovered that way, to salvage something from it? How did he find himself again and love himself again? I don't know.

H: You used the term "repetition" earlier referring to reoccurring themes in your works. In so many of your works you repeatedly explore similar events or choices from different perspectives, suggesting that, as stated in *In the Lake of the Woods*, "the angle creates reality."

TO: It's what I've tried to articulate now: I don't think the three books are an evolution. Each is a different angle on a central human concern that partly comes out of my autobiography, partly intellectual, partly just the fabric of the world as I know it. And I see it [the concern] through other people's experiences.

H: The things we do for love?

TO: And all the angles on it. It's a human thing. It's worth the exploration of a novel or a short story.

H: Despite, at times, the bleakness of the vignettes in all three of these books, what's the hope emerging in these works?

TO: "Maybe so." Those words are at the end of *Cacciato* where maybe Cacciato did make it to Paris. It's not an absolutism; it's a maybe so. It's what Faulkner, I think, was talking about—we can prevail. I don't think he meant it in an absolutist way. I think that he just meant the human spirit will keep trying, that kind of prevailing, not success. But we will prevail in that we'll just keep trying to walk away from wars and to better our relationships with other human beings and with ourselves. It's that kind of hope. . . . Humans somehow find a way to recognize their mistakes and plunge ahead, knowing they'll probably make more. But there's a kind of hope that prevents us from doing ourselves in: that thing we began talking about earlier, that little core of "me-ness" or "you-ness" that you find inside you and you hang onto it for dear life and hope it will suffice.

H: And hope also comes from the fact that we have the free will to make choices?

TO: Yeah, it's that quote in *If I Die* [epigraph], from Dante, "the greatest gift of God is freedom of will."

H: Shifting our focus back to one of the books, how do you explain the immense popularity of *The Things They Carried* among readers of all ages, genders, and backgrounds?

TO: Utterly shocking. I really don't know the answer to that. I think it's a hard book in some ways. Students find it frustrating and angering, "Oh, you're lying to me." And to convince them that I wasn't lying on purpose or for its own sake is hard. I spend half my time on college visits trying to justify what I did using myriad examples and some life events, but ultimately not succeeding. Maybe that's the reason [for the book's success]; it engenders frustration. But that's not the whole of it because I'll get letters from people and in conversations with kids, they'll say, "It's the only book I've ever read." So there's something happening in it that goes beyond the frustration.

H: Does this novel reach people at that gut level, that emotional level—"makes the stomach believe"?

TO: I think it is; something's happening. *Catcher in the Rye* falls into that category of books that get to people of all age levels. It gets to good writers; it gets to old people. But to put your finger on it, you can't. It's like Jell-O. In terms of books, I don't think [*The Things They Carried*] is my best book. I think that *Cacciato, In the Lake of the Woods,* and *July, July* are probably my best books. I don't mean to denigrate *The Things They Carried*. I like the book in all kinds of ways, but I don't think it's, by my standards, my best. It's in the top four.

H: Within the context of this interview, can knowing details about you as a person help readers in any way appreciate your writing more?

TO: I think really, not. I don't know what Larry, Phil, and Bob have said or other writers say, but I really don't think so. I know in my heart, in my head, and in all other ways that when I go into that [writing office], sit down, look at the page, and start typing sentences, I'm not the guy you're talking to now. My history is irrelevant. What's to know is what appears on the page, and even I don't know that until it's written.

H: Does an interview like this one introduce readers to incidents and concerns from your own life that are transferred and transformed in your writing?

TO: Sort of, but only to a point. You think of Conrad (we started there and I'm obsessed by him now); you could know all the facts of his life and read his letters, and you still wouldn't have *Heart of Darkness*, *Victory*, or *Lord Jim*. They're so imagined. I think there's an intent when you try to create art to not be yourself, but to be maybe your best self, or the self you almost were, or the opposite of yourself. There's an "un-selfness" where you intentionally are breaking the cord. You start with your own concerns, but then you move into a story that's not what you would do or have done. Instead, it becomes this otherness thing. It's this other life you're following that's related to yours, and you care about it deeply because it started with you. I've had many debates about this with people, and I know I've not utterly convinced everybody. But that's how I feel about it.

H: In an interview, Philip Caputo says, "One thing that tends to drive people to become writers or to need to be writers—Hemingway talks about this—is some sort of wound. Really happy, well-adjusted people don't become writers. At least they don't become what we think of as literary writers." How do you respond to Phil's observation in terms of your own writing career?

TO: I'd say I think he's right.

H: What's the wound in your own life?

TO: Well, everything we've talked about throughout the course of the interview: 'Nam, family life, Worthington, America—all falling ultimately into that main river of the love issue, people loving themselves and people wanting to be loved and trying to adjudicate the tension between those two things.

H: How might you respond to students in your MFA class who say they don't have a wound to drive them?

TO: I don't believe them if they say that to me. You wouldn't be a human being if you hadn't been wounded. They don't think with simplicity about it. They think it almost has to be a big climbing-a-mountain or going-to-war kind of thing. Your parents get divorced, or your dog dies, or a friend betrays you. Millions of things happen in our lives. I think a writer is one who is so moved by [these things] and disturbed that it's like a scab that you start picking. And you pick at it with this novel, and you pick at it with that novel. What I'd say to a student is that you've just got to pick at the scab, not be afraid of it. Probably that means acknowledging it, but it partly means just the courage to expose your own vulnerabilities.

H: Do you ever get a sense, and maybe this happens with the reviews of July, July, that critics, as well as some readers, don't want you to succeed at anything other than picking at your Vietnam scab?

TO: Part of me does think that at times. But I think it's more expectation than not wanting. . . . What if Shakespeare did a slapstick pornography thing with lots of onstage fucking? It'd be so jarring based on one's expectations coming from Hamlet or even Taming of the Shrew. But in the hands of say Henry Miller or a Mailer (exactly the same words), the response may be, "There's a good piece of Henry Miller." I really think it's more expectation than anything, and the thing about a career, thank God, is I'm still relatively young. I've got twenty, thirty years ahead of me.

H: Larry Heinemann in talking about his war experiences noted that they made him a writer; without them he probably would be driving a bus. Phil Caputo noted that without the war experiences he would be a full-time journalist with maybe a couple of books under his belt. Did the war make you a writer?

TO: I can't say that. It didn't make me that. I think if my father had not been my father, I wouldn't have been a writer. I would have found some other way to salvage something from the wreckage. If it hadn't been for the county library and my mom being a schoolteacher. If it hadn't been that I was hooked on books from the time I was five. Vietnam was a big part of it, but without those other elements, I doubt that I would have become a writer. As I mentioned earlier in the interview, I'd dreamed of [becoming a writer] from a time when I was very young. That desire to write just collided with Vietnam. So it took all these tributaries to make me sit down one day and begin Going After Cacciato, my first serious book. With If I Die, I wasn't a writer then. I was a graduate student who wanted to get Vietnam written about. And I don't mean to denigrate the book. It's honest, straightforward, and more or less accurate. There are things I like about it, but it's not a literary book. It wasn't the work of a conscious writer. When I started Cacciato, I was starting an effort to be a literary writer. By that I mean trying to write nice sentences, the tone of which would carry freight, not just the content of the words but the plot and whatnot, and becoming conscious of structure and what structure does to a story: how it matters and makes the story better, richer, and more memorable. Vietnam didn't cause any of that literary stuff to happen. That was caused by reading *Alice in Wonderland*; that was caused by reading Hemingway, Faulkner, Dos Passos, and the modernists.

H: Do you still have your military dress uniform with battle ribbons on it?

TO: Yes, it's in my closet.

H: What does the uniform represent for you?

TO: It's an artifact of history in the same way that, say you robbed a bank and went to jail, you'd want artifacts of your own mistakes around—a newspaper clipping or something from your jail cell to remind you of the person you were and don't do it again. Say you broke your leg in a sandbox when you were a kid. You wouldn't love the sandbox, but if you went back and revisited it, you'd look at that sandbox and it'd be part of your history and you'd be grateful to have seen it again. It's that kind of feeling. I wish I had more artifacts from that time. Most of them I lost along the way or maybe in anger disposed of. I've got maybe four photographs or five from that time. At one time after I came home, I must have had a hundred of them, either given to me or I'd taken. During a really bad time of my life I remember getting rid of a lot of that stuff, throwing it in the wastebasket, dumping it out, and being very proud of myself and angry. Now, I regret it. I do wish I had more artifacts, reminders.

H: Is there also a sense of a pride in endurance represented by the uniform and ribbons?

TO: No, pride isn't the word. I wish I could say yes because most veterans would really disagree with me. They'd say "you idiot" and "you asshole," but pride is not the operative word. It's a thing I've gone through, a bad thing. It's akin to having had cancer. Pride's not the word you come up with, at least not the first word anyhow. What the word is, I don't know, but it's just my "me-ness."

WORKS BY & INTERVIEWS WITH TIM O'BRIEN

"Faith." *New Yorker*, February 12, 1996: 62–67.

Going After Cacciato. New York: Delacorte, 1978.

If I Die in a Combat Zone: Box Me Up and Ship Me Home. 1973. Reprint, New York: Dell 1983.

In the Lake of the Woods. New York: Houghton Mifflin, 1994.

July, July. New York: Houghton Mifflin, 2002.

"Loon Point." *Esquire*, January 1993: 91–94.

Northern Lights. New York: Delacorte Press, 1975.

The Nuclear Age. New York: Alfred A. Knopf, 1985.

"Step Lightly." *Playboy*, July 1970.

The Things They Carried. 1990. Reprint, New York: Penguin, 1991.

"Tim O'Brien Interview." By Tobey C. Herzog. *South Carolina Review* 31 (1998): 78–109.

Tomcat in Love. New York: Broadway Books, 1998.

"The Vietnam in Me." *New York Times Magazine*, October 2, 1994: 48–57.

conversation with
ROBERT OLEN BUTLER

Butler reviewed my edited transcript of our October 2005 interview and made a few changes that he described as follows in an email: "Corrected some factual errors, cleaned up some awkwardness, clarified some unclear stuff, and made a few other editing changes." He had this to say about the final version of the interview: "This is, hands down, the best interview anyone has ever conducted with me."

My interview with Robert Olen Butler occurred during the afternoons of October 15 and 16, 2005, at the author's restored art-and-antique-filled, two-story antebellum home. At the time, Butler shared the home with author-wife Elizabeth Dewberry (recent novel, *His Lovely Wife*), three Bichon Frise dogs, and two cats. In a *very* small town about twenty miles west of Tallahassee, Florida, the home sits on an acre of property surrounded by extensive acreage owned by media mogul Ted Turner. Hanging prominently inside the entryway to the home is an 1840 plat of the property with the surveyor's fitting name, Robert Butler. The home has a satellite dish so that, among other offerings, Butler is able to watch St. Louis Cardinal baseball games. For both sessions, we met in Butler's multiroom writer's cottage located a short distance behind the house; Dewberry's writing space is on the home's second floor. The restored cottage, which doubles as a guest quarters, is filled with art works and shelves holding multiple copies of Butler's books. The main room is organized around Butler's computer and writing area on one side and on the other side a rectangular conversation-reading table, which we used for the interview. Prominently displayed in this room are copies of old magazines, including a *Life* magazine issue with a picture of Ernest Hemingway on the cover, and antique typewriters, including one of the same model given to Hemingway by his first wife, Hadley. One interesting feature of the cottage is the bathroom, where guests, instead of signing a guest book, write their names and comments on the walls. Our scripted conversations lasted about three hours each day. Butler, throughout the son, soldier, and author sections, related personal stories and anecdotes. He also included numerous examples from his book *From Where You Dream* in talking about his development as a writer, his views on the creative process, and befittingly for someone who has been teaching creative writing for over twenty years, the joys and struggles of teaching emergent writers. At the beginning of our first session, as we discussed details for the chronology section, Butler warned me that he personifies Graham Greene's description of a good novelist having a bad memory: "I have a novelist's memory. Graham Greene once said that 'all good novelists have bad memories. What you remember comes out as journalism; what you forget goes into the compost of the imagination.' So throughout this interview you will have this problem with me: my memories of childhood and the past are very sketchy."

SON

H: Describe the town (Granite City, Illinois) you grew up in; how did living in this town contribute to your growth as a person and a writer?

RB: It is on the cusp of North and South. The steel mill drew people from the upper Midwest, as well as a lot of deep Southerners. There were a lot of immigrants, especially Eastern European immigrants. And so my hometown obviously represented the kind of collision of cultures that eventually interested me in Vietnam. It was a working-class town with one high school.

H: Describe some of your activities and interests as a child and teenager.

RB: I was interested in baseball; I am a live-and-die Cardinals fan to this day. I played Little League baseball. At age twelve, I hit 525 and was an all-star first baseman. I was an avid reader, and I loved the theater. That is how I got into playwriting. My father was chairman of the theater department at St. Louis University. My first chance to get onstage was in eighth grade, and the ham sizzled hotly in me from then through Northwestern. And even to this day, I still get struck by that when I go out reading. But for a long while, theater was my professional ambition. For two summers in high school I was an apprentice at the Canal Fulton Summer Theatre in Canal Fulton, Ohio. I actually got a few parts in addition to painting scenery and so forth. I got a fairly nice speaking role in the play called *End as a Man* by Calder Willingham with Sal Mineo in the lead.

H: During your childhood and teenage years, did you have any particular heroes, including political figures?

RB: Wally Moon. When I was eight years old and I started getting interested in the Cardinals, he was the rookie center fielder and my favorite player. He was a left-handed hitter and developed this great inside-out swing. Other heroes were my dad, John Kennedy, Ernest Hemingway.

H: Was your father in the military? Did he talk about his war experiences with you?

RB: My father was an infantry captain under Patton in WWII and to this day bears dozens of pieces of shrapnel in his legs. But he did not talk a lot about the war, like many men of that generation, a few war stories. I remember two of my father's war anecdotes. I must have asked him when I was eight or ten about the moment he felt closest to death. It was not when he was wounded, but he had been in a building and had gone out of the building when fifteen or twenty seconds later the building was hit by an artillery shell and blew up. I also remember a story he told about when, after the war, he stayed as an officer in charge of displaced persons camps. At some point, it was winter and there was not a lot of food. He was in the line going into the mess hall, and a rabbit appeared in the field. He remembered everybody in that line quietly going out and surrounding the rabbit to enhance the pot that night. Those are the only two anecdotes that I remember; he did not talk much about his war experiences.

H: Did you play games of war as a child?

RB: Sure. When I was eight or nine years old, my favorite toys were these sets that Sears sold of different locales with little figures, like a cowboy scene or medieval fort. There was an army version that I played with. Also, you went through those motions with your kid friends in the empty lots at the end of your block making dirt-clod grenades. When I was playing gun games, it was probably more cowboys than war. I loved planes, and the war things I was particularly interested in were the F-86 and MiG-15 clashes in the Korean War. I could draw pretty well, and I was drawing MiG-15s and F-86s fighting in the air all the time. I had model airplanes, and I even glued a water gun onto the bottom of a plastic Thunderbolt propeller fighter so that I could walk around holding the handle of the water gun. I would walk around as if flying the airplane trying to squirt dragonflies, which reminded me of Mitsubishi Bombers, with my machine-gun Thunderbolt model. That was probably the most fun and completely a solo game.

H: Did you envision yourself joining the military and becoming a pilot?

RB: No, I don't think I ever did.

H: Are there any particular historical or social events—national or international—that you remember from your days through high school that impacted you at the time?

RB: Kennedy was not assassinated until I had just gone to Northwestern. As a child of the Cuban Missile Crisis, I remember being personally quite concerned about that—my own safety and the world's. Even if Granite City and St. Louis were not targets of an A-bomb, I felt concern for the world's equilibrium.

H: What role did religion play in your upbringing?

RB: As a child, the role of religion was very low key. We were not avid evangelicals; my parents were very relaxed about the forms of religion. They were not dogmatists or doctrinaire. The church I most remember going to for the longest time was the First Presbyterian Church. . . . This was a kind of mainstream, relaxed and low key, nonpolitical nondoctrinaire kind of Presbyterianism.

H: Describe your relationship with your father.

RB: Very, very close. He and I were good pals, and he was very much present in my life all the time. We were both interested in the theater. He was a wonderful director. I would go to his plays, and we would sit up at night talking about dramatic theory, plays, and books. We would watch TV together and talk about that. It was a very close, very warm and very communicative relationship, and it still is today. My dad is eighty-six and my mom is eighty-eight; we talk everyday. They live in Tallahassee.

H: Did your father's position in the theater department at St. Louis University influence your interest in the theater?

RB: Certainly. It is a wonderful art form; I loved performing and was good at it. It was not as if I felt I needed to get out of my dad's successful track and be my own person, because I was still doing something different in the theater from what he did. So there was never the taint of competition in the mutual interest. I have learned a lot through my theater experience that I bring to writing fiction.

H: What did you learn about life from your father?

RB: I think, in terms of a broader sense of life, the great virtue of intensely attending to the feelings of other people and being alert to the nuance of how those people's feelings are expressed.

H: Such an attention to people's feelings seems to influence your writing in terms of your use of an array of first-person narrators.

RB: Sure. Whoever the character is that I'm writing through, I feel my first responsibility is to be utterly compassionate and deeply embedded within the way that character sees the world. And the key to compassion is to understand the other in the other's terms.

H: What did you learn from your mother?

RB: The primary thing I learned from my mother was the dogged assertion of what you believe in and what you are striving for. She has always been a fierce advocate for me and my father, and she strongly encouraged me to assert my own sense of what to do and what to be.

H: How would you describe your years in high school?

RB: A happy high school career. It was the only high school in a town of forty thousand. I was student body president, very active in theater, valedictorian. I probably had the chance to exercise some of that pay attention to other people's feelings stuff I was learning about from my dad. It was not a strategy; I have always liked a very wide range of people. If you think about it, I grew up in a household with a very smart artistic guy, my father, and I was around him and his colleagues at the university. But I was just as comfortable with my fellow workers on the labor gang at the steel mill. The high school was a very working-class school. My affections for a wide range of people, which I was able to express, were quite genuine. And that is why high school was great for me.

H: How did this pre-college period of your life contribute to your development as an author?

RB: The compassion I learned was a main thing, as well as my activities in the theater. I am a big believer, at least in the kind of writing I do, that inhabiting the character I am giving voice to is crucial to my process. That notion would be refined in my university years in the discipline called oral interpretation, but it certainly began in my high school years with my acting.

H: How did you end up attending Northwestern University?

RB: It was a big theater school, and I wanted to be an actor. It was reputedly the best theater school in the country. I was on scholarship there and started out as a theater major.

H: How active were you in the theater community at Northwestern during your four years?

RB: I had significant roles in four of the six major productions in my freshman year. And then I was in a play or two during my sophomore year, but halfway through that year I felt that I would rather write than interpret. I felt what I wanted to express artistically had to do with *creating* the words, not inhabiting other people's words. By the way, when I began as a theater student, the great acting teacher Alvina Krause had just retired from Northwestern, and a number of us freshmen went and took private lessons from her. So I did have some lessons from one of the great method actors in my freshman year, and I was a student of the art form. Method acting would eventually shape my aesthetic theory in how I write and how I teach writing.

In the middle of my sophomore year I shifted from theater to oral interpretation. It is no longer called oral interpretation; it is a broader discipline now. Oral interpretation is a critical approach to literature through performance. You examine the text, to some extent with traditional literary analytical tools, but most important, you examine the text for an understanding of the narrative persona. And oral interpretation is based on the presumption that all written language has an embedded narrative persona; even your cereal box in the morning has a narrative persona—a single-minded, chirpy and insufferable sort of fellow. So as an oral interpreter, you get into the text and deduce that personality from the way the language is used in all its forms, word choice, rhythms, and so forth, as well as in overt emotional cues. Then you literally embody that persona in performance. For me, that was a wonderful bridge between my impulse to perform and my impulse to write. The inhabiting of the persona in the text is a kind of working out of the essential writing process where you inhabit the narrative persona you are putting on the page.

H: Once you understood the persona and began the performance, were you using a text?

RB: Yes, it is also great training for writers because you look exactly the way you look standing up behind a lectern at the Elliott Bay Bookstore on a book tour. You give a reading from the work. The text is part of the experience, so you don't get rid of the text. There are oral interpretation modes called chamber theater where you can divest yourself of texts, but primarily in oral interpretation, the text is prominently featured.

H: While at Northwestern, were you doing any creative writing?

RB: I graduated with the best grade average of my graduating class, and the process of doing that won me special privileges. In every class that I took in oral interpretation for the last two years, I was able to throw out the standard papers and assignments and write plays. I probably wrote half a dozen plays at Northwestern.

H: During this time, didn't you write a play about the boarding house in which you lived?

RB: I did—"The Rooming House." One of the people I lived with there I later discovered died in Vietnam. He was in Navy ROTC.

H: You describe some antiwar activities at Northwestern in your novel *Alleys of Eden*. Describe the actual attitudes toward the Vietnam War while you were enrolled at Northwestern.

RB: Not significant. I knew a guy who was an early founder of SDS there, but even SDS was seen as pretty tame—another student activity.

H: While at Northwestern, did you think about being drafted into the military once you graduated?

RB: I didn't even think about it. At that time, I thought I was going to go through [a graduate program] to get a Ph.D., and student deferments were holding up at that time, at least for undergraduates (that was the rumor I heard). But some people got a different story; local draft boards were all different. At my local draft board at that time, things seemed fine; of course, it was my local draft board that later [after Butler's graduation from Iowa with an M.A. degree] sent me into military intelligence. In the fall of '68, I got the greeting letter, which told me that my draft board was in need of general assistance, that my student deferment would be expiring upon my graduation from Iowa in February [1969], and that I would be welcomed into the U.S. Army. But as an undergraduate, I really did not give it much thought.

H: Why did you enter the graduate program at the University of Iowa?

RB: They had a very good playwriting program, and I was interested in playwriting at that point. I was wooed by a very prominent playwriting teacher there. He saw a copy of "The Rooming House" and loved it. They were anxious about getting me, and they did. I had a teaching assistantship. I entered there in the fall of '67 and finished in a year and a half because I thought I was going into the Ph.D. program.

H: Are there some additional details from your days as a student at Northwestern and the University of Iowa that might help people understand you better as a writer, as a thinker, and as a person?

RB: The oral interpretation people at Northwestern were important. I also had two workshops there with Steven Spender, the great British poet. He loved "The Rooming House," but I also started writing a little fiction then. My notions about film and fiction—I owe a lot of my insights there to Robert Breen, who introduced me to those concepts. I developed them somewhat after that, but the basic stuff was there with Breen. Spender would come every spring, and I took two consecutive spring creative writing workshops with him. The first time I did the play, and the next I did some experimental film-technique-driven fiction, just little pieces.

The literature classes I took at Northwestern were good, too. It was before the theorists got their grip on so many English departments and disastrously altered the pedagogy of literature in many universities in this country. I started my ravenous reading of fiction at Northwestern, so that was an important influence. I did so certainly at the instigation of the oral interpretation classes. Also, I had enough credits for a minor in English literature. I read mostly modern British and American literature. But I even loved Samuel Richardson's *Clarissa* and found myself liking things I would not have expected to like. *Clarissa* was a submersion in a first-person narrative. My tastes and appreciations were eclectic.

About my time in Iowa, there was the growing disintegration of a marriage. I've been married four times, and that is a considerable other kind of influence.

SOLDIER

H: Do you recall any particular events related to the war that you read about or discussed while you were in high school or college?

RB: The Tet Offensive occurred in February of '68 while I was at Iowa. That was another major sense of awareness. Then that fall, while we were still reading about the effects of Tet, I was told I was going to get drafted. So my consciousness was raised significantly in the fall of '68 by the warning from the draft board within the context of Tet.

H: What were your feelings about the war at this time?

RB: I was certainly intensely aware of the war, but my sense of personal engagement with it was somewhat remote. I was an avid despiser of Richard Nixon. I really loathed him, as all good right-thinking liberals did back then. The prosecution of the war seemed bungled and misbegotten. But the political focus was on Richard Nixon, just as now much of the focus is on Bush. My sense of our country being somehow profoundly flawed was not there. Instead, it was Nixon and Kissinger.

H: Did your family discuss the Vietnam War while you were in high school or college? Did these discussions influence your thinking about the war in any particular way?

RB: No, I think my father and I shared the same liberal attitudes about Nixon. Let's not forget it was John Kennedy who said, "we shall pay any price, bear any burden, meet any hardship, support any friend, oppose any foe, in order to assure the survival and the success of liberty." We were both Kennedy fans. The sense of what liberalism really implies now about our position in the world was not strong then. It still had its roots in another attitude about all that. I did not have, by background or political persuasion, a place to stand to separate myself politically from the war in any significant way.

H: In the fall of 1968 after receiving your notice about your draft status, did you, as many of your peers did, consider joining the reserves or National Guard?

RB: No, I just went to the local army recruiter, and he said he had the perfect job for me, counter-intelligence special agent. It sounded as if I would certainly be in some field office where the war was not going on, doing background investigations on military people seeking top-secret security clearances or advising military bases about handling classified documents. And that seemed like a reasonable job. But the only deal from the recruiter was, "We will assure you of that MOS [military specialty] if you sign up for three years instead of two."

H: As you later discovered, this counter-intelligence pitch seemed to be one that many recruiters were using.

RB: The empirical evidence of that was getting to Fort Holabird and finding so many people waiting for a counter-intelligence class to open. Consequently, we all just sat around and painted rocks for six months while the clock was ticking away on our three years.

H: Did you have any adventure fantasies about performing counter-intelligence, or was your enlistment decision simply the most practical way of dealing with your military obligation?

RB: For a writer it was an intriguing job on the civilian side. I'd always been interested in jobs that connected me to the real world. That's why I was forty years old before I ever started to teach creative writing. That's why I did not come back under the GI Bill and get a Ph.D. My writer self has always ravenously sought real-world, in-the-moment, sensual experience. The halls of academe in some ways do everything they can to undercut both of those things. I had worked in a steel mill and driven a taxi, and those jobs weren't just economic necessity. It was like "wow, what interesting work." In high school, one of the things that struck me was that in an anthology of the great writers, no matter how short the biography, you would see a line like "he picked grapes in California" or "he drove an ambulance in Italy" or "he worked in a power plant in Mississippi." It was always understood that an essential part of a writer's education and authenticity came from what was done in the world. If I had, apart from the army, a chance to go into people's homes and sit down with them, glance at the framed photos on the mantelpiece, hear the ticking of the clock, smell whatever's cooking, watch the nervous hands of the woman in front of me, ask her about her son, and write it down—if people would have paid me to go into people's homes and enter their lives like that—it would have been a perfect job. So this counter-intelligence was not just a way to get through the military. This opportunity sounded fascinating to me and, as a writer, very interesting.

H: Once you entered the military, what was your basic training experience like? Was it a humiliating experience or a valuable experience? Are there certain people—good and bad—you remember from these days?

RB: I could play baseball pretty well at age twelve. But at age thirteen, I was off doing other things and had gotten involved with the theater. I was very thin, like 135 pounds through most of my young manhood, and was not an athlete in school. But here I am in basic training. We had the third-most-decorated enlisted man in the country, who was the top sergeant in the company. My drill sergeant McKinney was a wonderful guy, a tall, gangly African American guy. The top sergeant was this intense, solid, tough, black sergeant who was kicking people in the formation, calling them out, and getting in their face. This was before things got easy on recruits. This was the height of the war, right after Tet; this was a tough basic training. For one thing, I was the guy who the whole platoon trusted to be the last guy out of the barracks, to do the final touch up on my hands and knees, walking around getting every scrap of dust before inspections. So our platoon won the barracks competition. And I did well in basic training in other ways, too. I'm proud of this: getting on the bus after basic training, coming from where I came from, that top sergeant came up to me and said, "Butler, you are going to be a hell of a soldier." Of all the things I've forgotten, I remember that. It was a good review. I felt as good about that as I did about Anatole Broyard's praise about *Alleys of Eden* in the *New York Times*, because I worked my ass off to be the best soldier I could be. In that restricted, utterly hostile, utterly alien world, it was an exercise in persona. I took on the persona of what was an admirable person in that enclosed world and got it right.

H: So your performance in basic training had nothing to do with supporting the war; it had everything to do with personal achievement.

RB: Yes, it did, and in a realm of experience where I had not demonstrated "chops" in my previous life. It was a part of that really intense rapport with that top sergeant. He appreciated what I did. The implication was not beyond that. It was like a frame around a painting or the structural boundaries around a novel; it was a closed, distinct world with its own set of values, and you did what you did. There are twenty million teenage boys sitting in their rooms, even as we speak, getting validation from video games, which is the same fundamental human impulse that I am describing in regards to basic training.

H: Overall, then, basic training was a positive experience because of that personal validation.

RB: Sure, because I was put into a hostile environment, which on the face of it should have overwhelmed me but didn't, and I excelled there.

H: What did you learn about the military during this experience?

RB: Again, it was an exercise in point of view and identification with persona. I did understand this much: if you yielded to abuse and to the unexpected assault on your person and your identity in that refined world, then in a combat situation you would also break. If you condition yourself to understand what the group requires, and you learn how to respond to those things (once you accept the premise as to what an army must do), you understood why the training went as it did. That much seemed clear to me. Of course, all the while I thought I would be in a field office in Des Moines doing background investigations. So my sense of pleasure at succeeding in this world did not supersede any humanitarian sense I might have about the philosophical basis of any war, or war itself. At the point when I went into the army, I had already made that decision. Did I have political beliefs such that I would right then exile myself from America for seemingly forever? I did not have the basis, politically or morally, to do that. I had no doubt that the country was flawed and prosecuting the war in inappropriate ways. But I also believed that the North Vietnamese had the same attitude. I also believed, at that point, that the people of South Vietnam saw themselves as a separate, distinct nation with separate values. And I can tell you that a million Vietnamese living in the U.S. will reaffirm that right now. Because of those mitigating factors and because I thought I had effectively gotten myself out of a killing role (and I harmed *no one* while in Vietnam), I could not say that I was part of a military machine doing terrible things and I would leave the United States forever because of that. I did not have the basis to do that.

H: Therefore, your decisions to enter the military and later to go to Vietnam, unlike Tim O'Brien's, were not traumatic?

RB: No.

H: While in counter-intelligence training at Fort Holabird, were you learning to be a spy?

RB: It was counter-intelligence, so we had a few light classes about the spy stuff. There was another MOS that was the spy thing. In practical terms, when I got to Vietnam, spying is what I did, but that is not what I was trained to do. We took classes in handling classified documents. A group of actors came in, and we had training with scenarios where they knew something and we had to interview and get it out of them. So we did practical type of interview things, which I excelled at. We had to ferret out information. I was training to do the things that the army recruiter said I would have to do, so his promises were not bullshit for the MOS I was filling. What was not said at the time of my enlistment was that they will train you for this MOS, but may use you in a different way somewhere else. But the training was how to handle documents, how to carry on background investigations.

H: Why were you selected to go to the Vietnamese language school in Crystal City, Virginia?

RB: I have no idea. We took aptitude tests. When they sent me to language school, I knew something was up. Why would I need Vietnamese in Des Moines? I didn't think Des Moines had a big Vietnamese community.

H: Were you angry at being sent to language school, or did you view the situation as another learning experience?

RB: I don't remember. I must have been angry and frightened. But my fate was cast. I would just do the best I could do. Again, going to Vietnam knowing the language was a great benefit. I spent a year at the school with a young Vietnamese woman who taught ten of us in our class, and her attitude was that this was a righteous war. She got nostalgic at the cannons going off at Fort Meade across the river, thinking of her country. She was young enough to have grown up with the war, and so cannon fire made her think wistfully of home, and she wanted the war to end.

H: I read that you were in language class seven hours a day, five days a week for a year. Was it a difficult language to learn?

RB: A difficult language in one fundamental sense, and that is its tonality. Second, there are no cognates. All the vocabulary you learn is out of thin air; you have nothing to hold onto from other languages that you know. The tonality is the tricky thing. There are five different tones that differentiate the meaning profoundly. The five Ba's, for instance, mean a cypress tree, father, grandmother, poisoned food, and a state of confusion. The scary thing in Vietnamese is that a certain word is not only the word for grandmother but also is the mode of address for an older woman who could potentially be a grandmother. So when you see her on the street, you say "Chao Ba," with two falling tones. In a sense, you understand it as a question like "how are you?" If you think of it as a question and your habits in English return to you, as most people do when you don't understand the tones, you're going to say "Choa Ba . . ." with an elliptical reflection at the end. And now you have clearly said to the woman "Greetings poisoned food." The Vietnamese understand the tones as we understand vowel sounds; they just hear it and have no reason to question it. That is the word they hear. So that is the hard part. The grammar is very simple, no verb conjugations, very simple.

When I got to language school, there was one of those wonderful army rumors running around that if you flunked out, they would send you to Korea instead. I didn't believe it, but virtually all the other guys in my cell of ten chose to believe it. It took them about twelve weeks to figure out that *nobody* flunked out, by which time it was too late. Of the ten people in my class, I was the only one who could speak the language. The others couldn't find their way to a latrine in Vietnamese, and yet we were all sent to Vietnam into jobs where we had to know the language. If that same percentage of guys not knowing the language applied down along down the hallway, and it probably did, you can see the eventual mischief sown by language training.

H: Upon arriving in country at Long Binh in January 1971, what were your initial impressions of the land, Vietnamese people, fellow soldiers, and overall atmosphere of the place?

RB: One first impression: all the Vietnamese prostitutes who were signed onto the base at night. In our tin hooches [barracks], I shared a room with another guy, and across the hall a guy and his Vietnamese "girlfriend" were having at it. Certainly, as with many prostitutes in Vietnam, they took on the veneer and attitude, and even the intent, of girlfriends. There were very few hardcore professional prostitutes in Vietnam; they all had romantic fantasies of falling in love and going back to America with some GI. So that was striking.

There was a big old dog who befriended me and I befriended him; also the smell of nuoc mam [fish oil sauce] in the air from the Vietnamese housekeepers making their lunch; the smell of wood fire; and out on the edge of the base the smell of shit fires burning with jet fuel in the pans of shit from the latrines. A morning formation, not mine, on my second or third day took a rocket, and a couple of people were killed. Just the look of the place outside the fence. That first drive from the airport with the metal grills on the buses' windows. But I was glued to that window, watching, looking into every little house, at every palm tree and rice paddy, just ravenously taking this place in.

H: You were approaching your Vietnam tour of duty less like a soldier and more like a writer?

RB: Absolutely, but as a writer in the purest sense. I was approaching it the way I approach life. It's this intense, complex, primarily sensual experience. Life in that way is filled with a wide range of people who are fascinating, and it's worth getting under their skin. That happens to be the best attitude for a writer. When I was self consciously a writer, I would lose touch with the things that make me a writer. I was still writing plays while in Vietnam. But in between, it was life—an unconscious taking in of all that intense, complex, humanity-based, sensual experience.

H: What were your military duties at your first assignment (Plantation)?

RB: I was an enlisted man, as you know. I was a hard-striped sergeant E-5, until eventually after five months at Plantation, I went to Saigon and turned into a specialist-5. That [change in rank designation from combat to support services] pissed me off. But I still have my hard stripes somewhere. While at Plantation I was out in the field. I had a little card in my pocket that said I was a USAID [U.S. Agency for International Development] worker, not an army guy. So I was in civilian clothes, a PX [Post Exchange] sport shirt and PX chinos, the tail of the sports shirt out so I could hide a .38 [pistol] on my hip. They gave us an army jeep to drive around the countryside with "219th MI [Military Intelligence] Detachment" stenciled on the sides. We had two agent handlers who controlled networks of local people who observed and reported. We were near the Bien Hoa airbase, so most of the intelligence we gathered was tactical: "The airbase is going to be rocketed at dawn from such and such coordinates." A typical event would be that one of the agent handlers would sign onto the base around dusk. He would give me the information, and I would create eleven copies of the spot reports and give one to the Tactical Operations Center at Plantation, which would call in the air force the next day to blow away the coordinates. I would take the other ten copies, alone in this jeep and driving the same damn path every night through the rice paddies, out to the local police chief, the provincial chief, and eventually to the air base. For five months, I was driving around at night, alone in the jeep, sometimes with another guy. I had to inform all the local people and the air base that there's word there will be a rocket attack at dawn.

H: Given that you were driving a marked military jeep, you must have thought that you were an obvious target for the enemy?

RB: Of course, which just made more fascinating and intense my experience of the kerosene lamp in the little hooch I passed, the face of that woman turning off on the side of the road, and needless to say the child up there ready to roll a grenade the VC had given him. But the fact is, that kind of ever-present, intense sense of your own well-being, the threat of death, and the intensity of the unknown heighten your senses. Works of literary art are sensual objects. Artists are not intellectuals; they are sensualists. So, yes, I was a sitting duck. Part of me was scared to death, but part of me was exhilarated.

H: You worked in this position at Plantation for five months.

RB: I had gotten into Saigon a couple of times and met a guy named Hatcher James, who was a diplomat. He was the American Foreign Service officer who was the advisor to the mayor of Saigon. At the time when our unit stood down in 1971 (the 219th MI Detachment was going home and I was not going with it; I was slotted for reassignment), there were rumors about going up to the DMZ and going here and there. And I just said to Hatcher James, who was a powerful guy, "Man I'd sure like to work for you." His assistant had just been arrested for dealing with black market stuff, or some other serious trouble, and he had an opening. So he asked for me, and he got me. I spent seven months as his administrative assistant. It was again a civilian-clothes job in Saigon City Hall, and I lived at the Hotel Metropole. As I have said many times before, my favorite thing in the world was that every night after midnight I would wander alone into the steamy back alleys of Saigon, where nobody ever seemed to sleep. And I would crouch in the doorways with these people and talk to them, and they were wonderful. Invariably, they invited me into their homes and into their culture and into their lives. I was conscious of the fact that in some respects I was in every bit as much danger walking around the back alleys of Saigon as my counterparts were out in the jungles. But the people were there, and the culture was there. So I went looking for it. I was patrolling out there trying to learn who these people were.

H: Was this patrolling in any way related to your job?

RB: No.

H: Basically, were you simply translating for your boss?

RB: Yes, and other odd jobs. One very odd job was that at some point he called me and said, "Sergeant Butler, I need to ask you a big favor." I said, "Sure." He said, "I'm going home on leave for three months; would you please live in my villa and watch it." So for three months, this E-5 specialist lived in an old French villa with servants, living in a house behind it, making my dinners. I lived alone, and the only thing I had to do was at 4 P.M. go into my room, close the door, and not go out for a while because the mayor brought his mistress and they had at it in my boss's empty bed down the hall. This was in Yen Do Street in Saigon, not far from one of my favorite soup restaurants, which I learned years later was Vietcong central. So my sense now is that I was surrounded by the Vietcong, and they tolerated me and embraced me somehow. I really think that it was the Vietnamese language that did it for me. Whatever was said behind my back and whatever easing off or tolerance of my continued life that happened, I think happened because I clearly spoke the language and clearly loved the Vietnamese and the culture. The language saved my life in a situation that I should not have been in.

H: Describe the people in your unit at Plantation—highly motivated, apathetic, scared?

RB: I don't remember. They were just doing their job. The catch phrase at the time was "there it is." That was the general attitude.

H: Tell me about the relationship you had with your commanding officers.

RB: My relationship was with a diplomat. I had a warm father-son relationship with Hatcher James, who was a career diplomat—sort of the equivalent of a two- or three-star general in the hierarchy. He was an advisor. He had been in Vietnam for a long time.

H: Did you encounter drug use in your unit?

RB: No. My unit was two or three guys for five months, and then I was alone in Vietnam.

H: While in Vietnam, did you think about the politics (validity) of the war?

RB: If you want an assessment of what we were protecting there, I was there during the last presidential election when [incumbent] Nguyen Van Thieu ran for president against Big Minh [Duong Van]. Mr. Binh, a Vietnamese friend of mine, had been inveighing against the corruption of Thieu for months, profound corruption. Election day came; Mr. Binh went off to vote and then came back. I asked what I thought was a rhetorical question. I asked who he voted for, and he said, "Well, I voted for Thieu." And I said, "Mr. Binh, how could you vote for Thieu?" And he said, "Well, Thieu has already made his fortune. If we vote in a new guy, he would just have to start from scratch." It was a pragmatic approach; the Vietnamese are pragmatists. But that is the democracy we were supporting.

H: You include a few scenes of intense physical interrogation of Vietnamese in some of your Vietnam-related books. Are such scenes based on real events from your tour?

RB: I did not see any of that. An event described in *On Distant Ground* comes from my experience. I did go to an interrogation center; I did go into a horrific little cell; I did move a little tray for the rice bowl; and indeed in the cell, just as described in *On Distant Ground*, someone had scratched in the wall in Vietnamese "hygiene is healthful." I was indeed extraordinarily struck by the mind, the sensibility that would in that circumstance write that. But I did not take part in any intense interrogations.

H: Was there a particularly acute moral dilemma you faced during your tour of duty?

RB: You face a moral dilemma every day of your life, almost anywhere. I presume you are asking for a moral dilemma that really troubled me. No. I had put myself into a position, for reasons we have discussed, that I didn't opt out of. I had put myself in a position where I was harming no one. Indeed, my feelings were warm and even loving for a wide range of people: from my favorite leper beggar on the street—who was one of the happiest, most cheerful people I have ever met and was telling me how he had been keeping track of how much his business had improved since his nose fell off—to the mayor of Saigon. So the moral dilemma was to maintain my sense of being in this place, connected to it, open to it, compassionate to it, and doing it no harm. That was an ongoing dilemma, but it was never seriously challenged.

H: Many excellent pieces of war literature focus on heart-of-darkness experiences among soldiers, in particular, episodes of soldiers losing control and in a primitive fashion revealing the dark, evil side that resides in them and in us all. Did you experience or observe any of these situations?

RB: That is an absolutely important and terribly intense and fruitful kind of theme. But it is the theme of the writers who were shaped by combat experiences in the Vietnam War. I was not. Only 18 percent of the men who went to Vietnam ever saw any combat. For the 82 percent who did not, it was a different war. For the 18 percent, the ravenous sensuality of combat will create an artist in someone who has the potential for it. You see it in Tim, Larry, Phil, and in a lot of other people. For them, what they were shaped by, thematically as artists, had to do with the heart of darkness and the human capacity for evil and destruction, as well as the human capacity for courage. Those are wonderful literary themes, and those guys explore those themes brilliantly. For me, it was a different experience. And I think that for all those people who stayed home yet were shaped by the Vietnam War, it was a different thing too. For all the rest of us, the experience was not about the heart of darkness, as much as it was about the collision of cultures. The central human issue is this: I stand here, and I have to decide where I draw the line around myself. Inside that line is my own; outside that line is the other. That was what the Vietnam War was about for all the rest of us. I think America redefined for itself where it drew the line, and we see the effects of that today. At that point, we thought the line was as wide as the whole world, which I guess grew out of the longstanding sense of America as a melting pot, open to all who would become part of us. But the melting pot also implied losing some of your own particularities, and now, the line is actually tighter. The current sense of finding who you are in an exclusive way by your gender, race, culture, ethnicity, religion, or whatever is the same large question that Vietnam raised for us—where do you draw the line? That is why I described the moral dilemma as I did. For me in Vietnam, in a personal way, the line was cast to the farthest horizon in a way that, in practical terms, had not effectively been done for me before. For others, it generated a "let me draw that line more closely, so that I do not have to go out of it; I can recognize the people within it more clearly, and everything is fine." By the way, this dilemma is at the heart of the religious wars of the twenty-first century. I am already nostalgic for the political wars of the twentieth century. Religion is now becoming the way you draw the line.

H: What did you learn about love in Vietnam?

RB: I learned that I found the opportunity and the capacity in myself to love a wider range of people with striking surface differences from me. I have been writing from that place of love since, not only about Vietnam, but also about all the characters in my books.

H: What did you learn about individual courage and cowardice during your time in Vietnam?

RB: Within my context, I don't know. Was it a courageous act for me to say, "Well, there is that dark steamy alley. I am in the middle of a war with no front lines; there are people there in the dark who would certainly want to kill me, or worse; yet there are also people who I can speak to with this language I have been given, who I am in the midst of. Let me just go down that alley way"? I am not trying to glorify myself by that. Is it a question of courage? Of course it is, and I understood that. I guess the real issue of courage is that it is impossible to have courage if nothing scares you. Real courage is to do the thing that is not natural to you: to do the job I had to do out there, to get in my jeep every night. For five months, I had no choice but to go into the dark where the people were. It was my job and duty to deliver messages to those places. I understood the dangers. And then for seven months, for my own purposes, I did the same sort of act. I did not have messages to deliver, and it was not my job. But I went out there, into the dark, where the people were. I am not glorifying that act, but in my own context that is what the issues of courage were.

H: Tell me a little bit more about your writing activities while you were there. Did these documents in any way become part of your later published writing?

RB: I did keep notes, but I have used them very little. I used them more early on, and I have used them little since—mostly for the name of a tree, a smell in the air, or the quotidian detail.

H: Upon leaving Vietnam, how were you a different person from the one who entered Vietnam one year earlier?

RB: I have pretty much described how I was different. I don't think I had fully realized it yet, although I would shortly after, but I had changed from a playwright to a fiction writer. What I had absorbed into my unconscious from the experience of Vietnam was the moment-to-moment sensual flow of experience. As a playwright, I am not responsible for that. The actors, production designer, director, all of those folks are. So I had been transformed from a playwright into a fiction writer by Vietnam, because the experience I had there could be expressed only by fiction, where I created the object that was fully in the moment and in the senses.

H: From this tour of duty, what are your lasting impressions of the Vietnamese people, the culture, and the land? Do such impressions make their way into your war writing?

RB: My lasting impressions had to do with a sense of the Vietnamese people, not of the people as exotic or drastically different in some basic way from Americans or anybody else. For me, the impression was of the human heart. When I won the Pulitzer Prize for *A Good Scent from a Strange Mountain*, a dozen prominent members of the Vietnamese literary community in Orange County, California [Westminster], had a lunch for me. The thing they praised the most and were most grateful for was that the stories did not make them into something exotic. Rather, they were humans sharing the matters of the human spirit that we all share: a yearning for self, identity, and a place in the universe; issues of family, friendship, loss and memory— these enduring universal human conditions. These are the things that the book is about, and the Vietnamese love that about the book. What I came away with from Vietnam was that the ravenousness of my experience there was not so much an experience of the exotic but of the *universal*.

H: When departing Vietnam, were you thinking that you would someday write about your Vietnam experiences?

RB: Yes, although I would not have put it into those terms because I was not writing *about* the experience. In fact, if you read *From Where You Dream*, you find one of the god-awful short stories, which was a Vietnam story, I wrote before I started writing well. Once I started writing fiction, I still wrote badly for a long while. I wrote five terrible novels and forty god-awful short stories, after a dozen dreadful plays. The first awful short story I wrote was called "The Chieu Hoi." I wrote that story six months after a certain event happened. When I was in military intelligence, I spent a couple of weeks working with the Australians. An incident happened then that I recorded in my notebook, and I used that as the basis for my first short story. You will see the ill effects of literal memory in staying too close to the notes. That same experience informed, but in a more legitimate, composted literary way, "Open Arms" in A Good Scent from a Strange Mountain.

H: From the late '6os on, there were veterans' protests going on in Washington, including those coordinated by the Vietnam Veterans Against the War [VVAW], led by John Kerry and others. Did you think about joining that organization upon your return from the war?

RB: No.

H: Did you experience PTSD symptoms upon your return?

RB: Not that I recognized. I came back to a divorce. In my second month in Vietnam, I got a letter from my then wife who said, "While you're gone, why don't we just both fool around." She had gone to graduate school and wanted to do something with an art teacher. So that precipitated that divorce. But it would have happened anyway, so that does not qualify as something resulting from the war.

H: Have you ever thought why you adjusted relatively well upon your return from Vietnam when other Vietnam veterans were having problems?

RB: I did not have to confront the evil that resides in my soul, as it does in every human soul. For me it was the antithesis of that. Vietnam helped open up my capacity to love people as opposed to opening up a glimpse into my capacity to hate and destroy. That is the hand that I was dealt. If I have any guilt, it is because I know some of my good pals just didn't get the kind of luck that I got. They did not get dealt the right hand over there and had to confront things in themselves that were really tough. I was a lucky man, a very lucky and blessed man. I went there and was subject to the same kinds of possibilities that everybody else was, but ended up having an experience that was drastically different from what all my writing pals had. That is the hand I was dealt.

AUTHOR _____

H: After returning from the war and working as a reporter and editor for Fairchild Publications, what was the turning point in your own efforts to get your fiction published?

RB: Well, the turning point had to do with my coming to the basic insight that I have (and that I have been teaching ever since) about what a work of art is:

works of art do not come from the mind. They are not created from the rational, analytical faculties; they are created from the place where you dream, from your unconscious. Actually "Moving Day" was the first thing I wrote well, and that, interestingly, was in the first person. It was about two Vietnam veterans, and it was my first published work [*Redbook*, October 1974: 92–93]. It was a good story that came from the right place in me. But then I wrote two more stories for *Redbook* and one for *Cosmopolitan*, and they were purely willed into being. All of the bad stories that never got published and all the bad novels that never got published were written from my head. So the crucial turning point was with *The Alleys of Eden*, basically from the first sentence: "The dogs had fled." All of a sudden I was in the right place, writing from my unconscious.

By the time I started *The Alleys of Eden* I was seven years out of Vietnam. But the Graham Greene insight is applicable here because I had finally forgotten enough from my literal memory that I could access that aspect of my life, and the other aspects of my life, to create a work of art. That was the turning point. Instrumental to that was the influence of a great teacher and a wonderful man of letters, one of the most perceptive book reviewers who has ever reviewed a book—Anatole Broyard. In 1978 I took two semesters of fiction workshops from Anatole at the New School in New York City. Anatole enlightened me about the fact that the stuff I had written so far was dreck, yet he seemed to believe in me and my possibilities. I started *The Alleys of Eden*, which he loved. The end of the book, what I called "Book One," was getting onto a helicopter leaving Saigon. It was literally a book, and Anatole said, "You have to follow them back to the States." I said, "Okay." "Book Two" came into being because Anatole said I want to know what's next. He loved the novel.

When I tried to get *The Alleys of Eden* published, I got turned down twenty-one times. One major editor at a major publishing house wrote, "This is a fine novel about Vietnam, except there aren't enough battle scenes." Anatole finally whispered in the ear of Ben Raeburn, who owned a small independent publisher, Horizon Press, in New York City, and Ben published the book and my subsequent two books. I owe a lot to Ben Raeburn as well. But in Anatole's presence I came to make that turn. I do not remember exactly the flash or the moment when it happened, although as I say, de facto writing that first sentence of *The Alleys of Eden*, because the book flowed beautifully after that. Interestingly, the central characters in the novel, Cliff and Lanh, were characters in the last play I ever wrote, which I wrote in Vietnam, but they were just miserable failures in the play, as well as was the play itself. These characters in prototype began in my last god-awful play, and then there was a lot of god-awful fiction in between. Finally, I came back to those characters. But they were not recognizable any more.

H: After returning from Vietnam, did you ever consider writing a memoir about your war experiences?

RB: No, never. It's pretty much agony for me to write nonfiction. I love to read nonfiction, but it just does not feel like the place I need to write from. For me, everything that comes out of my fingertips must come from the welter of my unconscious where the literal true things have vanished into the larger universe of the universal truth. Tim [O'Brien] talks about the lies that are stories, and I've always talked about exactly the same thing. For years I've quoted Carlos Fuentes, who defined the novel as "a pack of lies hounding the truth." And so I'm drawn solely to that mode of expression.

H: In a 1983 interview for *Contemporary Authors* ("Interview," Detroit: Gale, 1985, 112: 91) you noted that certain biblical writers (Daniel, Jeremiah, Isaiah, and Luke) influenced your early writing. How so?

RB: My second wife, the mother of my son, whom I gained complete custody of when he was eleven—when I married her [1972], she was a nonreligious New York Jew who was a pretty good poet. When I divorced her [1987], she was a radical right-wing, 1880s-style Marian Catholic. The arc in there was harrowing. We did a Cooks tour of Christendom looking for a church that she felt could keep back the darkness that nothing else could. And so I had to go along for that ride, because I was not going to get custody of our son in those years. When the interview for *Contemporary Authors* was done, I was still married to this person and, though I certainly felt a literary influence from the Bible, I had to speak in those terms so as not to lose my son. However, I am profoundly disaffected from organized religion, and I think that organized religion is now being used—with a certain philosophical inevitability flowing from the parochial absolutism inherent in the holy books and traditions—to generate much of the violence and hatred of the twenty-first century. We see that every day in the news. But organized religion is a necessity in the world because most people can be comforted only if they have clear, externally derived answers to the great questions of our existence. Artists ask the same questions, but with the utter openness of the maker of parables, the storyteller, that Jesus, in fact, was. The world would be a better place if we could understand the great religions of the world as massive objects of performance art, with their truths metaphorical truths, as in great works of art. When metaphor turns into dogma, really bad things can happen. Certainly, in that long search for a religion I experienced with my second wife, the way I consoled myself in the pews of many churches, while the preaching was going on in front of me, was to sit there and read the Bible. So I read the entire King James Bible word for word, making my own covert sort of index of it, which finally came to good use in the short story "Up by Heart" in *Had a Good Time*. But certainly the power of storytelling, the power of language, the richness of the long sentence, even the cinematic techniques of the Bible's storytelling—for example, in those crucial moments of slow motion violence in the story of Deborah and Sisera in the book of Judges—those things all certainly influenced my writing, no doubt.

H: How do you begin a writing project? Is there usually a moral, thematic, or character center that inspires you to begin a story?

RB: With a character who yearns. That is the other central insight in what I teach and what I understand about this process. Again, if you look at all the awful stories and novels I wrote, one thing almost always missing is a character who is built around a yearning, a deep desire. The essence of fiction is that it is a temporal art form; it exists in time. Poetry can be exempt from time, for example, because the length of line is part of the form, and so it is a kind of object on the page. You can have a poem that is out of time. Even so-called prose poems are less than a page long and still objects on the page. But as soon as you let the line length run on and you turn the page, you are, as they say in fairy tales, "upon a time." Buddhists will tell you, and this is one of the great truths of their religion, that as a human being with feelings (which are the other inescapable elements of fiction) you can't exist for even thirty seconds of time on planet Earth without desiring something. My favorite word in this regard is yearning, because it suggests the deepest level of desire, which is what literary writers explore. Fiction inevitably is the art form of human yearning. Yet in virtually every student manuscript I have seen in the last twenty years from students before I get my hands on them (and you look at my early work and I was struggling with the same problem), you'll find the characters have problems, they've got attitudes, they've got a voice, they've got a point of view, they've got a sensibility, and they may have a vividly evoked milieu, but all of those things put together do not automatically add up to the dynamics of desire. The dynamics of desire make stories go. And so I begin with the character, absolutely. I always have characters kicking around in me—lots of them—but I'm ready to let them speak only when I have a strong enough intuition about what it is at their deepest level they yearn for.

H: How do you intuit the character's yearning; is it by simply starting to write?

RB: No, I don't start writing and looking for the yearning. It's a process, but it is an unconscious process. It is a thing that's going on in my imagination.

When the characters there are ready to write, then I'm ready too. That first sentence is always important. I may sit and fiddle with that and listen for a long while before it is clear. But if I feel the character is close, then there is some working out on the page.

H: Once into a writing project, what are your writing habits?

RB: I write every day; that is crucial, no matter where I am. When I began my career [living in Sea Cliff, Long Island, and commuting into Manhattan], I realized—because of that marriage I described earlier and because when I was home I was constantly buffering my son from the proselytizing that was going on (he and I had a kind of covert separate life, where tolerance ruled)—if I wanted to be a novelist, I would have to write on the train, which is where I wrote. I wrote three hundred polished words going in and three hundred polished words coming home on the Long Island Railroad, before laptop computers, on a legal pad on a Masonite lap board. Having done that, I'm fine to write anywhere. So yes, I write wherever I am if I am in the midst of a project. Now, sometimes, I can take one day off if I need to. And on the next day, I can come back, and everything is fine. But if I take two or three days off, on the third or fourth day when I go back, it is as if I had never written a word before in my entire life. That is the nature of the unconscious. It is awful to get in there and scary as hell. When you are in there, if you go back day after day, it's still always scary and difficult, but it yields. However, if you give it a chance, it will seal itself again and erase any traces of where the entry point was. So writing every day is crucial, and I prefer to do it first thing in the morning on a computer.

H: When you write, do you have any notes nearby or an outline?

RB: Well, these days it is an oversimplification to call it an outline. I don't work with this anymore, but if you read my book [From Where You Dream], I refer to the system; it's a way of getting at my unconscious. I used to work with a kind of scene list that I put on three-by-five cards and could juggle around, and it was very important that the list would never be cast in stone. These days, even with novels, I basically sit down and write the book out, but having done a lot of meditating and note-taking. I have a little moleskin sketchbook beside my desk, and I am constantly writing a few quick impressions of what's coming up, or what may come up later. I do that in ink with my vintage fountain pens. But the composing is done on the computer.

H: What is your chief asset as a writer?

RB: My access to a wide range of voices. Even third-person narrative voices have personae, something I learned in oral interpretation. But in recent years it has been first-person voices, and I think my asset is that I can find a wide range of voices in my own unconscious that feel authentic to most people. Women, for instance, are constantly telling me how the women's voices are utterly authentic, and the Vietnamese people (I still don't have my picture in either of the paperback editions of *A Good Scent*) are constantly telling me that they are shocked to find that I am not Vietnamese. I suppose if I have to list an asset of my own, it's that.

H: Why are you so successful in creating authentic women's voices?

RB: Well, I've been married four times. And listened to my wives very carefully. Obviously, I didn't say the right things, but I listened very carefully. And I have known many other women in my life and listened to them in lots of different ways. For an artist, all people—both men and women—are to be entered into imaginatively and compassionately and heard and attended to. In that process of just living my life in contact with all these people, I have discovered that it's not a willful journalistic enterprise, but I have continued to be surprised at how many of these people have taken up residence in my unconscious.

H: One criticism occasionally leveled at some American soldier-authors writing about the Vietnam experience is the dearth of authentic Vietnamese voices in their books or the absence of significant female characters. Certainly, that criticism doesn't apply to your writing.

RB: I think it's an utterly unfair criticism of some of the fine writers who came out of Vietnam, because it's a matter of point of view. The world in those books is often seen through the eyes and sensibilities of men who were in combat, who did not know Vietnamese, and whose encounter with the Other, necessary in war, would make it impossible to have that kind of fully fleshed-out rendering of those kinds of characters in a legitimate work of art about such an experience. Actually, I think there are some characters in the works of those men who are fully developed; I'm not necessarily buying the premise of the criticism. But if there are opaque characters in the works, that trait is artistically necessary given the vision of those works.

H: What sets you apart, then, from many American writers who write about the Vietnam experience is your extensive encounters during your military tour with the Other facilitated by your ability to speak Vietnamese and your familiarity with the Vietnamese culture.

RB: Also, we talked about it earlier: my experience, as a result of superficial things, was that, in my unique military situation, I was dealing with a different aspect of the human condition—the collision of cultures as opposed to the essentials of warfare.

H: Despite your antipathy toward memoir, you said earlier that when writing *The Alleys of Eden*, you drew upon memories of your Vietnam experiences—perhaps more so than in any other work.

RB: Well I say that in a conditional way. *The Alleys of Eden* was written entirely from my unconscious. Now, that does not mean that everything I write is utterly untraceable; it's not a matter of I either remember it, or I don't. At the moment of creation, the artistic contingencies of that moment make organically appropriate these sensual impressions and these events, and they appear. Occasionally, once they are on the page and used in this new way through the sensibility of this other character, if I step back, I can identify which experience in my personal life brought forth those insights or those particular sense details. That is appropriate. What makes literal memory inappropriate occurs if I create a character (and I've got a model for that character), bring him into the story, for example, and then work the story out of the remembered characteristics of that character. That is working backwards, because a work of art is utterly organic. Every tiny detail resonates into everything else in a pure work of art. So everything has to be malleable. Everything is negotiable and changeable. If you work from literal memory in that inappropriate way, certain things in the remembered character won't allow themselves to be changed, and the work of art begins to fall apart. Then you get a mixture of memory, autobiography, and created fiction. The lies and truths get all mixed up, and the work of art suffers. The object of this sort of process might be fascinating, intellectually provocative, and politically, sociologically, or anthropologically brilliant, but ultimately, the object it creates breaks down aesthetically.

H: Continuing this memory-imagination thread, talk about the relationships between truth and lies in your writing.

RB: All fiction is a lie in some sense, but I'll go back to the Fuentes quote. Calling literary fiction a "lie" is a certain semantic trick, a kind of pose that we writers take sometimes: "Oh, I'm a writer; oh, this is a lie." Well, of course, it is. That's why it says fiction; that's why it says novel. But it's not a lie, really. It's imagined. If it's convenient or rhetorically effective to call that a lie, that's fine. But we understand that it's a lie of a different sort. What we are doing is saying that in the chaos of moment-to-moment real life on planet Earth, as artists we sense an order behind the chaos. And the only way to express this order is to manipulate the sequencing, the ordering, and the interconnection of moment-to-moment sensual reality in this artistic object. So when readers encounter the object, they encounter it as if it *were* life. But that pattern, that vision of order, shines true. That's the relation of truth and lie. That vision of order is a deeper kind of truth; it's the truth of the human condition, as opposed to the truth of quotidian chaos.

H: Are the truths in your writing, truths about the world's sensual reality?

RB: They're the truths of the human condition perceived through the organic ordering of that sensual reality.

H: Over the years, several of your books, including The Alleys of Eden, Sun Dogs, On Distant Ground, The Deuce, and The Deep Green Sea, have Vietnam connections. Is there a reason for this return as an author to the Vietnam experience?

RB: Well, it's not a matter of going back to that as it is a moving towards. It's a matter of what characters with what yearnings in what situations yield themselves up from my unconscious. So it's not a conscious going back. Once I finished The Alleys of Eden, Wilson Hand (who was by the way a secondary character in that book) lingered, and he had his own story. At the time, I had been at Energy User News as the editor in chief. I had visited Alaska and had even gone up to Deadhorse up on the North Slope; that had gone into my unconscious. Wilson and Alaska got hooked up together, and he just needed to tell that story [Sun Dogs]. Then, On Distant Ground was published in 1985. About 1983 I started hearing David Fleming [central character in the novel], who was coming out of The Alleys of Eden, but the central event that instigates David's story occurred in my first unpublished novel, a Vietnam novel called "What Lies Near." [The unpublished novel] is essentially about a character who is in military intelligence and encounters writing on the wall [see earlier comment about "hygiene is healthful"], becomes obsessed with the writer, tracks him down, and as the novel ends, sets him loose. That was the first novel I ever wrote. It didn't work. It probably comes closer to working than the subsequent bad novels, but it was not enough. Then the Vietnam babylift occurred ["Operation Babylift," April 1975] with the images of all those children. And just a couple of years earlier my son was born, and he looked very much like me. So from '73 to '83, ten years of absorbing the birth of my son and meditating on the way your child is a part of you, and from '71 to '83, twelve years of absorbing that writing on the wall. And, of course, I knew a number of Vietnamese women while I was there, some intimately. There was that whole realm of experience, and I thought, when I saw my son as an infant, there are men who returned from Vietnam who have just such a part of them back there. But given the nature of the relationships they were in, many of them left the country and had no idea that a child was coming into the world. So all that kicked around in me for a decade and finally, the two things came together—the writing on the wall and the child—and On Distant Ground happened.

H: Was *The Deuce* similarly influenced by your connecting your son with Amerasian children in Vietnam?

RB: Of course. I had been living in New York for a long time and commuting every day past the street people. I was very familiar with that pre-Giuliani [as New York City mayor] scene on 42nd Street at the same time that the street kids of Saigon that I had known were kicking around in my unconsciousness. Father-son issues were also kicking around, so *The Deuce* started talking to me. Tony Hatcher [Amerasian boy born Vo Dihn Thanh] started talking to me directly, and as you know that was the first book I wrote in the first person. So he insisted on speaking. Again, this wasn't a conscious going back to Vietnam, but these were the issues that were brewing in my unconscious.

H: Earlier you noted that of all the books you have written linked to the Vietnam experience, *The Deep Green Sea* is "my best work centered on Vietnam."

RB: If I had to choose one, that book would be it because it has both the Americans and the Vietnamese. Its central metaphor has to do with what we left behind, and what we left behind is an essential part of ourselves. What the Vietnamese have is an essential part of us. That's the central metaphor. The beauty of that and the tragedy of that intermingle in a framework that feels Sophoclean to me. . . . For me that novel embodies the essence of all that I've been seeing, I think, about that whole experience.

H: During your return trips to Vietnam after the war, have some memorable experiences occurred reaffirming your ongoing connection to the Vietnamese people, language, and culture?

RB: When I got to Saigon my first time [1993], I was staying at the Hotel Majestic at the river, and within twenty minutes of going out two things happened. First of all, two blocks from my hotel, there was a shop that was a combination bookstore, ice cream parlor, and book pirating operation. The ice cream was there, the books were there, as were two guys sitting at tables by the wall with exacto knives disassembling books. And of course, there was a big stack of pirated copies of *A Good Scent from a Strange Mountain*, and it was beautifully done, in signatures even. I met the guy and introduced myself. He sort of blanched. But I showed him that I was okay with the book operation, and he gave me a 30 percent discount on my own pirated book and a free ice cream cone.

Then there was a guy who I started an ongoing relationship with that week. He was on the street selling lapel pins from the Soviet era, and he had only a stump of a left arm. This guy was probably about my age. I spoke a Vietnamese greeting to him. He was really nice and friendly, and we exchanged pleasantries every morning. Then one morning, five days into the trip, I went by him, and he waved a magazine at me. So I came over to him, and he had a literary magazine that had just been published that day. It had a translation of "Crickets" [story from *Good Scent*] in it with my picture, and he had recognized me. He loved the story, and we started talking in more depth. He was a former Vietcong soldier. He was very excited about the story. He said that "you are absolutely right about us catching these crickets [for fighting]. And you know what else you got right? No matter whether the cricket was ours or not, if there was a charcoal cricket against a red fire cricket, we'd root for the fire cricket." If there are unconsciously driven literary symbols in my work, in "Crickets" the fire cricket represents the Vietcong and the charcoal cricket represents America. Here was a real ex-Vietcong soldier very excited and delighted by the story I had written. Without making a literary symbol out of the incident, which given my aesthetic I am opposed to, he was genuinely and directly responding to the sensual object in a special way because, of course, it had that resonance for him. He saw himself.

H: Have you incorporated or will you incorporate experiences from your postwar travel in Vietnam into your writing?

RB: Except for *The Deep Green Sea*, not yet. As you know, I probably by now have a significantly lower percentage of my work involved with Vietnam than most of the other writers that are identified by Vietnam. Once you have seen Vietnam as a kind of Sophoclean tragedy, there is not much else to say.

H: What makes a good war story?

RB: Ask Tim and those guys. I don't see myself writing war stories where war is the instigator. Much more interesting to me, war is simply a backdrop for the playing out of some deeper human condition unconnected to war as such.

H: Tim, Larry, and Phil each make a similar point: "I don't write war stories; I write stories in which war is present, but I am focusing on these universal human truths."

RB: And that is true, because human beings either have courage or cowardice in them in all realms of experience. We all carry around the heart of darkness or a potential for evil and violence in ourselves, and we deal with it or we don't. And so those are universal conditions that Tim, Larry, and Phil are getting at. Those, of course, don't have anything do to, necessarily, with war.

H: Are your books containing Vietnam-related experiences political or apolitical?

RB: I see them as utterly apolitical and therefore profoundly political. And this paradox has to do with the issues of writing from your head or writing from your unconscious. I think that virtually all political opinions are irrational. The things that people get heated about in politics, the most strongly held political beliefs, almost none of them have been arrived at by a careful, dispassionate, objective examination of issues and then choosing the position. The proof's in the white knuckles and the quavering voices. Politics are emotions. And Jonathan Swift once said, "You can't reason a person out of a position that he didn't reason himself into in the first place." So the writer who writes from the mind, from political ideas, with a political agenda and intent, inevitably creates an object that will speak from his mind to the reader's mind. Consequently, he'll make real sense only to someone who already agrees with him. However, the artist—by ignoring politics, by putting any sense of political agenda or intent aside, and focusing on, strictly, the moment-to-moment sensual reality of the one yearning soul at the center of the novel or story—will create an object that has the potential of getting around the mind of the reader and down to the place where political beliefs are actually held. What is political about Shostakovich's 4th Symphony or a Cezanne painting? Joseph Stalin knew. All of the prominent dictators of history have been much smarter about what works of art are—how they operate through the emotions, through the senses—than many of the academics in university lit departments. The dictators always go after the artists right away. They know works of art cannot be counteracted by propaganda, that the works of art get to the place where real political beliefs are held. So, no, my works aren't political; therefore, they are profoundly political.

H: Why is the American public still so fascinated with the politics and literature of the Vietnam experience?

RB: I don't think the culture in general is fascinated by the Vietnam War. I think the political commentators keep it alive in public forums that you and I look at. And they are happy to bring it up with their own political agendas to try to throw their own light on Iraq, or whatever, and with some good reason. But the culture in general, I just don't know how widely conscious we are of the Vietnam experience. So why do the commentators keep going back to it? Because it is a politically useful point of reference.

Some people are fascinated by it because they go home and play a video game where people kill each other, and so war has a kind of innate fascination for people. Also Vietnam is an exotic culture, and there are now over a million Vietnamese living in the U.S. So this exoticism is often right next door. It's like any realm of otherness; those realms are visited. Some visit them just to escape; others visit them to learn something about a deeper self; and we all—even the most book-ignorant, hormonally overwrought teenager—face the human question of where do I draw the circle around myself? It's the essence of teenage life in this country today that there are groups: goths, geeks, jocks, preps, and whoever. Every human being on this planet is always engaged with the issues that I feel are the most important about Vietnam and about the Vietnam War: who do we identify with as our own, and who do we see as the outside other. Ultimately, that's the thing that energizes anybody's engagement. The white kids simulating hip-hop gangsta rap or Colin Powell putting on his white shirt and tie and acting like George Bush's lackey—we're all trying to figure out who's our own and who's the other.

H: Differentiate between the two types of writing you classify as genre-entertainment-didactic writing and literary writing.

RB: The most important difference is process. The Stephen Kings of the world and even the Jean Paul Sartres of the world—Sartre as novelist, that is—the entertainment novelists and the didactic novelists share this: they have a preconceived effect that they wish to have on their readers. They know ahead of time the effect they wish to have. Stephen King wants to scare the hell out of you. Jean Paul Sartre wants to scare the hell out of you and also convince you of the cosmic verities of existentialism as a mode of philosophical thought. And then they construct an object to produce those effects. But the artists [literary writers] do not have a clue as to what the effect will be on a reader, nor do they care. The artists have an innate intuitive vision of the order behind the chaos. The only way that they can not only express what that order is but also find it for themselves is to go back to the chaos of moment-to-moment sensual existence, pull bits of pieces out of it, and reshape it into this sensual object that is a work of art. So creating the work of art is as much an act of exploration as it is of expression. That is the essential difference, and the difference is identifiable in the objects that are created. There are lots of textual effects that you can look at, but that is the basic difference between the two.

H: As part of your own literary writing you continue to write screenplays, as well as novels. Do you approach the writing differently?

RB: The essential difference is not unlike the difference that I encountered when I was studying playwriting. The screenwriter is involved in a collaborative art form in which the writer is even less important, by a long margin, than the writer is in the theater. But along the way, I have learned the differences. When I was failing as a playwright, because of my inability to come to terms with the collaborative art form, it was my only form of artistic expression. (As a playwright my most impassioned writing was going into the stage directions, which is a bad sign for a playwright.) Writing fiction takes care of that. Writing screenplays is a secondary and separate kind of activity for me. The essential difference is that in this collaborative art form you are not responsible as a screenwriter for the final moment-to-moment artistic experience of the object that is the film. That is far more the province in the direct experience of the actors, the director, the production designer, and so forth. As a writer, you are responsible for two things: the structure of the movie, or the plot (which, by the way, gets reordered and shuffled around by the editor anyway), and the dialogue, which eventually gets rephrased by the actors. As a screenwriter, you have to learn to create fruitful blank spaces in the screenplay for your collaborators to come in and fill. You have to make yourself comfortable with that. You also have to understand that the process cannot simply be from the unconscious, because you are always subject to notes, suggestions, and rewrite requirements from the people up the line from you—the producers and the studios who are paying the way. You are simply a writer for hire, and you have to deal with whatever it is that they see in the work or fail to see in the work. And the work they are looking at is not the finished work. They have to imagine a movie out of this object, and you are imagining a movie out of this object. So those two imaginings can be quite different. Either one could possibly come out of the object, but those people who are actually paying the money and, therefore, own the object require adjustments to fit how they are seeing the movie. You have to adjust to that. So you get into your unconscious when you can, but much of the time you have to write as a kind of willful act.

H: Consequently, like the genre-entertainment-didactic writer, the screenwriter has to have a strong sense of audience throughout this process.

RB: Sure, and knowing what the effect must be.

H: In writing screenplays, do you have the opportunity, as you do in your fiction, to get into the dream space and listen to a character's emerging voice?

RB: A little bit. To some extent you do, and you have to use as much of that part of yourself as you can to make it good. But you can't stay there. This [Redford screenplay (see Chronology, 2006)] is my ninth screenplay for hire. The universal process is that you tell people what you are going to do in some detail. They sign off on that and say, "Wow, that sounds like a great idea. Here is a bunch of money; go do that." You go do that, and then they say,

"Well, yes, you did what you said you were going to do, but now we see that's not what we want to do. Let's do it this way." Which, of course, is a drastically different way. That is something you just have to deal with.

H: How many of your screenplays have made it to the screen?

RB: None. I made a shitload of money; I spent twelve years in WGA [Writers Guild of America]; at age sixty-three I can retire with a very large pension; and it's possible that I will never have made a movie.

H: Along with your writing career, you also teach creative writing at Florida State. What are the joys and frustrations as a teacher of creative writing?

RB: I see students who have the potential of becoming artists, but the thing standing in their way is that they are writing from the wrong place. Because of the pedagogy of creative writing in the United States, which is so focused on craft and technique, the students have never been told that craft and technique have to be forgotten as well. Those things have to go into the compost heap along with their life experiences. The students think—and they often have been given the official impression—that all they have to do is consciously and analytically apply their craft and technique over and over and they can end up with a work of art. And that just isn't true. To see students like that unfold artistically because you are able to guide them from their head and into their unconscious, of course, is a joy. That is the pleasure of teaching. But the terrible danger of teaching is that I have to read a lot of bad writing, and I have to use my bad memory to get the ill effects of that out of my head when I sit down in my chair to write myself. Also, especially when I teach process as I do (which I feel I must do to take students' artistic ambitions seriously), I run the grave danger of becoming too self-conscious of my own process— sitting down and thinking about going into my unconscious instead of simply doing it. And so, again, I draw heavily on my good bad-novelist memory and put all of that away too. But make no mistake about it, I think, on balance, the dangers of teaching creative writing outweigh the joys, but I am able to deal with the dangers and focus on the joys. That's fine.

H: It seems to me that a very strong piece of advice you might give to students, in addition to writing from their unconscious, is to learn more about life rather than learning just craft and technique.

RB: Oh, *absolutely*. As I said earlier, artists are not intellectuals; we're sensualists. When I was teaching at McNeese State, I kept hanging outside my door a poster with tear-off coupons for the Peace Corps. I would say to my students, "You basically went from your undergraduate career to this MFA and now you want to go straight to a Ph.D. program in creative writing? Stop! Don't do that yet! Take a coupon and go off somewhere and live a real life.

Your unconscious is going to learn more." It depends on the background that person has. Although I think there is a grave danger in overemphasizing craft and technique, I think certain things in that realm are useful to learn. You can learn them in classes, and you can learn them from the ravenous reading of great literature—you can learn it by example. But these things will never replace a life intensely lived.

H: How does a writer get into his or her dream space and out of the mind?

RB: There are a couple of things. One is to describe something we all do that is similar to this. We are all capable in the presence of a bore, usually a public bore, to throw a switch in our head and leave the room, leave the building. We daydream into another place, and it is like literal dreaming, like a movie going on in our head. We see somebody; we hear them talk; we feel something or smell it. In our heads, we are having an ongoing experience somewhere else. We all are capable of that, and we do it readily. To enter the dream space, you flip a different switch on the same plate on the wall. The switch connects you to the intense, profound deep daydream coming from your imagination, your unconscious. You are doing it, not to escape a bore, but to enter into the place where your own white-hot center is burning. In practical terms, I often tell my students that they should try to write the first thing in the morning. You go straight from your literal dreams, your actual sleep dreams, and into your writing space and into the waking dream of artistic creation.

One of the problems that literary writers face is the medium. For all other artists, their media are irreducibly and inescapably sensual already: movement in dance, sound in music, moving pictures in film. Even in painting, what we call abstract painting is not abstract at all; it is color and form. But the literary artist, alone, deals with this terrible problem: our medium, language, is not irreducibly, inescapably sensual. Every word has a sound. But the sound is immediately overwhelmed by meaning, and most meanings are conceptual. I always face that paradox in my teaching, which is why I did the Internet Web cast ["Inside Creative Writing"]: I inveigh against abstraction, analysis, and ideas. How do I do it? Well, abstractly, analytically, and through ideas about that. So I say to my students, "Get up from bed, do not turn on CNN, do not check your email. If you have to pee, fine, but don't pick up the New Yorker beside the toilet bowl. If you must have coffee, put it on a timer or make a little sensual ritual out of making it. Then go and start writing before the other abstract uses of language intrude upon your consciousness." That is helpful, I think.

H: How does your related notion of thrumming ("tuning up the enhanced aesthetic instrument") facilitate the reading of literature?

RB: Since a work of art is created from the unconscious and since a work of art in its primary and only necessary mode of encounter is a sensual thing, the reader encounters it as a moment-to-moment sensual experience. And since the object created is a sensual object and exists in a sensual moment-to-moment flow, as a reader, then, the appropriate way to read a work of literary art is by bringing your own dream space into correspondence with the dream space of the book and experience the work sensually and in the moment. That is, in the primary and necessary way to experience a work of art, you are not meant, as a reader, to understand a work of art abstractly, analytically, or thematically. You are meant to thrum to a work of art. Like the vibration of a string on a string instrument, there is a harmonic resonance set up with this. That is the aesthetic response; that is the appropriate, primary, and only necessary response of a reader to a work of art.

Unfortunately the way we are taught to read is often drastically at odds with such an approach. The higher you go in the educational hierarchy, the worse this gets. Often, the impression a literature teacher will give a student reader is that the literary artist is a kind of idiot savant. The writer really wants to say these abstract, analytical, theoretical, philosophical, and sociological things, but somehow he can't really do it (that's the "idiot" part), so he creates this story or novel instead. It is, therefore, the reader's responsibility to fulfill the creative process by translating this object into abstraction, theory, and idea. You hear it all the time. Teachers say, "Well, what does this work mean?"—as if it did not have a meaning on the page. Or worse, "What is the author trying to say?" Trying. This is, of course, utter bullshit. But I'm not saying that every literature course should be taught drastically differently; necessarily, some will be more useful than others. It is okay to teach the way that literature teachers teach as long as two things occur. First, at the beginning of the class, it must be made clear that what we are going to do this semester to these works of art is a purely artificial and strictly secondary thing. But that's okay. Why? Because we'll try to tune up the instrument inside us that thrums. We'll add some strings in the upper and lower registers; we'll tune up all the strings to perfect pitch, so that when you encounter a work of art after this class you will thrum more harmoniously and completely to it. Second, the last assignment in any literature class in this country should be as follows: "Now that we have done this artificial secondary thing to tune up your thrumming instrument, your last and perhaps most important assignment is to forget everything we've said. Do not do this anymore. Because if you encounter a work of literary art and as you read you are asking "what does that mean?"

what's that theory? what's the idea here? what does that symbol mean?" then what's happened is your ability to have an aesthetic response (that is your ability to actually read a work of literature in an appropriate way) is totally destroyed."

H: I want to end our conversation by discussing three of your books in more detail, ones from the beginning, middle, and current portions of your writing career: *The Alleys of Eden* (1981), *A Good Scent from a Strange Mountain* (1992), and *Had a Good Time: Stories from American Postcards* (2004). How should we talk about those three works, given what you just said about readers thrumming to literature?

RB: Well, you look at the characters, and you ask what they yearned for.

H: Let's talk, then, about yearning in those books.

RB: Well, I can't talk as I should about these because I am going to invoke the Graham Greene syndrome. I don't remember them well enough to talk about them. I do know that there may be a unified field theory of yearning. That is, in a work of literature, when you get down below the surface goals of characters, down deep enough into the realm of yearning, probably almost all the time the character yearns for self, for an identity, for a place in the universe. Who am I? What the hell am I doing here? Those are the essential human questions. Literature deals with that. If you look at Cliff [*Alleys*], if you look at any of the narrators in *A Good Scent from a Strange Mountain* and in *Had a Good Time*, I think you will find characters yearning for a self, for an identity, yearning to define themselves in the world. It's true with Tim, Larry, and Phil. Who am I? That is Tim's great question, Larry's great question, Phil's great question. The U.S. Army said, "This is who you are." The contingencies of war said, "This is who you are." And the parts of themselves that they confront say, "This is who you are." Therefore, the great struggle within the characters of all those stories is "That's not who I am!" or "My God, is that who I am?" The same question should be asked for every one of the central characters in those three books and in all of my books.

H: For example, in your award-winning story "The One in White" in *Had a Good Time*, how might we frame this who-am-I question for the narrator (an American war correspondent for the *Chicago Tribune*)?

RB: I would compare that story with "Open Arms" from *A Good Scent*, for example. There is often dramatic irony at work; we as readers know more about this character than he knows about himself. In "The One in White," that newsman is yearning to figure himself out and find his place in the world, but he doesn't have a clue as to how to go about it. And the decisions he makes have to do with operating out of a self that involves his own pose as a journalist and his own cynicism about the world, his job, and the policies toward Mexico of President Wilson, who displays the same kind of military adventurism that the "big stick" of Roosevelt implies. The journalist is drawn to that Mexican woman [laundry woman and revolutionary] because he senses there is something about her that he's got to understand implicitly in order to figure out who he is and what he's doing. And he misses it [the understanding]; he utterly misses it. The irony of that last sentence in the story sums up the American attitude. (And by the way, what I am doing with this analysis is artificial and secondary, you understand.) He has just totally blown it. She has threatened his life; she has pointed out that Mexicans are dead on the street; she has embarrassed him, humiliated him; he can't forget her. And still he thinks, "I wish there was something I could have done for her." His attitude parallels the lunacy of American foreign policy today. It is not so simple as "I'm just going to go in and kick ass." It's "gee, I wish I could do something for these people; let me go in and invade their country and kill a lot of them. That will help them out." But he is trying to decide who he is. How do I act in the world?

H: Is a similar yearning for self-understanding occurring with the narrator in the title story from Good Scent?

RB: Well, of course Dao is trying to figure out who he is. And the ghost of Ho Chi Minh is trying to figure out who he is. In the afterlife, the decisions you make on Earth that leave out part of who you must be to be completely human are going to haunt you. Dao is seeing that in the yin and the yang. He is living in the moment and without a sense of the larger political implications of what he does. Ho lived totally politically without the larger personal implications of what he did. And so Ho, in the afterlife, is trying to figure out that pastry glaze, and Dao is faced with how to deal with the political murder that his own flesh and blood has committed. Dao slips away into the next life still unresolved about that but hopeful that somehow he and his old friend Ho can help each other out. They are looking for the whole self because they are incomplete in their selves. So the pursuit of self is at the center of the story.

H: You have noted that in Good Scent the title story was consciously written at the end with an overarching vision of the whole collection. So what you have just described—that pursuit of self—is what all the narrators in the book are seeking.

RB: Absolutely. They feel incomplete because part of them was left behind in Vietnam, and they have to redefine themselves in this new place, the U.S. In the two stories I have added at the end of the 2003 edition [Grove Press], that is happening in Vietnam as well. It is happening with an American who stayed in Vietnam and tries to recreate himself as Vietnamese ["Missing"].

H: Talk about the second added story, "Salem," which I find to be such a rich and emotional story on so many different levels.

RB: Well, that is a war story, I guess, about the essence of war—about how we get caught up in the mechanisms of government and politics and end up cast in a role in which we must take other people's lives. The narrator of "Salem," a North Vietnamese Army veteran, yearns to figure out who he is by figuring out what to do with these objects—the pack of Salem cigarettes and the photo that he took off the body of the American he killed—and why he saved them to begin with. He has killed somebody who was subject to the same political forces, and what the narrator comes to understand is that there was this profound connection to the man he killed. People on both sides of the guns who are killing each other, indeed at the deepest human level, are in deep kinship with each other. The final act in that story is recognition of that connection. He understands why he saved these items: because this man was his brother, deeply connected to him. And he has waited for the right moment when he can be part of that guy again by smoking the American's cigarettes. That story is written in the voice of the guy who was going to kill me in the back alleys of Saigon, if he'd had the opportunity.

H: Besides the obvious change from the third-person limited viewpoints in *The Alleys of Eden* to the multiple first-person narrators in the other two books, what are other differences among those three books?

RB: Well, I have found I am able to range with authenticity into the consciousness of characters who are increasingly distant from me in surface demographic ways. Of course, I believe this is the nature of the artistic unconscious. If you do go into your unconscious and face down the terrors there, and you do not avert your eyes, and you do that day after day, story after story, book after book, eventually you break through to a place where you are no longer male or female. You are no longer white, black, red, brown, or yellow. You are not Christian, Muslim, Jew, Hindu, Sikh. You are no longer Vietnamese, American, Albanian, or Serbian. You are human, and you draw your authenticity from that universal human condition. Then you [the writer] can bring that authenticity up through the vessels of characters who, on their surface, might be quite different from you. Another thing, there is a lot more humor in my work now than there was early on. Again, it is not a preconceived effect, but the deeper I get into my visions of the world, the more interconnected the light and the dark have become. That is a major movement in my work.

H: Is another major development your introduction of popular culture into your books?

RB: I was just going to say that. This use of popular culture has become more and more frequent and, I think, more antic and more complex. I think *A Good Scent from a Strange Mountain* was a good turning-point book in that respect because popular culture was just there in the other books in some ways, but not as the kind of central element as in *A Good Scent*. As the Vietnamese exiles in *A Good Scent* deal with their new surroundings and the culture they are going to have to adapt to, they are responding in this fresh way to the pop cultural content. And so only two books later I wrote *Tabloid Dreams*, which embraces pop culture in a drastic way.

If you look, there are also a lot of parallels in the way my work has utilized the visual arts. The visual arts work a lot in found objects now. These found objects appear in my works *Had a Good Time* and *Tabloid Dreams*, for example. Although there was some original reporting in *Tabloid Dreams*, the tabloids did not get several of those stories; I scooped them. But those headlines are found objects. The postcards in *Had a Good Time* are also found objects. Now, I am writing this book on Weegee photographs, which are also found objects. And so that is a trend in my work. Obviously with *Severance* and the Weegee stories, I'm also exploring the compressed version of the fictional experience, although I will go back to longer stories and novels. People are responding to the *Severance* pieces. Albert Goldbarth, who is a National Book Critics Circle Award–winning poet, is teaching some of these stories that he found in a literary magazine. He thinks they are unlike anything else. In some ways they are. The Weegee book, I think, will carry what I have learned in *Severance* beyond just the premise of *Severance*. Again, in my short fiction there has always been a central unifying theme or concept, although I hate the word because, given my philosophy, I don't understand that. But it is not a trick. Those concepts happen to tap into characters who already exist in my unconscious, and it's a focal point for them, a way for them to speak within a context in which they can reveal themselves. So the postcards, the headlines, the severed heads, they stand in the same relationship to those characters that the Vietnam War stands in relationship to the characters in *A Good Scent*.

H: You have also noted that *Good Scent* isn't a collection of stories, but rather a postmodern novel. How so?

RB: I have used the term only because others have pointed that out. It was not an original notion with me. Some of the critics have said this, and the label strikes a chord with me because there is a gestalt in all the books of stories

I've written. A gestalt occurs, an overarching kind of vision and a cumulative effect if you read these stories in order.

H: Tim O'Brien's *The Things They Carried* and his more recent *July, July* are also collections of stories with an overarching vision. I asked Tim why he writes this way, and he said, "That's the way life comes to me. It comes in fragments; it does not come in this cohesive whole."

RB: Well, that is true. I could say something similar to that. Look at the way that media shape us in this era. With the overarching story of Hurricane Katrina, you get this little fragment, this report, and that report. They, then, double back and repeat this fragment. But there is a little difference, and the earlier report is no longer the case. The way we watch news and absorb the world, I think, conditions the modern sensibility to a number of fragments, even of separate people's stories that somehow then add up to something larger. With Iraq coverage, you've got this suicide bomber in this marketplace; then you've got an American soldier killed on the side of the road by a bomb; then you have Rumsfeld talking about elections; then you've got the Sunnis killing Shiites; and you've got the voting on the constitution. Those are all different stories, and they are presented in a way that suggests that this is what Iraq is about. I think that Tim and I are responding to the way in which we frequently perceive the world.

H: One of the things that Tim and Phil resist adamantly is the label "war writer" or "Vietnam writer." How do you respond to such labels applied to you?

RB: I sat on a panel in Washington, DC, with Larry, Tim, and Phil. It was covered in the *New York Times* in the early eighties. I had just that morning visited the National Gallery, and each of us was asked that question, "How do you see yourself as a Vietnam novelist?" My answer to them, and it has always been my answer, is that Tim, Larry, Phil and I, as well as many other Vietnam writers, who are in fact artists, use Vietnam as a metaphor and a source of action and characters. With our real focus on the human condition, to call us Vietnam novelists is like calling Monet a "lily pad" painter.

H: Within this group of four writers, you seem to have moved the furthest away from your Vietnam experiences in particular and war in general. Was this intentional, or did it just happen?

RB: Oh it just happened. It was not intentional. I write the stories that I am given to write; that's all. I use the characters that walk out of the shadows of my unconscious and say, "This is what I want."

H: With the three books that I've selected for this section, when a reader finishes those books, what do you want that person to feel?

RB: You understand, of course, you're asking me what effect do I want to have on my reader, and that is none. I'm not saying I don't want the books to have an effect, but I want the readers to have encountered some important truths about the human condition in a direct, aesthetic way. That is not a specific effect; that's just a flip side of having a vision of a way the world makes sense and trying to articulate it. Well, then, you hope the reader who reads that book walks away having a sense of the way the world makes sense behind its chaos.

H: Going back to your earlier comment, just like the writer is in a dream space, do you want the reader to be in a dream space?

RB: Yes, I want the reader to walk away thrumming and not thinking.

H: And that thrumming, it is not the response of the mind to this book; it is a response of the soul, the body, and the senses.

RB: Yes, absolutely. And the mind can be aware there are important implications to this story, but the reader should be going, "Well, I don't want to think about them for a while." I think it is a fruitful secondary activity to see the broad philosophical, theoretical, and political implications of this story's insight into the human condition. That is fine; that's great. But I don't want the reader to do that yet, in the immediate walking away. The reader should come into the work nakedly, saying, "I'm coming here unclothed. I do not know what the world is about; just tell me what it is."

H: Such an approach isn't linked to New Criticism of years ago in which the text is isolated from everything around it.

RB: No, the profound relationship of the text to the things around it is deeply rooted in the truths of the human experience and the human condition. And New Criticism was not much interested in that.

H: Do you read reviews of your books?

RB: My wife screens them. I enjoy the smart ones, and I skip the ones that aren't. I occasionally look at a particularly misguided one with a sort of morbid curiosity. *Had a Good Time* got a lot of great reviews, but it got a savage review from a very prominent reviewer (who, however, quoted not a line from the book and referred to none of the stories in specifics). From a source in the book world I happened to learn something about this man, and in some basic ways he's typical of a pretty widespread problem. The reviewer I'm speaking of is self-syndicated, spending much time on the phone each week, calling newspapers and pimping the reviews. And he often reads and reviews four books a week. He speed reads. He has to. Now this might be okay for nonfiction books, but if you speed read literary fiction, you are not reading at all. You cannot read literary fiction faster than would allow you to hear the narrative voice in your head, or you are missing absolutely essential aspects of the experience of the work. By the way, this particular reviewer is not alone; many book reviewers speed read, and they read under deadline pressure. And even if they try to slow themselves down, as they read, they are thinking as they go, "What am I going to say?" They are reading from their heads. Happily, there are some wonderful exceptions to this, but too many book reviewers do not know how to thrum to a work of literary fiction.

H: Now, the question that may lead to your negating everything we have done to this point: Is there any value in doing an interview like this, in learning something about how you view your life experiences and your writing?

RB: Yes, as long as it does not encourage the biographical fallacy, which is a serious problem. One of the ways you can misread is by not entering into the dream of the text and by not understanding that the text is a created thing and that you cannot draw a single valid inference about the writer's actual life from what you read in the work. That's what the biographical fallacy is, invalid inferences about the writer's life from his work of fiction, and that is one of the inappropriate ways you can read a book. On the other hand, we are interested in ways in which writers' unconscious selves are formed. To see the relationship of the writer's life experience to the way in which the writer invents other self-contained worlds is certainly interesting and can throw a light on the legitimate creative process that goes into the making of these works of art.

This interview is also a chance to air my aesthetic philosophy, which might help others. The things I have said, which came out naturally in this interview, would help educate readers and writers as to how to approach what I do. I think that is terrific.

H: In an interview, Philip Caputo said, "One thing that tends to drive people to become writers or to need to be writers—Hemingway talks about this—is some sort of wound. Really happy, well-adjusted people don't become writers. At least they don't become what we think of as literary writers." How do you respond to Phil's observation in terms of your own writing career?

RB: I know what he's getting at, and I would agree with it. To phrase it in a way that fits with the kinds of things we've been talking about: it's not as if you write for therapy; it's not as if you remember the wound and you write about it. But I have often said that if, at the age of eighteen, I'd had a list of the things that were going to happen to me in my life and if I'd had the power right there and then to remove whatever I wanted from the list, I would have certainly, for example, removed being forced into the army and sent to Vietnam and having three failed marriages. But if I'd done that, *absolutely* I would not be sitting here talking to you, no question about it. So, yes, I think that if you find a literary writer to be an exception to that [wound stimulus], then the biographer has not dug deeply enough. The writer has experienced significant suffering in a subtly nuanced way that has in fact created the work of art. The interesting thing about suffering is that it's not relative to anyone else's suffering. The people who suffer, and most people do, do it on their own terms and intensity: suffering from the worst battle experience in the jungles of Vietnam, suffering the silence at a dinner table between the guy who went straight through school and into a grinding quotidian job and the wife who was the sorority girl, married him, and has been raising two children ever since. The suffering of that man and woman in their own inner realms can be just as acute as the guy in the platoon in Quang Tri. So there are wounds, but there are also other wounds.

H: Thus, your Vietnam War experiences made you a writer?

RB: Yes. This made me a writer as did three broken marriages. And my time in the steel mill made me a writer. And raising my son. And all the rest of it. It's all life experience. Would I be nearly as good of a writer if I had not been to Vietnam? I seriously doubt it. I would have been writing, and maybe I would have found a way into my deepest unconscious to write things of great value if I had not been to Vietnam. Perhaps I would have, but it is hard to say. I may well not have. I could have made a very serious mistake if, for example, I would have gone straight on to get a Ph.D., as was my plan, and ended up teaching in a university. I would not have won a Pulitzer Prize. Who knows? I would not have been writing nearly as well, nearly as deeply, and I would be teaching somewhere. I am teaching now, but on my own terms.

H: A final question: Do you still have your dress military uniform with ribbons on it?

RB: We'll go into the house and I'll show you where my uniform is hanging. Within the last year, I found it in a closet somewhere, and I thought, perhaps with some irony, it would be interesting. I've got a hook on the back of the door to my office in the house, and it's hanging on that door. A Steely Dan concert cap is hanging on the hook over it, so that would be the hat I'd wear with it. I've got the hard stripes on it, I think. Let's go see.

H: Why do you have the uniform hanging in this room?

RB: Well, it's in the room where I also have my first typewriter with which I typed all my early novels. I've got my first laptop computer, the seventeen-pound Tandy, in there, which I used to write *A Good Scent from a Strange*

Mountain. The uniform is an artifact of my life and very much of my writer's life. As I've said, the experience of going to Vietnam turned me into the artist I am. I can't imagine what I would be without having done that, but it wouldn't be this.

WORKS BY & INTERVIEWS WITH ROBERT OLEN BUTLER

The Alleys of Eden. New York: Horizon Press, 1981.

Countrymen of Bones. New York: Horizon, 1983.

The Deep Green Sea. New York: Henry Holt & Co., 1997.

The Deuce. New York: Simon & Schuster, 1989.

"Fair Warning." *Zoetrope: All Story* 4.2 (2000): 1–10.

Fair Warning. New York: Grove Press, 2001.

From Where You Dream: The Process of Writing Fiction. Ed. Janet Burroway. New York: Grove/Atlantic, 2005.

A Good Scent from a Strange Mountain. 1992. Reprint, New York: Grove Press, 2003.

Had a Good Time: Stories from American Postcards. New York: Grove/Atlantic, 2004.

"Inside Creative Writing." Florida State University, October 2001. Archived at <www.fsu.edu/butler>.

"Interview." *Contemporary Authors*, 112: 89–93. Detroit: Gale, 1985.

"Moving Day." *Redbook*, October 1974: 92–93.

Mr. Spaceman. New York: Grove Press, 2000.

On Distant Ground. New York: Alfred A. Knopf, 1985.

"The One in White." *Atlantic Monthly*, July/August 2004: 181–88.

"Robert Olen Butler" (Interview). In *Conversations with American Novelists*, ed. Kay Bonetti et al., 201–16. Columbia: University of Missouri Press, 1997.

Severance. New York: Chronicle Books, 2006.

Sun Dogs. New York: Horizon Press, 1982.

Tabloid Dreams. New York: Henry Holt & Co., 1996.

They Whisper. New York: Henry Holt & Co., 1993.

Wabash. New York: Alfred A. Knopf, 1987.

CONCLUSION LIFE STORIES

> "As much as you have chosen four writers of the Vietnam era,
> in each of their cases . . . life events since then have joined the
> river of 'Nam and the river of childhood, and those events are
> mentioned in one's work."—Tim O'Brien

At the risk of ignoring the warnings of my four writers about the often counter-productive roles of reviewers, scholars, and teachers in responding to literature (especially Butler's notions about hindering readers from "thrumming to a text"), I want to perform some critical thrumming of my own to a few salient connections, themes, implications, and differences spread among the four conversations. Obviously, I hope that you—readers of this book—have responded in your own personal ways to the interviews, whether at the sensual or analytical levels, and have found the questions and answers illuminating. Personally, my sessions with these writers have helped me begin to understand who these four sons-soldiers-authors are and how the person and the writer overlap. More important, the conversations have convinced me that in various ways for each author his life and writings exist in a symbiotic relationship, a point implied in O'Brien's observation, quoted above. In fact, soon after making this comment in our 2005 interview, O'Brien interrupted our extended discussion about fact and fiction in his writing to recount a seemingly unrelated anecdote about an ongoing home remodeling project. At the core of this story were his frustrations with a shady contractor who neither appeared on time nor performed as expected. With a somewhat sinister grin, O'Brien concluded the account by confiding that the contractor would probably make his way, in one form or another, into the author's current novel in progress. This plan of literary revenge reminded me of Heinemann's remark that "writers always get the last word." Then, bringing us full circle, O'Brien observed that a writer must acknowledge that these life episodes, the noteworthy as well as these "daily little things," often appear in one's writing. Although O'Brien did not say so directly, I might add that several of O'Brien's and the other writers' remarks also imply that including such episodes enables authors to contemplate these transformed events, not as therapy but to gain a better sense of self on a literary voyage of discovery.

Certainly, these four interviews and chronologies *do* illustrate how the momentous and occasionally ordinary details and concerns in a writer's life directly or indirectly surface in both nonfiction and fiction—everything from specific events to overarching personal themes and moral dilemmas. While considering such links between life and art, I am struck by the central place the "river of 'Nam" holds in the lives and writings of Caputo, Heinemann, O'Brien, and Butler—what they saw in war, what they did, what they felt, and what war did to them. Specifically, all agree that in significant ways the war made them writers. Early in their writing careers, all four, to varying degrees, transferred (memory) or transformed (imagination) their war experiences and related personal issues into stories—fiction or nonfiction. Decades later, the Vietnam War in particular and war in general, as these subjects do for a significant segment of the American population, continue to interest these writers and, especially for Caputo, Heinemann, and O'Brien, to evoke angst. Nonetheless, the point these four soldier-authors emphasized about their war experiences is that as writers they view them within the broader context of life experiences. The best war stories, as Michael Herr writes in *Dispatches*, are nothing more, than "stories about people." Granted, war, as Caputo pointedly reminded me, is indeed a compelling crucible in which, under such horrific and intense circumstances, human pretenses are often stripped away and a participant's true self is revealed, often the disturbing side. However, the larger arena of daily life provides similar opportunities for writers to strip away human pretense and encounter the universal tensions between courage and cowardice, honor and shame, good and evil—in other words, to examine the war of the living. As O'Brien declared about his own war stories and life stories, "For me, the use of Vietnam and war in general is a way of getting at what all of us face all of the time, every moment of life." What follows are a few more reflections on each author's literal and literary wars of the living told in our conversations.

SONS

In formulating questions for the son section of the interviews, I particularly wanted to probe whether where and how the four subjects grew up affected their subsequent Vietnam experiences, as well as their development as writers. In their formative years, did they want to become soldiers; did they want to become writers? Furthermore, a question always in the back of my mind was whether we can identify themes emerging from this time period (for example, father-son relationships, views on war, or an emerging world view) that directly or indirectly appear in their later writing. In addition, for all four individuals, did growing up in small towns in the Midwest (three in Illinois and one in Minnesota) influence their personal histories and their value systems? During this time did specific national or world events leave a lasting impression on them?[1] Obviously, such links between their life stories as sons and soldiers and their later writings are subject to important caveats about biographical fallacy, pop psychology, and the scholar's pitfall of "making interpretation." Clearly, however, for each of these individuals, noteworthy events and feelings materialized during his pre-Vietnam years that later shaped some of his writing.

As described by Heinemann and O'Brien, their childhoods and adolescent years, particularly father-son relationships during these times, significantly affected their later lives. Heinemann characterized his childhood and teenage years as "not especially unhappy." Nevertheless, his description of his relationship with his father and the rest of the family suggests a difficult family life: brothers who did not get along; a home with no books; apparently little interaction between parents and children; and plenty of corporal punishment, particularly as administered by a father who consciously separated himself, physically and emotionally, from the family. Such an environment seems a potential breeding ground for a son's anti-establishment, anti-authority attitudes, which carry over into his writing, as well as form a world view of, according to Heinemann, "an optimist who has not arrived." Still, during this time, a series of diverse jobs, the presence of a grandfather who was an inveterate storyteller, and an emerging fascination with trains also became important underpinnings for Larry's later storytelling.

Overall, O'Brien's home life as he was growing up seems more stable than Heinemann's. However, Tim's early father-son relationship, as he described it, was more psychologically complex and might be characterized as a model-mystery bond. On one hand, during the young O'Brien's years in Worthington, Minnesota, his well-respected and supportive father was a mentor and model for him, taking him on business trips, teaching him to play golf, and introducing him to the world of books. On the other hand, Tim's alcoholic father made his son's life miserable—O'Brien's embarrassment when his father was institutionalized; his distress caused by his drunken father's dinnertime taunts. For O'Brien, his father's actions were and are a mystery ("I still don't understand what it was that didn't please him") and, as O'Brien readily admitted, the seed for one of his major recurring themes in his writing, the quest for love. Such tensions at home led the young O'Brien to escape into performing magic, something that as a writer he continues to practice, in a metaphorical way, through his fiction.[2] In assessing this early stage of his life, O'Brien acknowledged that "big chunks of my books have their sources in childhood."

Caputo and Butler, in contrast, grew up in more stable environments. Caputo's father brought his family with him during summers that he worked away from home, and he introduced Phil to the pleasures of camping, canoeing, and fishing. Involved with these outdoor activities (as well as physical sports, such as boxing, wrestling, and football), captivated by images of Hemingway's "living large" and Sergeant Stryker's daring acts in the *Sands of Iwo Jima*, and shaped by his traditional Catholic education, Phil as he grew up hungered for tradition, adventure, and heroic exploits. Because of his blue-collar upbringing, he also carried (and does to this day) a self-described "chip on his shoulder"; he was eager to prove himself in a world where he felt the advantages of name, status, and privilege trumped merit. I am not surprised, then, that although all four writers played war games as children and attended war movies and two (O'Brien and Butler) had fathers who were World War II veterans, Caputo is the only one of the four who wanted to join the military, in fact, right out of high school. Also not unexpected is Caputo's eventual enlistment in the Marine officer program, the branch of the U.S. military boasting of its elitism, tradition, physical challenges, and machismo.

Compared to Caputo's upbringing, Butler's years growing up in Granite City, Illinois, and later attending Northwestern were equally affirmative and, possibly, the most conducive to an eventual writing career. As an only child with a very supportive mother and father, the latter chair of a university theater department, the young Butler flourished in an eclectic lifestyle. In his early years, he played Little League baseball and engaged in imaginary MiG-15 and F-86 aerial battles. Later, he worked in a steel mill, performed in the theater, conversed with his father about dramaturgy, and chatted about baseball with fellow workers at the steel mill and students at his working-class school. He is the only one of the four writers to describe his high school experience as "happy," perhaps occasioned by his roles as student body president and valedictorian. During this prewar period of his life, Butler aspired to a career in the theater, initially as an actor and later as a playwright. This interest in the theater and his early exposure to a limited collision of cultures present in his hometown fostered a lifelong attention to other people's feelings and a strong sense of the other. These traits have since influenced Butler's extensive use of first-person narrative in his writing: "Whoever the character is that I'm writing through, I feel my first responsibility is to be utterly compassionate and deeply embedded within the way that character sees the world."

Thus, I can clearly locate the emerging artist in Butler's early life and later in his commitment to writing, initially playwriting, nurtured during his years at Northwestern and subsequently at the University of Iowa. For the other three writers, however, their pre-Vietnam lives only hint of future literary careers but definitely reveal the beginnings of a writer's sensibilities. Heinemann struggled as a student, was not an avid reader, quickly learned that he was not cut out to be an actor, and took only one poorly taught creative writing course prior to his military service. But his brief interest in architecture and his ongoing attraction to storytelling and the theater suggested a nascent aesthetic sensibility. At a young age, O'Brien, after reading his father's vignettes about his war experiences, viewed becoming a writer as a possibility, and at the age of ten he composed his first "novel" entitled "Timmy of the Little League." He also wrote a novel while in college and was on the staff of his college newspaper. However, although wanting to be a writer, he did not plan on it, believing that "some things were done in Philadelphia, New York, L.A., and Chicago . . . and not by a kid from the Turkey Capital of the World." Instead, O'Brien's involvement in politics (both national and campus), along with his admission to Harvard graduate school in government, presaged a career in politics or academia. Similarly, Caputo was interested in writing during his high school and college years, specifically journalism. But as he noted, such career considerations were not engaged in seriously because of the looming specter of the draft and military service. Oddly enough, for all four writers, their time in Vietnam propelled them into their current writing careers in different ways and for different reasons.

SOLDIERS

These four sons brought to their military experiences distinct motivations, interests, and concerns from the pre-Vietnam period of their lives. They carried, as well, a budding writer's sensibilities and different attitudes about war. Our conversations confirmed that what they did in the military, especially in Vietnam, and when they did it altered their earlier interests and concerns and created new ones. Specifically, their draft status, military specialty (MOS), rank, place of deployment, dates of service, and exposure to the enemy and civilian Vietnamese shaped their perspectives of war and of themselves, as well as caused the diverse moral crises they faced. Among the four, Caputo is one of two soldier-authors to enlist in the military (but the only one to enlist enthusiastically), the first to enter Vietnam when official American involvement was just beginning (March 1965), and the only commissioned officer. He brought to his military service a desire to prove himself a hero and to "see the action." His war story follows a soldier's paradigmatic path of innocence, experience, and consideration described by Paul Fussell in The Great War and Modern Memory.

Armed with patriotism, romantic images of war, and a typical naïveté coupled with bravado, Caputo embodied the American ethos of 1965 regarding Vietnam. Soon, however, as an officer leading a rifle platoon of Marines in a guerilla war, his experience stage quickly commenced. He confronted the horrors of war and the inevitable pitfalls of America's controversial path in this particular war: "There really was a lot of confusion as to what we were doing there." A mixture of disillusionment with the horrors and exhilaration with the adventure also marked this stage and generated the emotional context for Caputo's self-described defining moment of his war experience: his involvement with the botched seizure of Vietcong suspects at Giao Tri. With this incident, he found his Jesuitical approach to the world and his own constructed ideal of noble conduct and mission running counter to the chaos of war and the exigencies of combat. The result, according to Caputo, was a "moral failure" on his part and a guilt that troubles him to this day. This soldier-author labeled his combat experience "the most significant event of my whole life to this day, and as such, it's just woven into my very being." The war made him "too cynical, too suspicious of everybody's motives." Paradoxically, it also created a Conradian "fascination of the abomination" that has played itself out in his career as a war correspondent and as a literary writer whose nonfiction and fiction books have large-scale conflict at their core. Furthermore, this Vietnam experience redefined his prewar interest in moral issues of good and evil. Finally, I regard much of Phil's writing, journalistic and literary, since his time in Vietnam to be part of his ongoing consideration stage of what war did to him and what it does to all participants: "You can become something you never thought you would become, without being aware of the transformation" (Caputo).

If Caputo was the adventuresome romantic entering the military, Heinemann, a few years later in 1966, was the bitter and blunt realist who allowed himself to be drafted because he had no other options. With his anti-authoritarian and anti-military bias, Larry entered a world that he perceived as run by "lifers." Although he, like the other three soldier-authors, relished the physical fitness portions of his basic training and prided himself on his success in this area, his stateside experiences can be summed up by a characteristic Heinemann epithet—"bullshit." Later in 1967, as an enlisted man assigned to an armored personnel carrier in a heavily contested war zone in South Vietnam, his perspective of the military and its conduct of the war did not improve. In our interview, contrasted with Caputo's focus on his personal disillusionment and guilt associated with his performance in the war, Heinemann often delivered blunt and broad political assessments of this war. He cited, in particular, the general ineptitude and wrong headedness of the military's "winning-the-hearts-and-minds" policy and its human toll (drugs, alcohol abuse, officer-enlisted tensions, fraggings, combat numbness, soldier apathy, and many dead Vietnamese civilians). And in one of the most succinct assessments of what the war did to him, Heinemann confessed that upon his departure from Vietnam, "I was twenty-five pounds lighter. Lean and solid, the one-thousand-meter stare, and wrapped pretty tight." He also admitted that in his immediate postwar life he suffered from periods of serious post-traumatic stress disorder (PTSD) resulting from his tour of duty. For Heinemann, the entire military experience changed him, angered him, and radicalized him in ways that later shaped the blunt, angry, cynical voice emerging in his war writing and in his views on current U.S. military involvement in Iraq.

Two years after Heinemann's reluctant entry into the military, O'Brien also involuntarily went into the army (1968), but as a self-described "guilt." In contrast to the other three soldier-authors, the civilian O'Brien was the most political in terms of his initial attitudes toward the Vietnam War. He opposed it to the point that he participated in peace vigils on the Macalester College campus and worked to elect peace candidate Eugene McCarthy: "It seemed a barbarous, inhuman war, a war fought for uncertain reasons." Such strongly held views fed his contempt for the humiliating and mindless treatment afforded recruits in basic training and, similar to Heinemann's response, intensified his scorn for most of the individuals who administered this treatment. Despite such strongly held beliefs and feelings, O'Brien entered the military and served in Vietnam, admirably I might add, in a dangerous combat position (an RTO), in one of the most hostile areas of South Vietnam (Quang Ngai Province), at the height of American involvement. Why? O'Brien attributed his service to a failure of moral courage ("to not listen to my own conscience"). Notwithstanding, I think an additional answer can be found in this chapter's epigraph—a merging in O'Brien's life of the river of 'Nam and the river of childhood. Specifically, his craving for acceptance and love, which emerged in his childhood, surfaced again, this time not a father's acceptance but a community's acceptance: "It was the sense of the town watching me that made me go to war—the fear of embarrassment. I didn't want to feel embarrassed in front of not just the town but maybe Minnesota as a whole or maybe beyond that the whole country." Thirteen months after entering Vietnam, O'Brien departed, also changed by the war. He, like Caputo, had failed to live up to an ideal, albeit a different one from Caputo's. He, too, returned more cynical, but also a self-described "relativist" rather than an "absolutist" about moral issues and individual conduct, especially related to acts of courage and cowardice. He also reentered civilian life with his "guilt" intact, and like Caputo and Heinemann with a greater sense of self-awareness. Most of all, he returned home with a resolve "to try to make something good out of this horror called Vietnam." For Tim, this vow quickly manifested itself in a sustained period of writing about the Vietnam War and exploring the confluence of some of the key themes from his rivers of war and life experiences.

By the time Butler entered the military (1969) and Vietnam (1971), American involvement in the unpopular war was winding down. "Quagmire" was a label often applied to the war's stagnation during this time. A prolific writer with a dozen unpublished plays under his belt and more to follow while in service, Butler, perhaps, brought the most refined writer's sensibility to his military experience. Not having a strong political or moral opposition to the war, he displayed a writer's optimistic attitude of making the best of a bad situation: "it [my tour of duty] was an exercise in point of view and identification with persona." Furthermore, what differentiates Butler the most from the other three soldier-authors is that he arrived in Vietnam with a fluency in Vietnamese gained through his training at an army language school. Such a skill allowed him to cultivate his fascination with the Other that had emerged during his years in Granite City. Consequently, his duties in and around Saigon, coupled with this language facility, created war experiences very different from those of the other three soldier-authors. Such activities gave him a perspective of the Vietnamese people and culture that was simply closed off to Caputo, Heinemann, and O'Brien.

Because of their combat status, Phil, Larry, and Tim often interacted with the Vietnamese in a hostile combatant's role. Unable to speak the language or know the culture, the three viewed the Vietnamese with an understandable suspicion and a bias of difference. In contrast, Bob's contacts with the people and the culture, while driving through the countryside or wandering Saigon's back alleys, were more those of the curious writer-anthropologist: "Life in that way is filled with a wide range of people who are fascinating, and it's worth getting under their skin." Butler's opportunities allowed him more readily to see similarities rather than differences, and the universal human connections between Americans and Vietnamese appear in many of his books. These fortuitous circumstances of Butler's tour of duty (a good fortune he readily acknowledged in our conversation) led to very different moral dilemmas for this soldier when compared to those of the other three soldiers. His was not a troubling heart-of-darkness experience of confronting the evil within his and others' souls. Instead, his struggle, emerging from a collision of cultures, was "to maintain my sense of being in this place, connected to it, open to it, compassionate to it, and doing no harm." Not unexpectedly, then, Butler's response to the question of how he was a different person upon leaving Vietnam had nothing to do with cynicism, radicalization, or abiding guilt. It had everything to do with his change as a person, with an increased capacity to love, and as an artist: "I had been transformed from a playwright into a fiction writer . . . because the experience I had there could only be expressed by fiction."

AUTHORS _____

The great irony, of course, of these four soldier-authors' lives is, as Heinemann declared, that the Vietnam War, in different ways, made them writers. But certainly other rivers of experiences and emotions contributed as well. As Butler noted, "The ravenous sensuality of combat will create an artist in someone who has the potential for it." In Butler's case, the war converted him from playwright to novelist allowing him to "create the object that was fully in the moment and in the senses." Admittedly, four marriages have also provided him with perspectives apparent in his writing. With Caputo, Heinemann, and O'Brien, their tours of duty supplied them with stories that for public and personal reasons they simply have to tell, but each also has carried into his writing career emotional truths from his civilian war of the living. For all four, the evolution of their literary voices begun in childhood continued with their war experiences: Caputo's voice of the traditional storyteller focusing on the visceral details of human activity and the complexities of classical moral issues; Heinemann's politically motivated anger, cynicism, and blunt realism of a "pissed-off infantryman"; O'Brien's lyrical emotional and psychological introspection; and Butler's multiple voices of the Other. For these soldier-authors, the Vietnam War also helped refine early life themes into literary themes: Caputo's preoccupation with the difficulties of doing the right thing, Heinemann's ongoing quest for a spiritual and emotional "home," O'Brien's fixation on "the things we do for love," and Butler's interest in the collision of cultures.

After departing Vietnam at discrete points in the war, these four soldier-authors traveled different literary paths in telling war stories (theirs and others'), developing their literary voices, and exploring their war and life themes. Initially, both Caputo and O'Brien recast their experiences into war memoirs. Yet their books display significant fictional influences on structure, dialogue, and scene-setting to give readers a visceral feel for this war but, more important, to intensify the writers' and others' sins of commission and omission. For his first book, Heinemann produced a fictional memoir (more memory than imagination) by transforming his and others' war stories into a graphic, almost pornographic, intense portrait of war. And Butler in his first published book (a novel) focused on the collision of cultures in the aftermath of war as he portrayed the toll war takes on the survivors: combatants and civilians, Americans and Vietnamese. Each author, in his subsequent literary career, has drifted away from war (some further than others) and turned his writing interests to other subjects and settings. Nevertheless, all, at important places in their lives, physically returned to the country of Vietnam and have returned through memory and imagination to war as they tell war stories in wiser, more complex, and more artistically satisfying ways.

Over the span of these writers' careers, these war stories often have received the most critical acclaim. Such praise, however, has been a blessing and a burden. The burden for all four, despite their successful nonwar books, is the frequently applied label from critics and readers of "war writer," or worse—"Vietnam writer." They bristle at such classifications and a perceived demeaning of their writing because it is often about war. Furthermore, perhaps resulting from such critical predispositions rather than actual critical appraisals, all four have occasionally endured negative reviews when they have written about nonwar experiences. The four continue, however, to tell significant life stories beyond the battlefield, armed with what they have learned from writing war stories and possibly guided by Heinemann's conviction that "if you can write a good war story, you can write anything."

This last oblique recommendation to aspiring writers from Heinemann is just one of many insights about the creative process, the war story, and the storyteller surfacing in this book of stories about war, life, and writing. Spread throughout the conversations are additional writing principles, which I think all four authors would subscribe to as common goals for their own creative process. Caputo suggests, "Write about what moves you the most, what excites or engages your passions." Heinemann warns, "Let the story speak for itself. . . . You must 'speak straight to us so that your words will go like sunlight to our hearts.'" O'Brien urges, "Try as far as you can to pay heed to your own voice. And by voice I don't just mean language; I mean the values that are under the language." And Butler admonishes, "Works of art do not come from the mind. They are not created from the rational, analytical faculties; they are created from the place where you dream, from your unconscious."

During our conversations, I also received insightful answers to my question of what makes a good war story. Again, these four storytellers would probably agree on some common features. At a superficial level, the obligation for tellers of war stories is to find the appropriate language to present for the reader the images, sounds, and emotions of war in an authentic and honest fashion. But the story must rise above the settings, actions, and plot of such stories. According to these four soldier-authors, the best war stories present engaging characters, psychological realism, moral gravity, and situations where characters must make difficult choices and live with the consequences of those choices. Most important, these stories reach readers at the gut level, O'Brien's "make the stomach believe." The best war stories are also ones of meaningful loss (friends, ideals, and humanity) and gain (self-awareness and awareness of others). These stories are "lies" told to arrive at truths: emotional truths, truths about the human condition, and truthful answers to a character's fundamental question of "who am I?" Ultimately, then, the best war stories are the best life stories, transcending the battlefield and addressing the universal condition of the war and chaos of the living, something that the finest storytellers attempt to do regardless of their subject.

What is left, now, is answering the basic question with which I started this project: who are these four storytellers? Simple answers are impossible, made all the more so by the reality of O'Brien's comment that "there is a truth as we live it; there is a truth as we tell it." As the interviews reveal, these sons-soldiers-authors are complex individuals with diverse upbringings, values, interests, writing careers, life experiences, and literary voices. They have distinct views on, among other things, war, the military, religion, the creative process, and the nature of both physical and moral courage. Nonetheless, they are linked to other war veterans, tellers of war stories, and each other by a "brother-sisterhood of the battlefield." Their basic war stories and life stories, in some ways, are similar to the stories passed on from generation to generation, from my father and mother to me. But these four soldier-authors simply tell them better, both in person and in their writing. They also tell them for familiar reasons, one articulated recently by Anthony Swofford in his Gulf War memoir, Jarhead (New York: Scribner, 2004): "The men who go to war and live are spared for the single purpose of spreading bad news when they return, the bad news about the way war is fought and why, and by whom for whom" (253). Without question, for Caputo, Heinemann, O'Brien, and Butler their tours of duty in a controversial war during a time of political and social turmoil in the U.S. motivated them, as O'Brien noted, "to make something good out of this horror called Vietnam." The resulting stories in oblique ways may save some of their readers from "blundering like blind beggars into the spikes of the cactus fence." On a personal level, their war stories and their life stories, perhaps, have helped these four sons-soldiers-authors respond to a fundamental yearning to answer their own question—who am I? A partial answer is that each, as evidenced by the stories, the memories, the regrets, the losses, the gains, the emotions, and the physical reminders of his time at war, is linked forever to the Vietnam War, the country of Vietnam and its people, and this story truth expressed by Caputo: "You can't escape [the war]; you might as well try to deny you were born for that matter."

NOTES

1. For example, three of the writers (Caputo, O'Brien, and Butler) cited the 1962 Cuban Missile Crisis as profoundly affecting their sense of personal mortality and the fragility of international relations.

2. Interestingly, in O'Brien's self-described "most autobiographical novel" (see *South Carolina Review* interview), the central character, John Wade, in *In the Lake of the Woods* performs magic as a young boy to escape the taunts of his alcoholic father.

appendix a

CHRONOLOGY OF PHILIP CAPUTO

All quoted material in this chronology (as well as in the three subsequent chronologies) that is not followed by an in-text citation comes from the specific interview conducted for this book.

1941: (June 10) Born Philip Joseph Caputo to Marie and Joseph Caputo in Chicago IL. A sister, Patricia, born in 1943. Caputo's family lives in Berwyn, a Chicago suburb, until Caputo is ten and then moves to another suburb, Westchester. Caputo's mother, a housewife, occasionally works part time. His father rises through the manufacturing ranks with a series of jobs ranging from interior construction, machinist, shop foreman, and industrial trouble-shooter to finally plant manager for Continental Can Company.

1959: (June) Graduates from Fenwick Catholic High School in Oak Park IL. (Fall) Enrolls at Purdue University in West Lafayette IN, where he majors in aeronautical engineering, joins a fraternity, and wrestles. After two and a half semesters, leaves Purdue upon discovering that he has little aptitude for math and science; works as a brakeman for the Chicago and Northwestern Railroad.

1961: (Spring) Joins the U.S. Marine Corps Platoon Leaders' Class, motivated by patriotism and desire for adventure. (Summer) Attends Marine Officer Candidate School (OCS) Basic Training at Quantico VA. (Fall) Enrolls at Loyola University Chicago.[1]

1963: (Summer) Attends Marine OCS Advanced Course at Quantico.

1964: Commissioned a 2nd Lieutenant, U.S. Marine Corps. (May) Graduates from Loyola with a B.A. in English and enters Marine Officers' Basic School for six months at Quantico.

1965: (Jan.) Following graduation from Officers' Basic, commands the 2nd Rifle Platoon, C Company, 1st Battalion, 3rd Marine Division in Okinawa. (Mar. 8, 1965) Lands with his rifle platoon at Da Nang, Vietnam, with 3rd Marine Division attached to a battalion of the Marine Expeditionary Brigade (first U.S. combat unit sent to Vietnam). Unit's area of operations is within the immediate vicinity of

Da Nang, and its mission is to defend the U.S. airfield located there. (June) Reassigned as assistant adjutant in Regimental Headquarters Company in Da Nang. Among his various administrative duties is regimental casualty reporting officer ("The Officer in Charge of the Dead"). While serving in this position, he is promoted to 1st lieutenant. (Nov.) Bored with his relatively safe assignment, requests reassignment as commander of a combat rifle platoon.

1966: (Feb.) Authorizes a five-man patrol to capture two Vietcong suspects from the village of Giao Tri. During the operation, the two suspects are killed under questionable circumstances; one of the suspects is later discovered to have been an innocent civilian. The five U.S. soldiers on the patrol, along with Caputo, are charged by American military authorities with two counts of premeditated murder. (Jun.) After a lengthy investigation and trial of one soldier, who is acquitted, murder charges against the other defendants are dropped. Caputo pleads guilty to one count of making a false statement under oath and accepts a letter of reprimand as his punishment.

1966–67: Returns to U.S. and commands an infantry training company at Camp Geiger NC (part of Camp Lejeune) and later given an Honorable Discharge from the Marines at the end of his three-year active duty commitment. Among the medals awarded are the Marine Combat Action Ribbon and the Vietnam Gallantry Cross.

1967: Travels in Europe (Paris, southern Spain, and London), and possessing both an idea and the title "A Rumor of War," begins writing a novel, which will later become his nonfiction war memoir. (Fall) Upon return from Europe, applies to MFA program at the University of Iowa and submits chapters from his war novel in progress as part of the application. Caputo is not admitted to the program.

1968–69: Employed as promotional writer and staff member for in-house newspaper at 3-M Corporation in Chicago.

1969: Marries Jill Esther Ongemach (librarian). Son Geoffrey born in 1970 (currently a musician and music teacher); son Marc born in 1973 (currently a political reporter for the *Miami Herald*). Marriage ends in divorce in 1982.

1969–72: Works as local and investigative reporter for *Chicago Tribune*.

1971: (Apr.) During Washington protest of the Vietnam Veterans Against the War (VVAW), sends letter and military campaign ribbons to President Nixon protesting American policies in Indochina.

1972–77: Serves as foreign correspondent in Rome, Cyprus, Beirut, Saigon, and Moscow for Chicago Tribune.

1973: Awarded (along with three other reporters) the Pulitzer Prize for Investigative Reporting based on the reporters' series of stories emerging in 1972 from a three-month investigation of 1972 primary election fraud at all levels in Chicago.

1973: As Middle East correspondent for the Chicago Tribune, covers the Lebanese Civil War. Held captive in Beirut for a week by an extremist faction of the PLO. His captors torture him because they mistakenly believe him to be working for the CIA.

1973: Receives the Overseas Press Club Award for his reporting from Beirut.

1974: Covers events in Cyprus after Turkish invasion.

1975: (Apr.) Covers the fall of Saigon and South Vietnam and then visits Sudan for the first time on his way to report on the Eritrean rebellion in Ethiopia. (Oct.) In Beirut while on assignment, shot several times in ankle and leg by two Muslim gunmen.

1977: After a lengthy convalescence, leaves job with Chicago Tribune to become freelance journalist and devote more time to his personal writing. (May) A Rumor of War published. This Vietnam War memoir chronicles Caputo's, as well as his country's, loss of innocence and romanticism regarding the war. Caputo used letters to his family and an unauthorized diary kept while in Vietnam as raw material for the memoir.

1980: (May–June) Reports on the Afghan-Soviet conflict for Esquire magazine. (Sept.) Caputo's first novel, Horn of Africa, published. The central character, a Vietnam veteran and war correspondent, is recruited as a mercenary in a mythical country in northeast Africa.

1980: CBS makes a two-part miniseries based on A Rumor of War. Caputo involved with considerable script rewriting and consultation.

1982: Marries Marcelle Lynn Besse; they divorce in 1985.

1983: DelCorso's Gallery, Caputo's second novel, published. The title character, Nick DelCorso, a Vietnam veteran (army combat photographer) and war photojournalist, whom Caputo notes is "very autobiographical," returns to Vietnam during the battle for Saigon in April 1975 and one year later travels to Beirut to cover the civil war.

1987: Indian Country published. A central character in Caputo's novel is a Vietnam veteran, suffering from classic symptoms of post-traumatic stress disorder and struggling to keep his marriage together. Later in year, Caputo is hired by Paramount Pictures as a self-described "body and fender man" to help revise the script for a movie (*Distant Thunder*) about Vietnam veterans who have difficulty adjusting to civilian and family life and retreat into the wilds of the Pacific Northwest.

1988: Marries Leslie Blanchard Ware, currently managing editor of *Consumer Reports*.

1990: (June) Returns to Vietnam with other American writers, including Larry Heinemann, on a trip sponsored by the William Joiner Center at the University of Massachusetts–Boston.

1991: *Means of Escape* published. In this memoir, Caputo describes his days as a foreign correspondent and freelance journalist covering wars, insurgencies, and civil strife in Vietnam, Africa, Afghanistan, and the Middle East.

1996: *Equation for Evil* published. This novel, based on an actual event, describes the central character's ambush of a school bus carrying Asian American children on a field trip in California.

1999: *Exiles* published. The three collected novellas are directly or indirectly war related, with two—"Paradise" and "In the Forest of the Laughing Elephant"—involving the Vietnam War and its aftermath. (Oct.) *The Voyage* published. In this novel Caputo, drawing upon his own interest in sailing and influenced by Joseph Conrad's tales of the sea, creates a turn-of-the century sailing story with a coming-of-age theme and a crucial moral crisis.

2002: (June) Caputo's nonfictional *Ghosts of Tsavo: Tracking the Mythic Lions of East Africa* published. Caputo recounts two expeditions he accompanied to learn more about the facts and myths surrounding the well-known 1898 story of two male lions that killed and devoured 135 Indian and African workers constructing a railroad bridge over the Tsavo River in Kenya. (Aug.) *In the Shadows of the Morning: Essays on Wild Lands, Wild Waters, and a Few Untamed People* published. This collection of previously published travel and adventure essays includes one essay detailing Caputo's 1999 return trip to Vietnam and another written in 1980 about Afghanistan under Soviet occupation.

2005: *13 Seconds* published. This book of reportage, memoir, history, analysis, and commentary emerges from Caputo's stint as a *Chicago Tribune* reporter covering the Kent State Massacre in 1970. (May) *Acts of Faith* published. With echoes of Joseph Conrad's *Heart of Darkness*, Graham Greene's *The Quiet American*, and Caputo's own *A Rumor of War*, Caputo sets this complex novel of war, slavery, greed, missionary zeal, corrupted idealism, good versus evil, and a host of moral ambiguities against the backdrop of the current Sudanese civil and religious strife.

2007–: Caputo routinely contributes to the *New York Times Sunday Magazine, Washington Post Sunday Magazine, National Geographic* (contributing editor), *Esquire,* and *Field & Stream.* He is writing a novel ("Crossers") set in the present day on the Arizona-Mexico border. According to Caputo, "It's about a Connecticut man who flees the grief and fear resulting from his wife's death in 9/11 and who finds on the border, in different form, the violence and evil he had hoped to escape. But this time he will not be able to run from it."

NOTE _____

1. The dates and sequence of joining the Marines and enrolling at Loyola provided by Caputo conflict with related information in his memoir *A Rumor of War.*

appendix b

CHRONOLOGY OF LARRY HEINEMANN

1944: (Jan.18) Born Larry Curtis Heinemann, the second of four sons (all about two and a half years apart) in Chicago IL to Dorothy and John Heinemann. Dorothy runs a babysitting agency out of the home. John is a bus driver and, according to Heinemann, a "lifelong failed businessman," including a stint as owner of a bus company.

1949: The family moves to the northern Chicago suburb of Northbrook, which at the time is a small farming community. Larry's oldest brother, Jim, disappears from the family in 1970 and is never heard from again. The youngest brother, Philip, after dropping out of high school and enlisting in the Marines, serves two tours in Vietnam (wounded in his first tour) and also disappears from the family in 1982. The middle brother, Richard, also an army Vietnam-era veteran who received an early military discharge, commits suicide in 1999.

1961:(Summer) Travels to Japan with group of forty Sea Cadets from all over the country on a troop ship taking army replacements to Korea.

1962: (June) Graduates from Glenbrook High School. Works in mail room of an architectural firm with idea of becoming an architect by apprenticeship; leaves job after six months. (Fall) Enrolls at Kendall College (a two-year liberal arts college in Evanston IL) but flunks out after approximately one and a half years.

1963–64: Holds a series of menial jobs including mail clerk at the Sarah Lee Bakery and dishwasher at a "greasy spoon" restaurant run by a Guadalcanal Marine. Eventually returns to Kendall College where he becomes involved in theater and creative writing.

1965: Performs in summer-stock theater company in Lock Haven PA but discovers he isn't an actor. However, according to Heinemann, this theater experience will later influence the visceral and sensual nature of his writing.

1966: (Jan.) Graduates from Kendall College with an A.A. degree. (May) Drafted, along with his brother Richard, into U.S. Army. Completes eight weeks of basic training at Fort Polk LA and departs with a Military Occupational Specialty (MOS) of 11D (armored reconnaissance). His brother Richard is sent to Fort Sill and then

Germany as part of a Pershing Missile crew. (Oct.) Completes twelve weeks of advanced individual training (AIT) at Fort Knox KY in armored cavalry reconnaissance and is assigned to a unit at Fort Knox that trains armored cavalry officers in the OCS program.

1967: (Mar.) Upon arriving in Vietnam, assigned to the Recon Platoon of the 4th Battalion (Mechanized) of the 23rd Infantry in the 25th Division at Cu Chi (about twenty miles northwest of Saigon). He drives an armored personnel carrier (APC) and later serves as a track commander (TC) in charge of the four-man crew. (July) Transfers to a recon platoon of the 2nd Battalion (Mechanized) of the 22nd Infantry at Dau Tieng near Tay Ninh and the Black Virgin Mountain, an area that figures prominently in his recent war memoir. His unit's responsibilities include convoy escort, perimeter security, and fire support for line companies conducting sweeps and search-and-destroy missions. Achieves final rank of sergeant (E-5).

1968: (Jan. 1–2) Involved in a particularly bloody battle at Soui Cut, about five miles from the Cambodian border. Oliver Stone (the film director), in another battalion, also participates in this battle. The events of that night and next morning later make their way into the climactic episode in Stone's Vietnam War film *Platoon* and into two of Heinemann's books. (Mar.) Upon return to U.S. receives Honorable Discharge and the Combat Infantryman's Badge (CIB). "I was not ashamed of what I had done, but I was not proud either. . . . I possessed a bitterness that was almost unconscionable. . . . I felt as if I'd been used, wasted, and then dumped" ("Larry Heinemann" 89). (Apr.) Marries Edie Smith, whom he met while stationed at Fort Knox. They move to the same Chicago neighborhood (Edgewater) where various Heinemann family members have lived since the late 1800s and in which Heinemann and Edie (currently a social worker) still reside. (Summer) While driving a bus for the Chicago Transit Authority (CTA) on his downtown route experiences firsthand the antiwar protests linked to the 1968 Democratic Convention. (Fall) Enrolls at Columbia College in Chicago—a small private liberal arts school—and begins a mentor-student relationship with John Schultz, a creative writing teacher and former army medic during the Korean War. Heinemann begins writing "his story," which becomes *Close Quarters*.

1971: Graduates from Columbia College with a B.A. in English.

1971–86: Teaches writing at Columbia College.

1974–75: Excerpted chapters of *Close Quarters* appear in *Penthouse*.

1977: *Close Quarters* published. Father dies of cancer one week before the book is published. Novel receives Best First Novel prize from the Society of Midland Authors. In this dark and, at times, purposely cynical and vulgar fictional war memoir, Heinemann (influenced by one of his literary mentors—James Jones) focuses on the routines, psychology, and violence marking the battlefield lives of two soldiers, both members of an APC crew. (Nov.) Daughter, Sarah Catherine, born (currently a studio artist).

1980: Son, Preston John, born (currently works in the food service industry).

1985: (Apr.) Publishes "'Just Don't Fit': Stalking the Elusive 'Tripwire' Veteran" in *Harper's*, an article about post-traumatic stress disorder (PTSD) and Vietnam veterans living on the Olympic Peninsula in Washington state.

1986: *Paco's Story* published. In this haunting, as well as at times cynical and ironic, war-aftermath novel (begun in 1977), Heinemann uses a ghost narrator to tell the story of Paco Sullivan, a Vietnam veteran patterned after the author's youngest brother. Paco, an interstate nomad, wanders the country to find a home and a livable peace while struggling with the physical and emotional scars of his war experiences.

1988: *Paco's Story* wins 1987 National Book Award for Fiction. Other finalists are Toni Morrison's *Beloved* and Philip Roth's *The Counterlife*. For this novel, Heinemann also receives the Carl Sandburg Medal, Vietnam Veterans of America Tu Do Chien (Freedom to Express) Award, and the Fiction Prize from the Society of Midland Authors. (Spring) Travels on two-week writers' junket to China headed by Harrison Salisbury.

1988–89: Supported by a Guggenheim Fellowship, begins novel *Cooler by the Lake*.

1989: (Dec.) As a member of group of American Vietnam War veterans, travels to Moscow to meet with Afghanistan War veterans.

1990: (June) Returns to Vietnam with other American soldier-authors (including Philip Caputo) on a trip sponsored by the William Joiner Center at the University of Massachusetts–Boston. As a result of this trip and two trips in 1992, begins book about the railroad system in Vietnam. Portions of this unfinished book later appear in *Black Virgin Mountain*.

1992: *Cooler by the Lake* published. Set in Chicago, this comic novel, marked by numerous digressions, often on the origins of Chicago streets and landmarks, recounts a central character's efforts to return a lost wallet to its owner.

1997: (Spring) Travels with American soldier-authors to Vietnam where they are hosted by the Vietnam Writers Association and meet with NVA soldier-author Bao Ninh (*The Sorrow of War*). (June) Publishes short story "Fragging" in the *Atlantic Monthly*, which describes a phenomenon of popular Vietnam War legend and literature—the killing of hated American officers or NCOs by disgruntled enlisted men in their units.

2003: Receives Fulbright Fellowship for study (Vietnamese folktales) and travel in Vietnam.

2005: *Black Virgin Mountain: A Return to Vietnam* published. This Vietnam memoir bluntly chronicles the author's military tour of duty and postwar experiences; contains passionate political commentary on the Vietnam War and its aftermath; and features significant lyrical portions of Vietnam travelogue based on the author's numerous return visits since 1990 and his genuine love for the cities, countryside, modes of transportation, and people of Vietnam. The memoir ends with Heinemann's emotional and symbolic visit to the Black Virgin Mountain and with the words "I'm home, I say to myself; I have arrived home; this place is home. . . . and I am almost embarrassed at the discovered clarity. Home. Well" (243).

2005–: Teaches at Texas A&M University as a writer in residence.

2007–: Writing a murder mystery novel (begun in 2003) set in Chicago during the time of the Chicago Fire (1871). The central character, a Chicago detective, is based on Heinemann's one-armed maternal grandfather (Grampa Denton) who lost an arm in a pit-mine accident and later lived with the Heinemann family.

CHRONOLOGY OF TIM O'BRIEN

1946: (Oct. 1) Born William Timothy O'Brien, Jr., to William T., Sr., and Ava E. (Schultz) O'Brien in Austin MN. A sister, Kathleen, born 1947, and a brother, Greg, born 1956. His mother, a WAVE veteran of WWII, is an elementary school teacher; his father, a Navy veteran of WWII who served on a destroyer off the coasts of Okinawa and Iwo Jima during the two major Pacific campaigns, sells insurance.

1956: Family moves to Worthington MN, a town of about ten thousand in the southwest part of the state.

1964: (Fall) Matriculates at Macalester College in St. Paul MN. Majors in political science but takes several courses in philosophy and English. Participates in student government, serving as student body president during his senior year, and takes part in a few small peace vigils and campus debates related to the Vietnam War.

1967: (Summer) Studies in Prague, Czechoslovakia, as part of a student program called Student Project for Amenity among Nations; writes an unpublished novel as course project (spy novel with political overtones).

1968: (Spring) Works as a "weekender" in the Democratic presidential primary campaign of peace candidate Eugene McCarthy. (May) Graduates from Macalester *summa cum laude* and Phi Beta Kappa. Accepted into a graduate program in government at Harvard University. (June) Receives draft notice. (Aug.) Although believing the war to be "ill-conceived and wrong," O'Brien reluctantly enters the U.S. Army. (Oct.) Completes Army Basic Training at Fort Lewis WA and receives an MOS of 11B (infantry).

1969: (Jan.) Completes AIT at Fort Lewis. At one point, considered going AWOL from his training company, crossing the border into Canada, and eventually fleeing to Sweden: "I simply couldn't bring myself to flee. Family, the home town, friends, history, tradition, fear, confusion, exile: I could not run. . . . I was a coward" (*If I Die* 73). (Feb.) Enters Vietnam as a Private First Class with 46th Infantry, 198th Infantry Brigade, Americal Division at Firebase LZ Gator along Highway 1, south of Chu Lai in Quang Ngai Province. Spends first few months as a rifleman with Third Platoon, Alpha Company, during which time (May) he is wounded (shrapnel from a grenade). For the next three months, he serves in the dangerous position of a Radio-Telephone Operator (RTO) carrying first the platoon and then the battalion radio for his commanding officers in an area of operations that includes the subhamlet of My Lai (site of the 1968 My Lai massacre). (Oct.) Assigned as a clerk in Battalion Headquarters at LZ Gator.

1970: (Mar.) Completes thirteen-month tour in Vietnam, and upon returning to the U.S. is honorably discharged with rank of sergeant (E-5). Military decorations include the Army Combat Infantry Badge, Purple Heart, and Bronze Star for Valor (rescuing a wounded solider in the midst of hostile fire). (July) Publishes nonfiction story "Step Lightly" in *Playboy*.

1970–76: Enrolled in Ph.D. program in government at Harvard University. Passes Ph.D. orals and completes fifty pages of his dissertation ("Case Studies in American Military Interventions") but leaves the program to become a full-time writer.

1971–72: (Summers) Interns at the *Washington Post*.

1973–74: During leave of absence from Harvard, works as general assignment reporter on national affairs desk at the *Washington Post*. Covers general politics, Senate hearings, and first oil boycott.

1973: *If I Die in a Combat Zone* published. In its structure, style, tone, and content, this nonfiction war memoir of a combat soldier who opposed the war serves as a prologue to O'Brien's subsequent war fiction. Some of the material for this memoir comes from an extensive personal journal compiled while in Vietnam.

1973: Marries Ann Weller, an editorial assistant at Little, Brown publishing house. After a lengthy separation, they divorce in 1995.

1975: *Northern Lights* published. O'Brien's first novel, written during his off hours as a general assignment reporter at the *Post*, is set in the woods and small towns of northeast Minnesota. It explores the relationship between two brothers (one of whom is a wounded Vietnam veteran suffering from PTSD) as each struggles with personal and family issues. O'Brien admits to an unmistakable Hemingway influence on the novel's style and content.

1976: Short story "Night March" (excerpt from *Going After Cacciato*) selected for *The O. Henry Prize Stories*.

1978: *Going After Cacciato* published, and his short story "Speaking of Courage" (will later appear in *The Things They Carried*) selected for *The*

O. Henry Prize Stories. O'Brien's first Vietnam War novel blends fantasy, realism, and travel narrative within a mix of past, present, and future time. O'Brien explores the heart and mind of central character Specialist Four Paul Berlin, who yearns to escape the war (in actions and daydreams), to control his fear, and to understand himself and his war situations.

1978–79: Writer in residence at Emerson College, Boston MA.

1979: *Going After Cacciato* wins National Book Award as O'Brien's novel is selected over John Irving's *The World According to Garp* and John Cheever's *Stories*.

1985: *The Nuclear Age* published. This dark comedy, which took seven years to write, focuses on narrator and central character William Cowling's obsessive fears of a nuclear holocaust. The novel also examines the Vietnam War from a new angle—an emotional, intellectual, and political battlefield situated within America's home front and involving the antiwar movement.

1989: Short story "The Things They Carried" wins National Magazine Award in Fiction.

1990: *The Things They Carried* published. Selected by the *New York Times* as one of the year's ten best works of fiction and receives the *Chicago Tribune*'s Heartland Prize. Finalist for Pulitzer Prize and National Book Critics Circle Award. In this fictional war memoir, influenced in its content and structure by *If I Die* and *Going After Cacciato*, O'Brien weaves together short stories, commentaries, confessions, character sketches, notes, and retellings of the same incidents from different perspectives. He also mixes facts and experiences from his life with those of his fictional character to counterpoint happening truth with story truth.

1991: Wins Melcher Book Award for *The Things They Carried*.

1992: Wins Prix du Meilleur Livre Etranger award in France for *The Things They Carried*.

1994: (Feb.) Returns to Vietnam for the first time since tour of duty and travels to Ho Chi Minh City and his former area of operations in Quang Ngai Province. (Oct.) Publishes "The Vietnam in Me" in the *New York Times Magazine*. The article chronicles O'Brien's emotional return to Vietnam, as well as the traumatic break-up of his relationship with the woman who accompanied him on the trip. According to O'Brien, this article is a companion piece for *In the Lake of the Woods*: "It [the article] was confessional about going to a war I hated. It was confessional about doing bad things for love, which is one of the essential themes both of the book [Lake] and of the article." (Oct.) In the Lake of the Woods published. Named by Time magazine as the best work of fiction published in 1994 and becomes a Book-of-the-Month Club selection. In this ambitious postmodern novel, which O'Brien labels "his most personal," the author focuses on the war and aftermath experiences of Vietnam veteran John Wade, as reconstructed and recounted by a fictional narrator, who is also a Vietnam veteran. O'Brien interweaves abundant research and historical facts related to the My Lai massacre and its aftermath, incidents and emotional crises from his own life, and a complex probing of his central characters' psyches.

1995: In the Lake of the Woods receives James Fenimore Cooper Prize for best novel based on a historical theme.

1996: (Mar.) Adaptation of In the Lake of the Woods, produced by Hallmark Entertainment, appears on the Fox Network.

1998: Tomcat in Love published. O'Brien's sixth novel features his recurring theme of "the things we do for love." The author returns to the dark comic tone and shifting time frames of The Nuclear Age in creating a story of loves gained, lost, and imagined as recounted by narrator/protagonist Thomas Chippering (Vietnam veteran and professor of linguistics), who O'Brien intentionally created to be an unsympathetic character. The novel's opening chapter has its origins in a real-life adventure of O'Brien's boyhood transformed into the short story "Faith" in the New Yorker.

1999–: Assumes the position of the Roy F. and Joann Mitte Chair in Creative Writing at Texas State University–San Marcos where he teaches one course (creative writing) every two years in the MFA program.

1999: Title story of The Things They Carried selected for Best American Short Stories of the Century, edited by John Updike.

2001: Marries Meredith Hale Baker, a professional actor/director who teaches in the theater department at Texas State University. First son, William Timothy O'Brien IV, born in June 2003. Second son, Trevor Hale O'Brien, born in June 2005.

2002: July, July published. In this novel, O'Brien explores what has become of his Vietnam generation through a series of twenty-two interrelated vignettes emerging from the thirtieth reunion of Darton Hall College's Class of 1969. Focusing on ten central characters, many of whom are female, O'Brien explores how the characters carry with them the war's aftermath, along with hopes, fears, ennui, anger, disappointments, affairs, love, loves lost, and physical changes ever present in their metaphorical "war of the living."

2003: "What Went Wrong" from July, July selected for *The O. Henry Prize Stories*.

2007–: Lives in Austin, Texas. Currently writing a novel in which the central character, a father who works at a JC Penney store, robs a bank out of desperation and concern for the well being of another person. According to the author, the book is influenced by his real-life role as a new father.

CHRONOLOGY OF ROBERT OLEN BUTLER

1945: (Jan. 20) Born Robert Olen Butler, Jr., to Lucille Frances (Hall) and Robert O., Sr., in Granite City IL, a blue-collar town of about 35,000 located east of St. Louis across the Mississippi River. Butler's father chairs the St. Louis University Theater Department, and his mother works occasionally as an executive secretary.

1963: (June) Graduates from Granite City High School where he was student body president and co-valedictorian of his graduating class. (Fall) Attends Northwestern University in Evanston IL on scholarship, where he initially majors in theater and has main roles during his freshman and sophomore years in several campus theater productions. Switches major to oral interpretation during sophomore year.

1967: (May) Graduates from Northwestern University *summa cum laude*. (Fall) Enters M.A. program in theater department at University of Iowa.

1968: (Aug.) Marries Carol Supplee.

1969: (Jan.) Receives M.A. in playwriting from University of Iowa. He continues to write full-length plays, which will number a dozen before he realizes he is a nascent novelist working in the wrong medium. (Feb.) About to be drafted, Butler enlists for three years in the army to secure "promised" stateside duty and an MOS as a counter-intelligence special agent. (Mar.) Completes Army Basic Training at Fort Lewis WA. (Dec.) Completes twelve weeks of training at the Intelligence School at Fort Holabird MD.

1970: (Jan.–Dec.) Attached to Fort Meade MD, attends Vietnamese language school in Crystal City VA.

1971: (Jan.–Dec.) During one-year tour of duty in South Vietnam and with fluency in Vietnamese, initially serves in counter-intelligence for five months while assigned to the Plantation, an American military base near Long Binh on Highway 1. As part of his duties, he travels into the countryside talking with a host of people—Vietnamese informants, village chiefs, farmers, and U.S. military personnel. Later, spends seven months assigned to Saigon City Hall as an administrative assistant/interpreter for the American counterpart to the mayor of Saigon. During this time he records his experiences in several notebooks. Achieves the rank of sergeant (E-5), and upon his Honorable Discharge receives the Meritorious Service Medal.

1972: Returning from Vietnam, finalizes divorce from Carol Supplee; later in the year marries poet Marylin Geller and joins Fairchild Publications in New York City as a section editor and reporter for *Electronic News*.

1973: Returns to Granite City as a freelance writer and substitute high school teacher. Finishes first unpublished novel called "What Lies Near," which is Vietnam-centered and portions of which are later incorporated into *On Distant Ground*. (Nov.) Son, Joshua Robert Butler, born (currently a writer, editor, director, and producer in film and television).

1974: Rejoins Fairchild Publications in Chicago as the Midwest reporter for *Electronic News*. First work of fiction is published in *Redbook* magazine—a short story titled "Moving Day" about two young men about to be sent to Vietnam.

1975–85: Returns to New York City to create Fairchild's business newspaper *Energy User News* and serve as its editor in chief.

1978–80: After writing five novels and numerous short stories between 1972 and 1979 (without any being published), enrolls in a writing class at the New School for Social Research (New York City) taught by Anatole Broyard, writer, *New York Times* critic, and significant influence in Butler's literary career.

1981: *The Alleys of Eden* published. In his first published novel (rejected twenty-one times), Butler explores themes of identity, displacement, and connections as he depicts the romantic relationship between a U.S. Army deserter (counter-intelligence) and his Vietnamese lover (a bar girl). After living together for four years in Saigon, they flee Vietnam for the U.S. immediately before Saigon's fall to the North Vietnamese.

1982: *Sun Dogs* published. Butler's novel is set on the North Slope of Alaska. The central character is a Vietnam veteran (counter-intelligence) and private investigator haunted by memories of his ex-wife's suicide and his brief time as a prisoner of the Vietcong.

1983: *Countrymen of Bones* published. In this novel, Butler examines the intersection of past and present as an archaeologist works under deadline near the end of World War II (before testing of an atomic bomb destroys the site) to complete a dig at an important burial ground in New Mexico's Alamogordo Desert.

1985: *On Distant Ground* published. The novel's central character (an army intelligence officer and minor character in *Alleys of Eden*), in the midst of his 1975 stateside court-martial for earlier helping a Vietcong officer escape from confinement, suddenly recalls his previous relationship with a Vietnamese woman. Convinced that he has a son in Vietnam, he flees the U.S. and returns to Saigon during its final days in April 1975 to search for his mistress and son.

1985: Hired as Assistant Professor of Creative Writing at McNeese State University, Lake Charles LA.

1987: Divorces Marylin Geller and awarded custody of their son; marries Maureen Donlan. Awarded the Tu Do Chinh Kien Award by Vietnam Veterans of America for outstanding contributions to American culture by a Vietnam veteran. (Mar.) *Wabash* published. In this novel, set in fictional Wabash IL (east of St. Louis), Butler explores issues related to marriage, work, violence, and labor unrest associated with this Depression-era steel mill (Wabash Steel) community in the summer of 1932.

1989: *The Deuce* published. With this novel, Butler explores one frequently neglected legacy of the Vietnam War—the plight of biracial children of American soldiers and Vietnamese women. The story is told through the first-person voice (used by Butler for the first time) of a runaway teenage Amerasian boy, who in 1974 at age six was brought to the United States by his Vietnam veteran father.

1992: *A Good Scent from a Strange Mountain* published. To date, this collection of short fiction is Butler's most popular and critically acclaimed work. Butler, inspired by his contact with Vietnamese communities in and near New Orleans, draws upon his fluency in the Vietnamese language and his extensive experiences with Vietnamese culture, folklore, the spirit world, and war veterans. In fifteen stories about the Vietnamese diaspora, he explores, through Vietnamese voices (young and old), how these displaced Vietnamese American characters live with the aftermath of the American War, adjust to life in America, and attempt to retain their individual and cultural identity.

1993: Awarded Pulitzer Prize in Fiction for *A Good Scent from a Strange Mountain* and the Richard and Hinda Rosenthal Foundation Award from the American Academy of Arts and Letters. Also receives

Guggenheim Fellowship for travel to Vietnam to research a proposed follow-up collection of stories to *Good Scent* containing the voices of Vietnamese who remained in Vietnam after the war. The book is never published, but two published stories—"Salem" and "Missing"—emerge from this trip.

1994: *They Whisper* published. In his seventh novel, Butler explores sexuality and love through the stream-of-consciousness narration of a public relations specialist and Vietnam veteran (counter-intelligence officer) who confesses to a lifelong passion for women.

1995: (Feb.) Travels to Vietnam. Upon return divorces Maureen Donlan; marries Elizabeth Dewberry, a novelist and playwright (separated, summer 2007).

1996: *Tabloid Dreams* published. In this collection of short stories, Butler incorporates the world of popular culture into his fiction. Inspired by real tabloid headlines, he creates his own outlandish headlines and comic, playful, inventive, and sometimes bizarre stories of exile, disappointment, self-discovery, love, and human yearning.

1997: *The Deep Green Sea* published. Butler returns in this novel to a scenario present in *On Distant Ground*. A Vietnam veteran visits Ho Chi Minh City thirty years after his tour ended to attain closure to this part of his life. During his quest, he becomes entangled in a very complicated and tragic romantic relationship (with Sophoclean overtones) with a young Amerasian woman, who works as a tourist guide.

2000: *Mr. Spaceman* published. In this inventive novel with multiple voices, Butler works with religious allegory and the genre of science fiction in exploring marital dynamics and mysteries of human yearning, as well as the power and limits of language. An alien (Desi) for years has been hovering over the Earth in his spacecraft and temporarily abducting Americans so he and colleagues can record their stories and understand the human race. (Summer) Travels to Vietnam on a State Department–sponsored trip to meet with Vietnamese writers and cultural officials in Ho Chi Minh City and Hanoi. (Fall) Appointed a Francis Eppes Distinguished Professor in English at Florida State University, a position that Butler currently holds.

2001: Receives National Magazine Award in Fiction for his short story "Fair Warning," which appeared in *Zoetrope: All Story*. (Oct.) Begins "Inside Creative Writing" via the Internet and an educational television channel. Over seventeen days in two-hour sessions, Butler creates and completes (in real time) for his viewers an unplanned piece of literary fiction and comments on the writing process. (Dec.) *Fair Warning* published. This novel, emerging from his award-winning short story, explores the world of wealth and upscale auction houses in New York City through the voice of an independent, beautiful, and successful female auctioneer.

2004: (July) *Had a Good Time: Stories from American Postcards* published. In this collection of short fiction, Butler again uses popular culture as his inspiration—specifically his own assortment of early-twentieth-century picture postcards. The short messages, or "little outbursts" as he calls them, written on the back of the cards by real people are the starting points for fifteen imaginative first-person stories set in the years 1906–17.

2005: *From Where You Dream: The Process of Writing Fiction* published. This collection of edited Butler lectures for graduate students in his fiction writing courses at Florida State University contains the author's ideas about the nature of fiction (exploring human beings and human emotion, with yearning as its compass) and the process of writing fiction ("art comes from the place where you dream"). (Apr.) Receives National Magazine Award in Fiction for his short story "The One in White," which originally appeared in *Atlantic Monthly* and is included in *Had a Good Time*.

2006: *Severance* published, a collection of sixty-two fictional monologues—each 240 words long—by historical, mythical, animal, or contemporary figures immediately *after* their beheading. Also finishes work on a screenplay for Robert Redford about an elder statesman TV anchor.

2007–: *Weegee Stories*, scheduled for publication in fall 2007, links short monologues with sixty Weegee (Arthur Fellig) photographs of New York City life. Working on a novel contracted *before* Hurricane Katrina and, *at that time*, described by Butler as a "New Orleans hurricane novel set in a speculative near future."

INDEX

Alighieri, Dante, 129

Aquinas, 98, 103

Bao Ninh, 74, 121; *The Sorrow of War*, 31, 80

Beattie, Ann, 28

Bellow, Saul, 33–34

Bible, 71, 155–56

Brothers Grimm, *Grimm's Fairy Tales*, 91

Brown, Rita Mae, *Ruby Fruit Jungle*, 86; *Southern Discomfort*, 86

Broyard, Anatole, 143, 154

Bush, George W., 57, 89, 109, 116, 141

Butler, Robert Olen, 45, 74, 121, 189–90; divorce, 153; and Elizabeth Dewberry (wife), 134; fatherhood, 155, 157, 160; and Marilyn Geller (wife), 155; marriage, 141, 158, 176; McNeese State, 166; on nature of love, 151, 153; on reading literature, 140, 167–69, 174; University of Iowa, 140
AS AUTHOR, 153–77; advice to writers, 156, 165, 166–67, 188; aesthetic philosophy, 138, 139, 141, 148, 153–54, 156, 158, 159, 163, 166–67, 173, 174; on artist's role, 148, 158, 163–64; Bible as influence, 155–56; book structure, 172–73; Fairchild Publications, 153, 160; "Inside Creative Writing," 167; memoir, 155; memory vs. imagination, 159; on nature of fiction, 156, 159; on nature of unconscious, 155, 157–59, 162, 167, 171, 175; New School for Social Research, 154; oral interpretation influences, 139, 140, 157; playwright, 140, 152, 154, 165; Pulitzer Prize, 152, 176; relationship between life and works, 175; response to reviews, 174–75; "The Rooming House," 139, 140; screenwriter, 164–66; on teaching in MFA programs, 166–67; return to Vietnam, 161–62; theater influences, 135, 137, 182; thrumming to a text, 167–68, 174, 175, 179; Vietnam War influences, 160, 175–76, 177, 180, 186; on war stories, 162; war writer label, 173; Weegee photographs, 172
AS SOLDIER, 141–53; arrival in Vietnam, 146; attitudes toward Vietnam, 139–40, 141, 144, 149; basic training, 143–44; counter-intelligence, 142–43, 144–45, 146–48, 149–50, 153; on courage, 151; culture collision, 148, 150–51; draft, 140, 142; drug use, 149; enlistment, 142; on evil nature, 150, 153; Fort Holabird, 142, 144; Hatcher James, 148, 149; heart-of-darkness experience, 150; language school, 145–46; military occupational specialty (MOS), 144–45; military uniform, 176–77; moral dilemmas, 150, 153, 186; on perception of military, 144; Plantation (Vietnam), 147; post-traumatic stress disorder (PTSD), 153; Saigon City Hall, 148–49; transformation during Vietnam War, 152, 186–87; Vietnam impressions, 146; Vietnam Veterans Against the War (VVAW), 153; Vietnamese language, 145–46, 149, 186; Vietnamese people, 146, 149, 152, 161–62, 186; writing activities, 147,

151–52, 154

AS SON, 135–41; childhood interests, 135, 182; Cuban Missile Crisis influence, 137; Granite City (Illinois), 135, 182; heroes, 135–36; high school, 137, 138, 182; mother's influence, 138; Northwestern University, 138–39; relationship with father, 136, 137, 141, 182; religion, 137, 155–56; war games, 136

THEMES AND SUBJECTS OF WORKS: culture collisions, 158, 182; father-son relationships, 160, 161; human condition, 152, 171, 174; humor, 171; life, 162–63; Otherness, 137, 151, 158, 186; popular culture, 171, 172; postmodernism, 172; self, 170; sensual reality, 160; truth, 159–60, 162; Vietnam War as Sophoclean tragedy, 161, 162; Vietnamese people, 158, 161; women's voices, 158; yearning, 156, 162, 169

WORKS: *Alleys of Eden*, 139, 143, 154–55, 159, 160, 169–74; "The Chieu Hoi," 153; "Crickets," 162; *The Deep Green Sea*, 160, 161, 162; *The Deuce*, 160, 161; *From Where You Dream*, 135, 152, 157; *A Good Scent from a Strange Mountain*, 152, 153, 161, 169–74, 176; "A Good Scent from a Strange Mountain," 170; *Had a Good Time, Stories from American Postcards*, 156, 169–74; "Missing," 170; "Moving Day," 154; *On Distant Ground*, 149–50, 160; "The One in White," 169–70; "Open Arms," 153, 169; "Salem," 170; *Severance*, 172; *Sun Dogs*, 160; *Tabloid Dreams*, 172; "Up By Heart," 156; *Wabash*, 46

Caputo, Philip, 51, 86, 121, 131, 150, 162, 169, 173, 175, 184, 185, 189–90; first wife, 9; Leslie Ware (wife), 1, 43; on nature of love, 18

AS AUTHOR, 25–43; advice for writers, 28, 39, 188; aesthetic philosophy, 29, 38–40; book content, 27, 28; Catholic imagination, 33; character development, 31; chip-on-shoulder mentality, 8, 40; development as, 3, 6–7, 19, 20, 36–37, 182, 187–88; on genres, 26–27; imaginative autobiography, 29; journalism influences, 7, 25; life-writing, 29, 31–32; memoir, 30, 32; MFA programs, 37, 39; poems, 20; relationship between life and works, 29–30, 31, 41; return to Vietnam, 24; truth detector, 31; Vietnam War influences, 24–25, 27, 34, 41–42, 180; on war stories, 32–33; war writer label, 27; world view, 40; writer's wound, 41–42; writers' influences, 7–8, 28; writing characteristics, 37, 38, 40; writing process, 25–26

AS SOLDIER, 9–25; arrival in Vietnam, 13–14; attitude toward Vietnam, 10, 12, 14, 16, 17, 20, 182; books as influence, 13; Camp Lejeune, 20, 21; and combat, 17–18, 23–24; enemy contact, 14–15, 182; enlistment, 6, 9–10, 182, 183; on evil nature, 17; Giao Tri (Vietnam) incident, 16, 22, 42, 184; guilt, 41–42, 182; heart-of-darkness experience, 16; impressions of Vietnam, 13, 16; Marine Corps image, 10, 182; medals, 43; military occupational specialty (MOS), 12; moral dilemmas, 42, 182; officer candidate school (OCS), 11–12; officer's basic school, 12–13; post-traumatic stress disorder (PTSD), 22; rifle platoon, 14, 15, 42; return to Vietnam, 19, 20; Vietnam Veterans Against the War (VVAW), 21–22; Vietnam War aftermath, 22–23, 43; Vietnam War politics, 15–16, 21, 22, 23; Vietnamese people, 19, 186; writing activities, 18–19

writing characteristics, 73, 78, 79, 80; writing process, 78–79
AS SOLDIER, 57–74; advanced individual training (AIT), 59; armored personnel carrier, 63, 64–65; arrival in Vietnam, 62; attitude toward Vietnam, 65–66, 80; attraction to combat, 71; basic training, 58–59; Bien Hoa, 62; Black Virgin Mountain (Vietnam), 69–70; brothers' war experiences, 58, 61; on courage, 71–72; draft, 55, 56, 57–58, 184; drug use, 68–69; on evil nature, 71; First Sergeant Alva, 60; Fort Knox, 59; Fort Polk, 58; fragging, 66–67; heart-of-darkness experience, 70; impressions of Vietnam, 63; love of nature, 71; lifers, 51, 61–62, 67, 75, 184; medals, 87; military perceptions, 58, 184; military uniform, 86; officer training school, 60; post-traumatic stress disorder (PTSD), 72–73, 185; race relations, 66; Soui Cut (Vietnam), 70; transformation during Vietnam, 63, 72, 185; Vietnam War aftermath, 74, 86–87; Vietnam War politics, 65, 72, 184–85; Vietnamese people, 69, 186; views of officers, 60
AS SON, 46–57; architectural interests, 54; childhood interests, 47–48; family life, 48, 52, 56, 181; grandfather Denton, 46–47, 52; heroes, 51; high school, 54; jobs, 48, 55; Kendall College, 55; relationship with brothers, 54–55; relationship with father, 52–53, 58; relationship with mother, 52; religion, 52; Sea Cadets, 49, 52; storytelling, 46–47; theater interests, 55–56; views on authority, 48–50; views on military, 49, 60; war games, 51–52; war movies, 51
THEMES AND SUBJECTS OF WORKS: anti-authority, 48–50, 181; emotional

truth, 81; irony of life, 81; path to wisdom, 81; quest for home, 70, 75, 83, 85, 123; realism of war, 75, 78, 80; soldier's life, 85
WORKS: *Black Virgin Mountain*, 60, 79, 81–86, 123; *Close Quarters*, 53, 66, 70, 74–75, 76, 79, 81–86; *Cooler by the Lake*, 79; *Paco's Story*, 70, 75, 76, 79, 81–86
Heller, Joseph, *Catch-22*, 50, 60, 116
Hemingway, Ernest, 4, 116, 136, 182; "Big Two-Hearted River," 32; *A Farewell to Arms*, 7; *The Sun Also Rises*, 7, 97
Herr, Michael, *Dispatches*, 121, 123, 180
Homer, *The Iliad*, 33

Iraq War, 35–36, 50, 63, 71, 72, 79, 80–81, 89–90, 100, 110, 170, 173
Irving, John, 127

Jones, James, 43, 58, 75; *From Here to Eternity*, 7, 60, 75; *The Thin Red Line*, 7, 75; WWII, 105
Joyce, James, *Ulysses*, 97

Kantor, Mackinlay, *Andersonville*, 48
Kerry, John, 21–22, 111, 153
Kennedy, John F., 92, 141
Komunyakaa, Yusef, 19
Kovic, Ron, *Born on the Fourth of July*, 51, 99

Le Minh Khue, 80
Lewis, Sinclair, 89
life-writing, 118, 179–80
London, Jack, 8

Mailer, Norman, *Armies of the Night*, 8; *Executioner's Song*, 8; *The Naked and the Dead*, 8, 75
McCarthy, Cormac, 117
McCarthy, Eugene, 96–97, 185
McEwan, Ian, *Atonement*, 28

courage, 95, 108, 126; father-son relationships, 95, 126; flee or fight, 126; free will, 129; happening truth vs. story truth, 30, 114, 120–21, 124; history and war, 95; hope, 128–29; magic, 95, 190n2; memory and imagination, 95, 114, 118–19, 124–25; multiple perspectives, 127, 128; mystery of human existence, 115; politics of life, 117, 118; quest for love, 125–26, 127, 128, 181, 185; time shifts, 124; war of the living, 117, 127, 180

WORKS: Going After Cacciato, 32–33, 102, 107, 113, 114, 119, 120, 121; If I Die in a Combat Zone, 99, 100, 104, 106, 108, 109, 111, 120, 124–32; In the Lake of the Woods, 88, 106, 111, 117, 119, 120, 121, 128, 129; July, July, 111, 121, 124–32, 173; "Loon Point," 117; Northern Lights, 94; The Nuclear Age, 94; "Step Lightly," 109; "Sweetheart of the Song Tra Bong," 118; The Things They Carried, 97, 114, 119, 120–21, 124–32, 173; "The Things They Carried," 27–28; Tomcat in Love, 127; "The Vietnam in Me," 88

Owen, Wilfred, 7

Patrick, John, The Curious Savage, 95
Pork Chop Hill (movie), 91
Pratt, John Clark, 67
Pynchon, Thomas, 38; Mason & Dixon, 39–40

Raeburn, Ben, 154
Reagan, Ronald, 35
Remarque, Erich Maria, All Quiet on the Western Front, 7, 99
Renoir, Jean, 84
Richardson, Samuel, Clarissa, 140
Roosevelt, Theodore, 3–4
Roth, Philip, 33–34

Rumsfeld, Donald, 50, 116
Rush, Norman, 40

Safer, Morley, 29
Salinger, J. D., The Catcher in the Rye, 129
Salisbury, Harrison, 29
Sands of Iwo Jima (film), 4, 51, 182
Sassoon, Siegfried, 7
Schell, Jonathan, 103
Sedaris, David, 171
Shakespeare, William, 116; Hamlet, 115, 131; The Taming of the Shrew, 131
Spender, Stephen, 140
Stone, Robert, 117
Swift, Jonathan, 163
Swofford, Anthony, Jarhead, 189

Theroux, Paul, 79
To Hell and Back (film), 101
Tolstoy, Leo, Anna Karenina, 31; War and Peace, 80
Trumbo, Dalton, Johnny Got His Gun, 78
Twain, Mark, 50, 77, 81; Huckleberry Finn, 91; Tom Sawyer, 91
Tzu, Sun, The Art of War, 12

Updike, John, 117

Vietnam Veterans Against the War (VVAW), 21, 111, 153. See also AS SOLDIER under individual authors
Vietnam War, 186; American policy, 185; attitudes toward, 10–11, 34–35, 60, 65–66, 80, 96, 98, 145, 184–85, 189; draft, 7, 140; drug use, 68, 103–4, 149; fragging, 66–67, 104; Gulf of Tonkin, 7, 12, 98; innocence lost, 35; literature of, 99, 111, 122–23, 158; My Lai, 104–05, 106, 119–20; nature of, 16, 17–18, 35, 63, 64, 103, 104, 105, 106, 109, 111, 149, 150, 185; ninety-day-wonders, 60; "Operation Babylift," 160; politics of,

21, 22, 23, 99, 149, 184–85; "Project 100,000," 21, 59; post-traumatic stress disorder (PTSD), 22, 63, 112; race relations, 66; Tet Offensive, 63, 65, 141; veterans' return from, 72; and William Calley, 60, 120. *See also* AS SOLDIER under individual authors

Vietnamese literature, 19, 31, 74, 80, 121

Vonnegut, Kurt, 77

Walzer, Michael, 113

war movies, 84, 91, 101. *See also* AS SON under individual authors

war stories, 32–33, 75, 78, 108, 180, 188–89. *See also* AS AUTHOR under individual authors

war writer, 27–28, 85, 158, 173, 188. *See also* AS AUTHOR under individual authors

Wayne, John, 4, 51, 101

Weigel, Bruce, 73

Willingham, Calder, *End as a Man*, 135

World War I, 17

World War II, 2–3, 10, 15, 21, 90–91, 136

Wright, Stephen, *Meditations in Green*, 80